The SHINE Framework

Samuel M. Y. Ho

The SHINE Framework

Fostering Resilience and Growth
in the Face of Adversity

Samuel M. Y. Ho
Department of Social and Behavioural
Sciences
City University of Hong Kong
Hong Kong, People's Republic of
China

ISBN 978-3-031-89105-2   ISBN 978-3-031-89106-9   (eBook)
https://doi.org/10.1007/978-3-031-89106-9

© The Author(s), under exclusive license to Springer Nature Switzerland AG 2025

This work is subject to copyright. All rights are solely and exclusively licensed by the Publisher, whether the whole or part of the material is concerned, specifically the rights of translation, reprinting, reuse of illustrations, recitation, broadcasting, reproduction on microfilms or in any other physical way, and transmission or information storage and retrieval, electronic adaptation, computer software, or by similar or dissimilar methodology now known or hereafter developed.
The use of general descriptive names, registered names, trademarks, service marks, etc. in this publication does not imply, even in the absence of a specific statement, that such names are exempt from the relevant protective laws and regulations and therefore free for general use.
The publisher, the authors and the editors are safe to assume that the advice and information in this book are believed to be true and accurate at the date of publication. Neither the publisher nor the authors or the editors give a warranty, expressed or implied, with respect to the material contained herein or for any errors or omissions that may have been made. The publisher remains neutral with regard to jurisdictional claims in published maps and institutional affiliations.

Cover illustration: © John Rawsterne/patternhead.com

This Palgrave Macmillan imprint is published by the registered company Springer Nature Switzerland AG
The registered company address is: Gewerbestrasse 11, 6330 Cham, Switzerland

If disposing of this product, please recycle the paper.

Acknowledgements First, I would like to thank my patients and clients who have used their experiences to teach me how to cope with difficulties. My deepest gratitude goes to my collaborators, many of whom I have mentioned in this book, for providing me with a fulfilling professional career. I am blessed to know you all. I enjoyed every moment of working with you.

Special thanks to my teammates for running resilience workshops and presentations on the SHINE framework, especially Christine, Ada, Bonnie, Nerrisa, and Darren. They made significant contributions to the materials in this book.

Donna provided initial editorial support for the presentation materials and provided feedback on the content from the perspective of a young reader with little formal education in psychology. I found her input invaluable.

I would like to thank the staff at Palgrave Macmillan, especially Clelia Petracca and Naveen Dass, for their great support in writing this book.

Most importantly, I sincerely thank my family, Georgiana, Joyce, and Kevin, for their support and encouragement over the years. Kevin contributed to this book based on his medical training background, too.

Finally, I want to thank you for your interest in this book. I hope it will help you manage and thrive in the face of life's challenges.

Competing Interests The author has no competing interests to declare that are relevant to the content of this manuscript.

Prologue

The topic of resilience has gained popularity in academia and among the general public in recent decades due to the increasing number of natural disasters, pandemics, and geopolitical tensions. The popularity of psychological research on resilience and disasters may have begun after the 9/11 attack in New York in 2001, with some new and 'unexpected' findings as a result. Most notably, George Bonanno and his colleagues (Bonanno et al., 2006) showed that most people can recover from a traumatic experience without any intervention. Furthermore, Richard Tedeschi (Tedeschi & Calhoun, 2004) reported that people can exhibit positive changes after trauma. Their findings are provocative and unacceptable to some clinical and therapeutic psychology experts at the time. The criticisms both Bonanno and Tedeschi received in the early days of their research were well-witnessed through my collaboration with them. Yet equally impactful to me was their great resilience, as they thrived in difficult situations. Today, Bonanno's resilience model and Tedeschi's posttraumatic growth framework have both become mainstream theories in trauma research.

My interest in resilience first began in the early 90s when I worked as a clinical psychologist in the paediatric oncology ward of a public hospital in Hong Kong. Seeing the psychological trauma cancer treatment left to so many young children and their parents stunned me at first. Looking back, my young self may too have been traumatised by my experience in the cancer ward because I was not ready for the job at the time, both developmentally and professionally. Nonetheless, what truly made

viii PROLOGUE

a deep impression on me was the resilience they developed through their traumatic experiences.

I did not stay in the hospital for long. However, my desire to better understand resilience never ceased. When I had the opportunity to pursue a PhD at the University of Melbourne in 1996, I enthusiastically proposed to study the experience of cancer patients undergoing a then-new and intrusive treatment called bone marrow transplantation. The study was conducted under the joint supervision of Professor David Horne, clinical psychologist, and Professor Jeff Szer, haematologist, which has truly paved the way for my life-long research and clinical focus on trauma and resilience, particularly cancer research.

This book adopts an evidence-based approach to introduce five factors related to resilience: S*trength-based habit-building*, H*opeful thinking*, I*nterpersonal Support and Communication*, N*oticing both positives and negatives*, and E*mbracing change*. Together, they form the **SHINE** framework, which contains my research findings and clinical experience over the past 30 years. This model includes elements of cognitive psychology (attentional bias, cognitive theory of hope, mindfulness) and positive psychology (character strengths, positive communication).

My focus in cognitive therapy originated from my Ph.D. supervisor Professor David Horne, and through collaboration with Professor Keith Dobson in Canada. I have benefited greatly from their input, as I mainly adopted a cognitive approach in my clinical practice, and have established a solid track record using Cognitive Behavioural Therapy to treat patients with depression and anxiety.

The positive psychology part mainly came from my involvement in the positive psychology movement in the US in the late 1990s. I am one of the first psychologists in Asia involved in Martin Seligman's positive psychology movement (Seligman & Csikszentmihalyi, 2000). I was first recognised as a Positive Psychology Summer Institute Scholar in 2003 in Philadelphia, and subsequently a Fellow of the Positive Psychology Templeton Fellows Programme in 2005 and 2006 at the Positive Psychology Centre in Washington, DC.

I previously described the SHINE framework in a book chapter (Ho et al., 2017). I also briefly mentioned the SHINE framework in the *New World Book of Happiness* (in Dutch), edited by L. Bormans in Belgium (Ho, 2023). The present book discusses in more detail the theories, research findings, and applications of the five SHINE components. A Practical Applications section after each chapter provides assessment tools and activities for self-learning, education, and intervention. This book, therefore, primarily aims at a general audience interested in resilience. Professionals and students in professional training may apply the tools to their clients. You are encouraged to practise the exercises and do the assessments for self-learning as you read along. However, the exercises and assessments are not for remedial purposes. In other words, they cannot treat your illness. If you are experiencing psychological symptoms and disorders, I advise you to seek professional help from a qualified practitioner.

SHINE is a new user-friendly framework that I developed with my research and practice experience in positive and cognitive psychology. This book contains both theoretical and research-based content as well as practical tips to facilitate resilience. It not only promotes self-learning and education but also long-term habit-building to increase resistance to adversity, post-adversity resilience, and constructive and positive changes.

I hope you enjoy this book and find it helpful to your resilience.

People's Republic of China   Samuel M. Y. Ho

CONTENTS

1 Resilience and SHINE — 1
  1.1 Adversity and Resilience — 2
  1.2 Positive Adaptation to Adversity — 3
  1.3 Factors Promoting Resilience — 5
    1.3.1 Personality Traits — 6
    1.3.2 External and Internal Resources — 7
    1.3.3 Dynamic Personal Factors — 8
  1.4 The SHINE Framework — 11
    1.4.1 Strength-Based Habit-Building (Chapter 3) — 12
    1.4.2 Hopeful Thinking (Chapter 4) — 12
    1.4.3 Interpersonal Communication and Support (Chapter 5) — 12
    1.4.4 Noticing Both Positives and Negatives (Chapter 6) — 12
    1.4.5 Embracing Change (Chapter 7) — 13
  1.5 Characteristics of the SHINE Framework — 14
    1.5.1 Theoretical Underpinnings — 14
    1.5.2 A Long-Term Habit-Building Model for Prevention — 16
    1.5.3 Less Is More — 17
  1.6 Summary — 17
  References — 17

xii CONTENTS

2 Distress and Psychopathology in the Context of Adversity and Resilience 29
2.1 *Distress and Psychopathology* 30
    2.1.1 *Acute Stress Disorder and Posttraumatic Stress Disorder* 30
    2.1.2 *Adjustment Disorder* 32
    2.1.3 *Prolonged Grief Disorder* 37
2.2 *Summary* 40
References 40

3 Strength-Based Habit-Building 47
3.1 *Virtue and Character Strengths* 48
    3.1.1 *Different Names, Same Three Strengths* 51
    3.1.2 *Assessment of Strengths in the SHINE Framework* 51
    3.1.3 *Character Strengths and Resilience* 52
3.2 *Vital Engagement = Flow + Meaning* 54
3.3 *Adaptive Habit-Building* 56
3.4 *Summary* 57
3.5 *Practical Applications* 57
    3.5.1 *Identify Your Character Strengths* 57
    3.5.2 *My Strengths for Overcoming Adversity* 60
    3.5.3 *Using Your Strengths in Daily Life* 60
    3.5.4 *Using Your Strength(s) in a Vital Engagement Activity to Create Habits* 61
References 62

4 Hopeful Thinking 67
4.1 *The Story of a High-Hope Person* 68
4.2 *The Adaptive Cognitive Triad of Hope* 68
4.3 *The Expanded Model of Hope* 69
4.4 *What Hope Is and Is Not?* 70
4.5 *Hope and Resilience* 73
    4.5.1 *High-Hope Individuals Are Better Prepared to Face the Unknown* 73
    4.5.2 *High-Hope Individuals Exhibit Resilience Even in Life-Threatening Situations* 74
    4.5.3 *High-Hope Individuals Are Sensitive to Both Positive and Negative Information in the Environment* 75

	4.5.4 High-Hope Individuals See Hope in Hopeless Situations	76
4.6	Summary	78
4.7	Practical Applications	78
	4.7.1 Measuring Hope	78
	4.7.2 Goal Setting	80
	4.7.3 Pathways (Waypower)	82
	4.7.4 Agency (Willpower)	84
	4.7.5 Cultivate Relationships Where You Can Get Functional and Emotional Support	86
References		86

5 Interpersonal Support and Communication — 93

5.1	Social Support and Adversity	93
5.2	Social Support in the SHINE Framework	95
5.3	Responding to Negative Experiences	97
	5.3.1 Prepare Yourself	97
	5.3.2 Find an Appropriate Place	98
	5.3.3 During the Conversation	98
	5.3.4 What You Can Offer	98
	5.3.5 Summary	98
5.4	Responding to Positive Experiences	99
5.5	Summary	101
5.6	Practical Applications	102
	5.6.1 Your Response Styles to Positive and Negative Experiences	102
	5.6.2 Tips on Practising the 4Ls and ACR	102
References		104

6 Noticing Both Positives and Negatives — 107

6.1	The Four Categories of Attention Deployment	108
6.2	Attentional Bias and Psychological Problems	110
6.3	Practical Applications	112
	6.3.1 A Starting Point	112
	6.3.2 Building a Bank Account of Good Things	112
	6.3.3 Savour Positive Experiences to Enhance Positive Attention	113
References		114

xiv CONTENTS

7 Embracing Change 117
7.1 *When Adversity Seems Never-Ending* 118
7.2 *Optimism* 118
7.3 *Explanatory Style* 118
7.4 *Rumination* 120
7.5 *Constructive Positive Changes* 122
    7.5.1 *The Five Dimensions of PTG* 123
    7.5.2 *Constructive Versus Illusory PTG* 124
    7.5.3 *Growth Versus Depreciation* 126
7.6 *Summary* 128
7.7 *Practical Applications* 128
    7.7.1 *Self-Serving Explanatory Style* 128
    7.7.2 *Constructive PTG: Expressive Versus Benefit-Finding Condition* 132
References 132

8 Epilogue 137
8.1 *Introduction* 137
    8.1.1 *The SHINE Framework Revisited* 138
    8.1.2 *Building Your Own Psychological Gymnasium* 140
    8.1.3 *Future Development of the SHINE Framework* 141
References 141

References 143

Index 175

List of Figures

Fig. 1.1	Possible responses to adversity	5
Fig. 1.2	The SHINE framework	13
Fig. 2.1	Cognitive triad of depression (Beck et al., 1979)	34
Fig. 2.2	Relationship between brooding, negative cognitive style, and depressive symptoms. "+" = significant positive relationship, ns = non-significant relationship. Adapted from Lo et al. (2008)	35
Fig. 2.3	The Chinese oracle character for "death" depicts a person crying next to the body of the deceased: The person has lost a loved one, leading to the emotional reactions of grief and mourning, which are the socially constructed ways of expressing grief (Cheung & Ho, 2004).	39
Fig. 3.1	The three core strengths of the BSS model (Ho et al., 2016)	51
Fig. 3.2	The quadrant model of flow shows the flow state occurring in high challenge and high skill situations	55
Fig. 3.3	Steps of the strength-based adaptive habit-building strategy of the SHINE framework	57
Fig. 4.1	The three cognitive components of hope proposed by Snyder (2000)	69
Fig. 4.2	The expanded model of hope proposed by Ho (2016)	71
Fig. 5.1	Learn, Look, Listen, and Link: The 4L principles of good communications based on PFA (World Health Organization et al., 2011)	99
Fig. 5.2	Ways of responding to positive and negative experiences	103

xvi   LIST OF FIGURES

Fig. 6.1	The four categories of attention deployment	109
Fig. 7.1	Optimistic versus pessimistic explanatory style	120
Fig. 7.2	Circular relationships between pessimistic explanatory style, brooding rumination, and depressive symptoms	121
Fig. 7.3	The five domains measured by the PTGI (Tedeschi & Calhoun, 1996)	124
Fig. 7.4	The inverted U-shaped relationship between PTG and PTD (Ho et al., 2021)	127
Fig. 8.1	The SHINE framework: A summary of key strategies	139

LIST OF TABLES

Table 3.1	The six virtues and 24 character strengths in positive psychology (Peterson & Seligman, 2004)	49
Table 3.2	The three strengths of the SHINE framework and their corresponding strengths in other three-dimensional models	52
Table 3.3	Brief Strength Scale (BSS-12) result	58
Table 3.4	Examples of using your strengths in daily life	61
Table 3.5	Use your strength(s) in a vital engagement activity to create habits	62
Table 4.1	Hope-based versus problem-focused strategies	72
Table 4.2	Interaction between hope and hopelessness on suicidal ideation, adapted from Huen et al. (2015)	77
Table 4.3	Hope profile by McDermott and Snyder (1999)	80
Table 5.1	Negative responses to negative experiences	96
Table 5.2	Active constructive communication matrix	100
Table 5.3	Examples of active constructive responses	101

xvii

CHAPTER 1

Resilience and SHINE

Abstract Resilience is characterised by positive adaptation to adversity. Adversity takes many forms, including catastrophic events, accidents, and daily hassles, and affects individuals from all walks of life. Positive adaptation involves the ability to bounce back or even thrive in the face of adversity. There are five possible responses to adversity: succumbing, survival with impairment, recovery, resistance, and thriving. The SHINE framework facilitates positive adaptation after trauma, including recovery, resistance, and thriving. It comprises five key elements—Strength-based habit-building, Hopeful thinking, Interpersonal communication and support, Noticing both positives and negatives, and Embracing change—designed to cultivate resilience through habitual practice. By integrating principles from cognitive and positive psychology, the framework equips individuals with practical strategies to enhance their resilience in the face of adversity. The chapter concludes by advocating for a simplified, preventive approach to resilience that is accessible to diverse populations.

Keywords Resilience · Adversity · Positive adaptation · Cognitive psychology · Positive psychology · Preventive approach · Conservation of resources

© The Author(s), under exclusive license to Springer Nature Switzerland AG 2025
S. M. Y. Ho, *The SHINE Framework*,
https://doi.org/10.1007/978-3-031-89106-9_1

1.1 Adversity and Resilience

In psychology, resilience can be conceptualised as a trait, a process, or an outcome (Cornwell et al., 2024; Herrman et al., 2011). The trait approach views resilience as a dispositional characteristic, while the process approach emphasises the dynamic and evolving ways individuals respond to adversity over time. In contrast, the outcome approach focuses on the end results of resilience, such as successful adaptation, recovery, or positive functioning despite challenges. This perspective acknowledges that resilience encompasses not only inherent qualities (traits) and ongoing efforts (processes) but also the achievement of positive outcomes in the face of adversity.

The SHINE resilience framework offers practical strategies to maintain positive functioning under adverse conditions, aligning well with the outcome approach. Hence, I adopt the outcome approach to conceptualise resilience in this book. Accordingly, resilience has two key elements: adversity and positive adaptation (Fletcher & Sarkar, 2013; Herrman et al., 2011; Shoychet et al., 2023).

Adversity is the first key element, which can be understood as a state of suffering and discomfort triggered by challenges, misfortunes, or potentially traumatic experiences (Jackson et al., 2007; Sisto et al., 2019). Different types of events can cause adversity. The most common events are catastrophic events, including natural disasters such as earthquakes, floods, heat waves, drought-induced famines, as well as major storms and man-caused disasters, such as nuclear meltdowns, wars, underwater oil fracking, and terrorism. Adversity caused by disasters is becoming more and more common these days. In 2022 alone, 387 natural disasters occurred worldwide, killing 30,704 people and affecting 185 million people (Centre for Research on the Epidemiology of Disasters, 2023). Other negative events, such as accidents and unemployment, can also cause adversity. In a year-long prospective study, Dorfman et al. (2022) identified seven types of adversity, namely (1) social conflict, (2) personal health (including mental health), (3) economic hardship, (4) daily hassles, (5) others' health, (6) academic/work setbacks, and (7) major trauma. Accordingly, every person can face adversity, irrespective of age, gender, nationality, or socioeconomic status. In fact, when I began writing this book, the world was just recovering from a mega-adversary situation due to the Coronavirus Disease 2019 (COVID-19) pandemic, which was classified by the World Health Organization (WHO) as a public health emergency of international concern from 30 January 2020 to 5 May 2023 (World Health Organization, 2023b). Although vulnerable and at-risk groups were more likely to be infected with COVID-19, we were all adversely affected by associated control measures such as face mask wearing, social distancing, and lockdown policies (stay-at-home orders, quarantines) (Famodile et al., 2023; Snook et al., 2023). A preliminary study of 1000 young adults reported that 69% of the sample had experienced at least one trauma in their lifetime and 21% had experienced one traumatic event in the past year alone (Norris, 1992). A recent study reported that 40% of children and 51% of youth referred to mental health clinics experienced four or more types of adversity (Meraj et al., 2023). These figures are likely to be much higher today because of the COVID-19 pandemic.

Accordingly, adversity does not apply to specific groups but affects people from all walks of life. This book prepares us for distress and hardship due to adverse external circumstances by cultivating ways to maintain our normal functioning or bounce back to our pre-adversary level of functioning afterwards. It aims primarily at a general audience interested in resilience and self-help. It also serves as a valuable resource for professionals and students in training, offering practical insights that can enhance their practice.

1.2 Positive Adaptation to Adversity

The second key element of resilience is positive adaptation. More than 20 years ago, Carver (1998) described four possible reactions to adversity. The first is *succumbing*, which represents a downward trajectory of deterioration, with the individual remaining in a continued impaired state of functioning after the adverse event. In the second possible outcome, the individual bounces back after a decline in daily functioning but cannot return to their pre-adversity level of functioning. In other words, the individual exhibits a *survival with impairment* outcome trajectory. In the final two possible outcomes, *resilience* and *thriving*, the individual returns to (resilience) or even exceeds (thriving) their pre-adversity level of functioning after a period of distress.

In Carver's (1998) above proposition, an adverse experience is demonstrated by a decrease in an individual's functioning; without this, the experience is not qualified as an adverse encounter. In later studies, Bonanno and colleagues (Bonanno, 2004a; Bonanno et al., 2005; Bonanno et al.,

2006) challenged this concept and reported that some people maintain their daily functioning without severe negative psychological reactions even after an extreme traumatic experience, such as 9/11 attack in New York. The authors called this pattern *resilience* and used the term *recovery* to label the trajectory pattern illustrated by an initial decline and then a return to the premorbid level of functioning (i.e. resilience in Carver's model). My collaborative studies with Bonanno (Bonanno et al., 2008) among survivors of severe acute respiratory syndrome infection in Hong Kong and people undergoing intrusive medical screening for colon cancer (Ho et al., 2010) also showed that some people can maintain their normal level of functioning after an adverse encounter. Other researchers (Hobfoll et al., 2009; Layne et al., 2007) have suggested that *resistance* may be a more appropriate term for Bonanno's no-symptom resilience pattern. Bonanno and Mancini (2012) seemed receptive to the suggestion and adopted *resilience–resistance* to label their original resilience pattern. Bonanno and his collaborators recently proposed a 'resilience quadrant' to classify the four outcome trajectories in their resilience research (Lunansky et al., 2024). The quadrant has two axes: (1) healthy versus dysfunctional and (2) stable versus unstable. Resilience is the healthy and stable domain of the resilience quadrant. The resilience quadrant can help improve our understanding and conceptualisation of resilience, which merits further investigation. Finally, Bonanno and colleagues (Bonanno, 2004a; Bonanno et al., 2006; Bonanno et al., 2007; Bonanno et al., 2008; Bonanno & Mancini, 2012) used potential traumatic events to frame their studies to address the concern that an event without resulting symptomatology or a decrease in functioning should not be considered a type of trauma or adversity in the first place.

There is another possible outcome in Carver's (1998) model called *thriving*. This outcome is sometimes referred to as posttraumatic growth (PTG) in the contemporary psychological literature based on the work of Tedeschi and colleagues (Kang et al., 2023; Tedeschi & Calhoun, 2004; Tedeschi et al., 1998a, 1998b). Chapter 7 of this book discusses PTG based on my research experience with Tedeschi and other collaborators (Cheng et al., 2018; Cheng et al., 2020; Ho, 2011; Ho & Cheng, 2023; Ho & Yu, 2010; Ho et al., 2008). It is important to acknowledge that authentic positive changes and growth during and after adversity should be viewed as a resilience outcome.

Figure 1.1 summarises the possible outcomes after adversity and the labels used in this book. The outcome patterns of recovery (i.e. symptoms

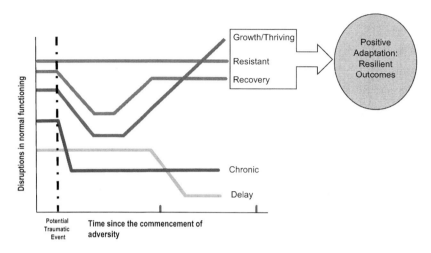

Fig. 1.1 Possible responses to adversity

followed by a return to pre-adversity level of functioning), resistance (i.e. a stable level of functioning despite adversity), and growth (i.e. an increase beyond the pre-adversity level of functioning) are all considered positive adaptation and hence relevant to resilience. The SHINE framework in this book aims to facilitate any of these three outcomes to increase resilience in the face of adversity.

1.3 Factors Promoting Resilience

Given the complexity of resilience concepts, a combination of neurobiological, psychological, and social factors contributes to it. We focus on factors from the psychosocial domain, such as personality traits and coping strategies, because they are more relevant to the SHINE framework of this book. However, neurobiological factors, such as genetic and epigenetic makeup, brain structure, and neurotransmitters, play an important role in resilience. Interested readers may refer to publications on this topic for further information (Ayash et al., 2023; Russo et al., 2012; L. Zhang et al., 2023).

1.3.1 Personality Traits

It is well established that an individual's personality has a significant effect on the onset of psychological disorders. For example, individuals with high trait anxiety are more likely than their counterparts to develop anxiety disorders (Gidron, 2013; Morales, 2012). Bar-Haim et al. (2007a) reported that individuals with high trait anxiety exhibited an attentional bias towards emotionally threatening stimuli and that this tendency was independent of whether the stimuli were perceived consciously or subliminally. Furthermore, neuroticism (Eysenck, 1994), a personality dimension characterised by emotional instability, is related to maladjustment to stress and adversity (Bagby & Parker, 2001; Muris et al., 2004; Nolan et al., 1998; Scheier et al., 1994; Teasdale & Dent, 1987). For instance, Zinbarg et al. (2023) assessed the personality of 342 subjects aged 18–19before the COVID-19 pandemic in January 2017 and their psychological reactions to it six times during the pandemic. They reported that neuroticism was related to maladaptive adjustments indicated by distress and fear across all waves of their study.

If personality factors are important in the onset of psychopathology, they should also play an important role in resilience in the face of adversity. Matthews et al. (2017) proposed a trait–stressor–outcome (TSO) model for resilience to highlight the role of personality traits in resilience. This model acknowledges that neuroticism is an important personality trait that affects resilience across settings. However, this single broad personality trait is unlikely to explain individual differences in resilience outcomes. The model proposes to include specialised resilience traits. Hardiness (Maddi & Kobasa, 1991) is a well-known example of such personality traits in the TSO model. Hardiness is represented by three core dispositional attitudes: *commitment*, characterised by an attitude of viewing life and daily activities as meaningful and purposeful; *control*, an appraisal of self-control over the outcome of events; and *challenge*, characterised by an attitude of viewing change and difficulty as an opportunity to learn and growth (Maddi, 1999). In adversity, hardiness is manifested by the courage and motivation individuals demonstrate to cope with difficulties by proactively solving problems and interacting with others through support and encouragement (Bartone et al., 2023; Maddi, 2002). In a seminal paper on resilience after loss and trauma, Bonanno (2004b) suggested that hardy people tend to appraise adversity and potentially traumatic events as less threatening and are therefore better able to demonstrate resilience. A meta-analysis of 180 studies showed that hardiness was a significant moderator between life stressors and adjustment outcomes and explained variance in health outcomes above and beyond neuroticism (Sinclair & Tetrick, 2000). In other words, hardy people are more likely than non-hardy people to exhibit resilience in the face of adversity.

1.3.2   *External and Internal Resources*

Psychological models focus primarily on individual factors such as personality traits. However, socioenvironmental factors play such an important role in resilience that understanding them is necessary to gain a complete picture of resilience (Collette & Ungar, 2020; Li et al., 2020). The conservation of resources (COR) model (Hobfoll, 1989; Hobfoll et al., 2018) is used to discuss factors in this domain.

In short, COR theory posits that all human beings strive to acquire and protect the resources they value most. Adversity threatens these precious resources and causes losses, leading to negative reactions such as depression and anxiety. Successful adjustment to adversity (i.e. resilience) relies on the conservation and replacement of existing valued resources despite losses resulting from adversity (Bonanno & Mancini, 2012; Hobfoll, 1989; Hobfoll et al., 2018). There are several categories of resources in this model, such as *physical objects* (e.g. houses, cars), *personal characteristics* (e.g. hardiness, self-esteem), *conditions* (e.g. marriage, occupational status), and *energies* (e.g. knowledge, memory). Disasters like hurricanes can destroy our house, physical disabilities after a traumatic accident can damage our self-esteem, an economic recession can make us redundant, and dementia can rob us of our memory and knowledge. Such resource losses impact our adjustment to adversity.

According to COR theory, resource loss has a greater effect on the outcomes of adversity than resource gain. Therefore, we need to invest in building resources during good times to reduce the impact of resource loss when adversity strikes. An example is saving money to prepare for a future loss of income due to unemployment or retirement (Hobfoll et al., 2015). Finally, the model suggests cognitive strategies such as shifting attention from losses to potential gains in adversity to help combat the negative effect of resource loss (Hobfoll, 1989). One example of this shift in focus is the attitude of hardy people who interpret difficulties as challenges. We will return to this strategy when discussing attentional bias in Chapter 6. In the 30 years since Hobfoll's (1989) first paper, a large body of research has supported the COR model in predicting adversity outcomes after stressful events (Bell et al., 2020; Benight et al., 1999; Bonanno et al., 2007). Recently, Banford Witting et al. (2023) conducted a longitudinal study of 535 heterosexual couples in the US at the onset of the COVID-19 pandemic in 2020, showing that, consistent with COR theory, greater resource loss, both within and between partners, significantly predicted higher levels of posttraumatic stress symptoms over time. Kelada et al. (2023) used the COR model to examine anxiety and depression in 7013 Israeli university students in 2021, again showing that resource loss was positively associated with psychological symptoms.

It should be noted that the COR model also includes personal factors such as self-esteem, although it places more emphasis on external resources. Next, we discuss some models of psychological resilience that focus more on individual factors related to resilience.

1.3.3   Dynamic Personal Factors

Unlike stable dispositional factors such as personality traits, dynamic personal factors are individual characteristics that can change over time and are sensitive to intervention (de Terte et al., 2014). In psychology, dynamic personal factors related to resilience can be categorised into stress coping and emotion regulation approaches. The stress coping approach focuses on adaptive coping strategies in stressful situations, while the emotion regulation approach focuses on individuals' strategies to control emotions in stressful encounters. Both approaches generate key strategies and intervention programmes to promote positive adaptation to adversity. For example, coping effectiveness training for HIV + adults (Chesney et al., 2003) is based on the transactional model of stress (Folkman, 1984; Lazarus & Folkman, 1984; Park & Folkman, 1997). Similarly, mindfulness-based emotion regulation training has been developed with effective outcomes (Raugh & Strauss, 2023).

An example of a resilience model is the model proposed by de Terte et al. (2014), who selected *optimism, adaptive coping, adaptive health practices*, and *social support* from their original five-part model (de Terte et al., 2009) and grouped these factors into three components to form a three-part model (3-PR) of resilience. The three components are cognitions (optimism, adaptive coping), environment (social support), and behaviours (adaptive health practices).

Optimism is an individual's attitude of believing that good things will happen in the future (Scheier & Carver, 1985). Accordingly, optimism is a dispositional construct (Scheier & Carver, 1988), although people can learn to become more optimistic, which makes it appropriate to be considered a dynamic personal factor (Seligman, 1990). The next two factors in the 3-PR, adaptive coping and health practices, introduced below, are dynamic factors that can be cultivated through individual efforts.

There are two well-known approaches to categorising coping strategies:

a. Problem-focused coping (e.g. confronting, planful problem-solving) versus emotion-focused coping (e.g. distancing, escape-avoidance, positive reappraisal) (Folkman et al., 1986; Folkman et al., 1986) and
b. Active coping (engagement) versus avoidance coping (disengagement) (Carver & Connor-Smith, 2010).

Problem-focused and active coping strategies are generally expected to be related to better adjustment to adversity than emotion-focused and avoidance coping. Carver and Connor-Smith (2010) conducted a meta-analysis and showed that active coping was associated with positive resilience constructs, such as optimism, extraversion, conscientiousness, and openness, while avoidance coping was related to neuroticism. In contrast, Lazarus and Folkman (1984) proposed the goodness-of-fit hypothesis and stated that there are no adaptive or maladaptive coping strategies. The controllability of an event moderates adaptiveness. In uncontrollable situations, emotion-focused coping strategies may be more effective than problem-focused strategies. In contrast, problem-focused coping should lead to better outcomes than emotion-focused coping in controllable situations (Forsythe & Compas, 1987; Park et al., 2001).

In my studies of coping with cancer (Ho et al., 2013; Ho et al., 2003), I administered the Mini-Mental Adjustment to Cancer Scale (Mini-MAC) (Watson et al., 1988; Watson et al., 1994) to Chinese cancer survivors and found that cognitive avoidance, an avoidance coping strategy, as measured by the Mini-MAC, was positively correlated with fighting spirit (an active coping strategy) but had no significant relationships with depression and anxiety. Cognitive avoidance measures people's tendency to avoid actively thinking about their cancer experience. It differs from denial, which represents people's rejection of the cancer diagnosis and its negative impact

(Ho et al., 2003). Accordingly, cognitive avoidance is an emotion-focused coping strategy and may have a positive function in psycho-oncology, as proposed by the goodness-of-fit hypothesis (Lazarus & Folkman, 1984). My studies also revealed an interesting finding: fatalism combined with fighting spirit to form an active coping strategy to cope with the adversity brought by cancer. A similar finding that fatalism was positively associated with better outcomes was obtained in a more recent 7-year, three-wave longitudinal study of 248 women with breast cancer in Taiwan (Cheng et al., 2021). Fatalism may refer to the concept that current sufferings are the consequences of past actions or are due to predestined affinities or relationships. Fatalism helps people to attribute their suffering to external causal factors and make adversity more bearable (Ho et al., 2003). In summary, different coping strategies can facilitate resilience depending on the nature of the adversity and the sociocultural context.

The next component of the 3-PR is adaptive health practices, which include exercise, nutrition, substance use, and self-compassion. Perhaps more appropriately, some authors have sometimes called this component "self-care behaviour" (Chettiar & Terte, 2022). Self-care behaviours are preventive practices aimed at managing and maintaining one's psychological, social, and physical well-being (Chin et al., 2021). Habitual practice of self-care behaviours can cultivate resources (better health and emotion regulation, more friends) to cope with adversity, leading to greater resilience (Abdollahi et al., 2022).

The final element is social support, which comes from two sources: (1) family and friends and (2) work colleagues and supervisors (de Terte et al., 2014). Social support can serve both emotional and instrumental functions. Emotional social support fulfils an affect regulation function (e.g. a listening ear), while instrumental social support provides concrete help in solving problems (e.g. temporary accommodation) (Declercq et al., 2007). Furthermore, giving and receiving social support can contribute to resilience in the face of adversity (Shakespeare-Finch & Obst, 2011).

Other more comprehensive models containing a variety of factors have been proposed. For instance, Lahad et al. (2013) proposed an integrated model of resilience called BASIC Ph, which includes 6 elements: belief (B), affect (A), social (S), imagination (I), cognitive (C), and physical (Ph). The researchers reviewed more than 30 studies to identify factors that promote resilience and integrate them into their BASIC Ph framework (Lahad et al., 2013). The BASIC Ph model is comprehensive and provides practitioners with the flexibility to design an intervention plan. A survey of the factors in the BASIC Ph framework suggested that it includes the key factors, such as optimism, active coping, and social support, mentioned in other models and discussed above. Similarly, Southwick et al. (2023) proposed 10 resilience-promoting factors, namely (1) an optimistic belief in a better future, (2) an attitude to confront fears and treat them as a challenge, (3) a tendency to seek, accept, and provide social support, (4) a habit of learning from role models, (5) an inner moral compass, (6) stable religious or spiritual practices, (7) attention to health and well-being, (8) curiosity and a habit of learning new things, (9) flexibility to cope with problems and show acceptance when necessary, and (10) the search for meaning and growth during and after adversity.

The above models provide useful information to inform resilience promotion and intervention. Several common characteristics of these models motivate the development of the SHINE framework in this book. First, many models are comprehensive and contain various factors that may be difficult for people without a healthcare background to follow. Second, many models focus on developing intervention programmes after the onset of adversity rather than providing primary prevention training before adversity. Finally, many models are developed in specific populations, such as disciplinary workers, adolescents, and people with physical illnesses (Herrman et al., 2011). After the COVID-19 pandemic and the many natural and man-made disasters that have occurred around the world in recent years, we need a simple and easy-to-use resilience framework (i.e. with few dynamic personal factors) focused on primary prevention (i.e. building resilience-promoting factors for future adversity). I also agree with Herman et al.'s (2011) call for a generic resilience framework that can be applied to different groups of people in various cultures and across different types of adversity. Accordingly, the SHINE framework is proposed in this book.

1.4 The SHINE Framework

The SHINE framework contains five elements selected based on my clinical practical and research experience. These five elements are *Strength-based habit-building*, *Hopeful thinking*, *Interpersonal communication and support*, *Noticing both positives and negatives*, and *Embracing change*.

1.4.1 Strength-Based Habit-Building (Chapter 3)

In normal life, before adversity, we can find activities to exercise our strengths, do them regularly, and turn them into habits. It would be better if these activities could give us a "flow" experience. In adversity, we can exercise our strengths to overcome difficulties and obtain regular "time-off" periods to do something we are good at and enjoy. Many of us discover our strengths in adversity, that is, something we are good at. After adversity, we should engage in activities to develop these strengths and prepare for future adversity.

1.4.2 Hopeful Thinking (Chapter 4)

Snyder's cognitive theory of hope consists of three components (Snyder et al., 2005): goal, willpower, and waypower. In a previous study, I extended Snyder's model by adding goal disengagement–reengagement and sub-goaling strategies to cope with adversity (Ho, 2016a). Hopeful cognition helps us to see the future beyond adversity and enables us to plan for better outcomes after adversity.

1.4.3 Interpersonal Communication and Support (Chapter 5)

Social interaction and support are essential elements in many models of resistance and resilience. We should build (and rebuild) positive and nurturing relationships in the face of adversity.

1.4.4 Noticing Both Positives and Negatives (Chapter 6)

People who focus on the negative are prone to depression and anxiety. However, seeing environmental threats is essential to our survival and well-being. People who only see the positive can create an illusory world that will harm them in the long run. Attending to and remembering both the positive and negative events in our lives is essential to building resilience.

1.4.5 Embracing Change (Chapter 7)

The world will inevitably change. A pearl of wisdom from the ancient Chinese *Book of Changes* teaches us to embrace change and experience the flow of the positive and negative aspects of life cycles: yin and yang.

The above five elements constitute the SHINE framework (see Fig. 1.2). I discuss each of them in more detail in the following chapters.

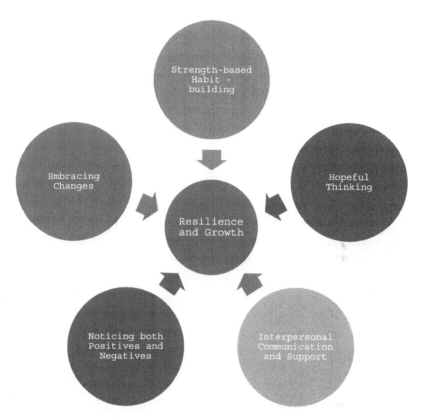

Fig. 1.2 The SHINE framework

1.5 Characteristics of the SHINE Framework

1.5.1 Theoretical Underpinnings

The five elements of the SHINE framework are based on two psychological approaches: cognitive theory and positive psychology.

a. Elements of Cognitive Psychology

Cognitive theory emphasises the role of cognition, accessible in the conscious awareness domain, in affecting psychopathology and adjustment outcomes (Dobson & Kazantzis, 2024). The conventional cognitive model is based on a realistic model of human functioning, which posits that adaptive functioning is achieved through accurate perception and interpretation of events in the objective world without distortion (Dobson, 2012). All individuals have unique cognitive structures, often called "schemas," developed based on their experiences and knowledge (Beck & Haigh, 2014). The cognitive triad of depression mentioned in Chapter 2 (see Fig. 1.2) is an example of schemas. Schemas play an active role in information processing: we attend to and remember new information that aligns with our schema (Dobson, 2012). Accordingly, there are two ways to facilitate resilience. First, we build an adaptive schema to prepare for adversity. The hopeful thinking element of the SHINE framework is an adaptive schema (Chapter 4). Second, we reduce biased attention to either positive or negative elements to achieve a more balanced (and hence more accurate) perception of our environment. The Noticing both Positives and Negatives element of the SHINE framework aims to accomplish this (Chapter 6).

The cognitive approach has recently integrated constructivism to create CBT's "third wave" (Kennedy & Pearson, 2021; Moorey & Greer, 2012). Unlike the conventional philosophy of absolute reality in CBT, constructivists posit that there is no such thing in the external world. The idiosyncratic meaning attached to an experience creates a subjective "reality" specific to an individual (Dobson & Kazantzis, 2024). In other words, if 100 people are affected by the same major disaster, there will be 100 external realities related to the disaster, depending on each individual's unique meaning assigned to it. Teasdale (1983) argued that the negative meaning assigned to a negative experience during adversity, but not the negative experience itself, is the main factor leading to non-resilience. The Embracing Change element of the SHINE framework (Chapter 7) aims to cultivate a mindful attitude of acceptance towards negative experiences and changes, fitting into the third wave of the CBT approach. It is worth mentioning that the constructivist approach adopted by the third wave of CBT is consistent with the philosophy of Zen Buddhism (Gash, 2016) and may be familiar to people of Asian cultural background.

b. Elements of Positive Psychology

The SHINE framework consists of two elements of positive psychology: Strength-based Habit-building and Interpersonal Communication and Support. Positive psychology is a movement initiated by Seligman to move psychology towards a balanced approach aimed at understanding strengths as well as weaknesses, at building the best things in life as well as repairing the worst, and at making the lives of normal people fulfilling as well as healing pathology (Seligman & Csikszentmihalyi, 2000). Positive psychology studies the conditions and processes that contribute to the optimal functioning of people, groups, and institutions (Gable & Haidt, 2005). The Strength-based Habit-building element of the SHINE framework adapts the two core concepts of character strengths (Peterson & Seligman, 2004) and flow (Csikszentmihalyi, 1994) from positive psychology.

Social support plays an important role in almost all resilience models, such as the 3-PR model (de Terte et al., 2014) and the BASIC Ph framework (Lahad et al., 2013). The SHINE framework cannot be complete without including this element. Rather than repeating what other models have covered, the SHINE framework adapts the active constructive responding (ACR) framework (Gable et al., 2006; Gable et al., 2018) from positive psychology to discuss ways to respond to positive experiences during adversity to increase resilience. In a meta-analysis of 51 studies using a positive psychology intervention to alleviate depressive symptoms in 4266 participants, hope, strengths, and gratitude were identified as the most effective treatment strategies (Sin & Lyubomirsky, 2009). The SHINE framework contains all three strategies.

1.5.2 A Long-Term Habit-Building Model for Prevention

The resilience models mentioned above, including the 3-PR model (de Terte et al., 2014), the BASIC Ph framework (de Terte et al., 2014), and to a lesser extent the 10-factor model of Southwick and Charney (2022), are intervention models; that is, they lead to the development of manualised treatment interventions for people suffering from psychological problems after adversity. Instead, the SHINE framework is a type of primary prevention (Reisig & Wildner, 2008), which, according to the WHO, consists of actions aimed at avoiding the manifestation of a disease (World Health Organization, 2024). Vaccination, such as that against COVID-19, is a common example of primary prevention. In stress management, primary prevention builds coping skills to prevent distress and negative reactions in stressful situations (Quick et al., 2013). In the context of resilience, the SHINE elements facilitate the resilience trajectories of resistance, recovery, and growth. As a primary prevention approach, the SHINE framework is a population-based intervention for ordinary people to prepare for future adversity. The strategies described in the Practical Applications sections of this book may not help those who have already experienced psychological disorders or symptoms due to adversity or other factors.

One of the important characteristics of the SHINE framework is that it uses a habit-building approach. I built the first prison-based psychological gymnasium (PSY GYM) for female offenders in Hong Kong (Mak et al., 2018). In a physical gym, individuals exercise regularly to strengthen different body parts to achieve physical fitness. After acquiring the necessary skills, individuals can practise independently and transform these new skills into habits. Similarly, PSY GYM equips individuals with the mental skills necessary for psychological well-being. Individuals continually practise the skills they learn through PSY GYM to transform them into automatic, habitual activities for mood management and positive living. The SHINE framework adopts the PSY GYM approach. In essence, all strategies described in the Practical Applications sections of this book require consistent long-term practice to turn them into automatic habits of responding to adversity before they can produce the desirable effects.

All elements of the SHINE framework are individual resources in the COR resilience model mentioned in Sect. 2.2 (Hobfoll, 1989; Hobfoll et al., 2015; Hobfoll et al., 2018). Consistent with the COR model, the SHINE framework promotes investment in resource building to reduce the negative effect of resource loss in the face of adversity. COR theory states that long-term effort is required to cultivate resilient resources, consistent with the habit-building PSY GYM approach of the SHINE framework.

1.5.3 Less Is More

Last but not least, the SHINE framework is not a comprehensive model of resilience. It only captures factors that effectively facilitate resilience based on my research and practical experience. I believe that a simple model that can be applied to the general public across the lifespan is important to prepare for potential disasters and adversities in the future.

1.6 Summary

Resilience involves the outcome trajectories of resistance, recovery, and growth. The SHINE framework aims to develop habitual skills to facilitate resilience in the face of adversity. It consists of five elements: Strength-based habit-building, Hopeful thinking, Interpersonal communication and support, Noticing both positives and negatives, and Embracing change. These elements are based on cognitive and positive psychology theories. It uses a PSY GYM approach to promote the cultivation of psychological resources through regular long-term practice to transform skills into automatic habitual responses to combat adversity.

References

Abdollahi, A., Alsaikhan, F., Nikolenko, D. A., Al-Gazally, M. E., Mahmudiono, T., Allen, K. A., & Abdullaev, B. (2022). Self-care behaviors mediates the relationship between resilience and quality of life in breast cancer patients. *BMC Psychiatry, 22*(1), 825. https://doi.org/10.1186/s12888-022-04470-5

Ayash, S., Lingner, T., Ramisch, A., Ryu, S., Kalisch, R., Schmitt, U., & Müller, M. B. (2023). Fear circuit–based neurobehavioral signatures mirror resilience to chronic social stress in mouse. In *PNAS Proceedings of the National Academy of Sciences of the United States of America* (Vol. 120, No. 17, pp. 1–7). https://doi.org/10.1073/pnas.2205576120

Bagby, R. M., & Parker, J. D. (2001). Relation of rumination and distraction with neuroticism and extraversion in a sample of patients with major depression. *Cognitive Therapy and Research, 25*(1), 91–102. https://doi.org/10.1023/A:1026430900363

Banford Witting, A., Tambling, R., & Hobfoll, S. E. (2023). Resource loss, gain, and traumatic stress in couples during COVID-19. *Psychological Trauma: Theory, Research, Practice, and Policy, 15*(3), 502–510. https://doi.org/10.1037/tra0001276

Bar-Haim, Y., Lamy, D., Pergamin, L., Bakermans-Kranenburg, M. J., & van Ijzendoorn, M. H. (2007). Threat-related attentional bias in anxious and nonanxious individuals: A meta-analytic study. *Psychological Bulletin, 133*(1), 1–24. https://doi.org/10.1037/0033-2909.133.1.1

Bartone, P. T., McDonald, K., Hansma, B. J., Stermac-Stein, J., Escobar, E. M. R., Stein, S. J., & Ryznar, R. (2023). Development and validation of an improved hardiness measure: The hardiness resilience gauge. *European Journal of Psychological Assessment, 39*(3), 222–239. https://doi.org/10.1027/1015-5759/a000709

Beck, A. T., & Haigh, E. A. P. (2014). Advances in cognitive theory and therapy: The generic cognitive model. *Annual Review of Clinical Psychology, 10*, 1–24. https://doi.org/10.1146/annurev-clinpsy-032813-153734

Bell, T. R., Langhinrichsen-Rohling, J., & Selwyn, C. N. (2020). Conservation of resources and suicide proneness after oilrig disaster. *Death Studies, 44*(1), 48–57. https://doi.org/10.1080/07481187.2018.1521885

Benight, C. C., Swift, E., Sanger, J., Smith, A., & Zeppelin, D. (1999). Coping self-efficacy as a mediator of distress following a natural disaster. *Journal of Applied Social Psychology, 29*(12), 2443–2464. https://doi.org/10.1111/j.1559-1816.1999.tb00120.x

Bonanno, G. A. (2004a). Loss, trauma, and human resilience. Have we underestimated the human capacity to thrive after extremely aversive events? *American Psychologist, 59*(1), 20–28. https://doi.org/10.1037/0003-066X.59.1.20

Bonanno, G. A. (2004b). Loss, trauma, and human resilience: Have we underestimated the human capacity to thrive after extremely aversive events? *The American Psychologist, 59*, 20–28. https://doi.org/10.1037/0003-066X.59.1.20

Bonanno, G. A., & Mancini, A. D. (2012). Beyond resilience and PTSD: Mapping the heterogeneity of responses to potential trauma. *Psychological Trauma: Theory, Research, Practice, and Policy, 4*(1), 74–83. https://doi.org/10.1037/a0017829

Bonanno, G. A., Galea, S., Bucciarelli, A., & Vlahov, D. (2006). Psychological resilience after disaster: New York City in the aftermath of the September 11th terrorist attack. *Psychological Science, 17*, 181–186. https://doi.org/10.1111/j.1467-9280.2006.01682.x

Bonanno, G. A., Galea, S., Bucciarelli, A., & Vlahov, D. (2007). What predicts psychological resilience after disaster? The role of demographics, resources, and life stress. *Journal of Consulting and Clinical Psychology, 75*(5), 671–682. https://doi.org/10.1037/0022-006X.75.5.671

Bonanno, G. A., Ho, S. M. Y., Chan, J., Kwong, R. S. Y., Cheung, C. K. Y., Wong, C. P. Y., & Wong, V. C. W. (2008). Psychological resilience and dysfunction among hospitalized survivors of the SARS epidemic in Hong Kong: A latent class approach. *Health Psychology*, *27*(5), 659–667. https://doi.org/10.1037/0278-6133.27.5.659

Bonanno, G. A., Rennicke, C., & Dekel, S. (2005). Self-enhancement among high-exposive survivors of the September 11th terrorist attack: Resilience or social maladjustment? *Journal of Personality and Social Psychology*, *88*(6), 984–998. https://doi.org/10.1037/0022-3514.88.6.984

Carver, C. S. (1998). Resilence and thriving: Issues, models, and linkages. *Journal of Social Issues*, *54*(2), 245–266. https://doi.org/10.1111/0022-4537.641998064

Carver, C. S., & Connor-Smith, J. (2010). Personality and coping. *Annual Review of Psychology*, *61*, 679–704. https://doi.org/10.1146/annurev.psych.093008.100352

Centre for Research on the Epidemiology of Disasters. (2023). *2022 Disasters in numbers: Climate in action*. C. f. R. o. t. E. o. Disasters. https://www.emdat.be/publications/

Cheng, C. T., Ho, S. M. Y., Hou, Y. C., Lai, Y., & Wang, G. L. (2018). Constructive, illusory, and distressed posttraumatic growth among survivors of breast cancer: A 7-year growth trajectory study. *Journal of Health Psychology*. https://doi.org/10.1177/1359105318793199

Cheng, C.-T., Ho, S. M. Y., Lai, Y., Zhang, Q., & Wang, G.-L. (2021). Coping profiles predict long-term anxiety trajectory in breast cancer survivors. *Supportive Care in Cancer*. https://doi.org/10.1007/s00520-020-05936-6

Cheng, C.-T., Wang, G. L., & Ho, S. M. Y. (2020). The relationship between types of posttraumatic growth and prospective psychological adjustment in women with breast cancer: A follow-up study. *Psychooncology*, *29*, 586–588. https://doi.org/10.1002/pon.5312

Chesney, M. A., Chambers, D. B., Taylor, J. M., Johnson, L. M., & Folkman, S. (2003). Coping effectiveness training for men living with HIV: Results from a randomized clinical trial testing a group-based intervention. *Psychosomatic Medicine*, *65*(6), 1038–1046. https://doi.org/10.1097/01.PSY.0000097344.78697.ED

Chettiar, S., & Terte, I. d. (2022). *The psychological resilience treatment manual: An evidence-based intervention approach*. Taylor & Francis Group. http://ebookcentral.proquest.com/lib/cityuhk/detail.action?docID=6939704

Chin, C. H., Tseng, L. M., Chao, T. C., Wang, T. J., Wu, S. F., & Liang, S. Y. (2021). Self-care as a mediator between symptom-management self-efficacy and quality of life in women with breast cancer. *PLoS ONE*, *16*(2), e0246430. https://doi.org/10.1371/journal.pone.0246430

Collette, A., & Ungar, M. (2020). Resilience of individuals, families, communities, and environments: Mutually dependent protective processes and complex systems. In M. Ochs, M. Borcsa, & J. Schweitzer (Eds.), *Systemic research in individual, couple, and family therapy and counseling* (pp. 97–111). Springer International Publishing. https://doi.org/10.1007/978-3-030-36560-8_6

Cornwell, H., Toschi, N., Hamilton-Giachritsis, C., Staginnus, M., Smaragdi, A., Gonzalez-Madruga, K., Mackes, N., Rogers, J., Martinelli, A., Kohls, G., Raschle, N. M., Konrad, K., Stadler, C., Freitag, C. M., De Brito, S. A., & Fairchild, G. (2024). Identifying cortical structure markers of resilience to adversity in young people using surface-based morphometry. *Social Cognitive and Affective Neuroscience, 19*(1). https://doi.org/10.1093/scan/nsae006

Csikszentmihalyi, M. (1994). *Flow and the foundations of positive psychology. The collected works of mihaly csikszentmihalyi.* Springer. https://doi.org/10.1007/978-94-017-9088-8

de Terte, I., Becker, J., & Stephens, C. (2009). An integrated model for understanding and developing resilience in the face of adverse events. *Journal of Pacific Rim Psychology, 3*(1), 20–26. https://doi.org/10.1375/prp.3.1.20

de Terte, I., Stephens, C., & Huddleston, L. (2014). The development of a three part model of psychological resilience. *Stress and Health, 30*(5), 416–424. https://doi.org/10.1002/smi.2625

Declercq, F., Vanheule, S., Markey, S., & Willemsen, J. (2007). Posttraumatic distress in security guards and the various effects of social support. *Journal of Clinical Psychology, 63*(12), 1239–1246. https://doi.org/10.1002/jclp.20426

Dobson, K. S. (2012). Theory. In *Cognitive therapy* (pp. 11–27, 154 Pages). American Psychological Association. https://doi.org/10.1037/17334-003

Dobson, K. S., & Kazantzis, N. (2024). Cognitive theory in psychotherapy. In F. T. L. Leong, J. L. Callahan, J. Zimmerman, M. J. Constantino, & C. F. Eubanks (Eds.), *APA handbook of psychotherapy: Theory-driven practice and disorder-driven practice* (Vol. 1, pp. 175–190, 553 Pages). American Psychological Association. https://doi.org/10.1037/0000353-011

Dorfman, A., Moscovitch, D. A., Chopik, W. J., & Grossmann, I. (2022). None the wiser: Year-long longitudinal study on effects of adversity on wisdom. *European Journal of Personality, 36*(4), 559–575. https://doi.org/10.1177/08902070211014057

Eysenck, M. W. (1994). *Individual differences: Normal and abnormal.* Lawrence Erlbaum Associates.

Famodile, E., Stovin, H., & Sumilo, D. (2023). *Impact of COVID-19 (2023)* https://www.nottinghaminsight.org.uk/themes/health-and-wellbeing/joint-strategic-needs-assessment/adults/impact-of-covid-19-2023/

Fletcher, D., & Sarkar, M. (2013). Psychological resilience: A review and critique of definitions, concepts, and theory. *European Psychologist*, *18*(1), 12–23. https://doi.org/10.1027/1016-9040/a000124

Folkman, S. (1984). Personal control and stress and coping processes: A theoretical analysis. *Journal of Personality and Social Psychology*, *4*, 839–852. https://doi.org/10.1037/0022-3514.46.4.839

Folkman, S., Lazarus, R. S., Cruen, R. J., & DeLongis, A. (1986). Appraisal, coping, health status, and psychological symptoms. *Journal of Personality and Social Psychology*, *50*, 571–579. https://doi.org/10.1037/0022-3514.50.3.571

Folkman, S., Lazarus, R. S., Dunkel-Schetter, C., DeLongis, A., & Gruen, R. (1986). The dynamics of a stressful encounter: Cognitive appraisal, coping, and encounter outcomes. *Journal of Personality and Social Psychology*, *50*, 992–1003. https://doi.org/10.1037/0022-3514.50.5.992

Forsythe, C. J., & Compas, B. E. (1987). Interaction of cognitive appraisals of stressful events and coping: Testing the goodness of fit hypothesis. *Cognitive Therapy and Research*, *11*(4), 473–485. https://doi.org/10.1007/BF0117 5357

Gable, S. L., & Haidt, J. (2005). What (and why) is positive psychology? *Review of General Psychology*, *9*(2), 103–110. https://doi.org/10.1037/1089-2680. 9.2.10

Gable, S. L., Gonzaga, G. C., & Strachman, A. (2006). Will you be there for me when things go right? Supportive responses to positive event disclosures. *Journal of Personality and Social Psychology*, *91*(5), 904–917. https://doi.org/10.1037/0022-3514.91.5.904

Gable, S. L., Reis, H. T., Impett, E. A., & Asher, E. R. (2018). What do you do when things go right? The intrapersonal and interpersonal benefits of sharing positive events. In H. Reis (Ed.), *Relationships, well-being and behaviour: Selected works of Harry Reis* (1st ed., pp. 39). Routledge. https://doi.org/10.4324/9780203732496

Gash, H. (2016). Zen and constructivist thinking. In G. E. Lasker & K. Hiwaki (Eds.), Personal and Spiritual Development in the World of Cultural Diversity. Vol XIII. (pp. 23-27). *International Institute for Advanced Studies*.

Gidron, Y. (2013). Trait anxiety. In M. D. Gellman & J. R. Turner (Eds.), *Encyclopedia of Behavioral Medicine* (pp. 1989–1989). Springer New York. https://doi.org/10.1007/978-1-4419-1005-9_1539

Herrman, H. M. D., Stewart, D. E. M. D., Diaz-Granados, N. M., Berger, E. L. D., Jackson, B. P., & Yuen, T. B. (2011). What is resilience? *Canadian Journal of Psychiatry*, *56*(5), 258–265. https://doi.org/10.1177/070674371 105600504

Ho, S. M. Y. (2011). Resilience, growth, and distress after a traumatic experience. In K. K. Y. Wu, C. S. K. Tang, & E. Y. S. Leung (Eds.), *Healing trauma: A professionals' guide in Hong Kong* (pp. 89–104). HKU Press.

Ho, S. M. Y. (2016a). Adapting goals. In L. Bormans (Ed.), *The world book of hope: The source of success, strength and happiness* (pp. 355–358). Lannoo.

Ho, S. M. Y., & Cheng, C.-T. (2023). Illusory versus constructive posttraumatic growth in cancer. In R. Berger (Ed.), *The Routledge international handbook of posttraumatic growth* (pp. 21–28). Routledge. https://doi.org/10.4324/9781032208688-4

Ho, S. M. Y., & Yu, B. (2010). Posttraumatic growth in Chinese culture. In T. Weiss & R. Berger (Eds.), *Posttraumatic growth: A cross-cultural perspective* (pp. 147–156). Wiley.

Ho, S. M. Y., Chu, K. W., & Yiu, J. (2008). The relationship between explanatory style and posttraumatic growth after bereavement in a non-clinical sample. *Death Studies, 32*(5), 461–478. https://doi.org/10.1080/07481180801974760

Ho, S. M. Y., Ho, J. W. C., Bonanno, G. A., Chu, A. T. W., & Chan, E. M. S. (2010). Hopefulness predicts resilience after hereditary colorectal cancer genetic testing: A prospective outcome trajectories study. *BMC Cancer, 10*, 279. https://doi.org/10.1186/1471-2407-10-279

Ho, S. M. Y., Law, L. S. C., Wang, G.-L., Shih, S.-M., Hsu, S.-H., & Hou, Y.-C. (2013). Psychometric analysis of the Chinese version of the posttraumatic growth inventory with cancer patients in Hong Kong and Taiwan. *Psycho-Oncology, 22*(3), 175–179. https://doi.org/10.1002/pon.3024

Ho, S. M. Y., Wong, K. F., Chan, C. L.-w., Watson, M., & Tsui, Y. K. Y. (2003). Psychometric properties of the Chinese version of the Mini Mental Adjustment to Cancer (Mini-MAC) scale. *Psycho-Oncology, 12*(6), 547–556. https://doi.org/10.1002/pon.3024

Hobfoll, S. E. (1989). Conservation of resources: A new attempt at conceptualizing stress. *American Psychologist, 44*(3), 513–524. https://doi.org/10.1037/0003-066X.44.3.513

Hobfoll, S. E., Halbesleben, J., Neveu, J.-P., & Westman, M. (2018). Conservation of resources in the organizational context: The reality of resources and their consequences. *Annual Review of Organizational Psychology and Organizational Behavior, 5*(1), 103–128. https://doi.org/10.1146/annurev-orgpsych-032117-104640

Hobfoll, S. E., Palmieri, P. A., Johnson, R. J., Canetti-Nisim, D., Hall, B. J., & Galea, S. (2009). Trajectories of resilience, resistance, and distress during ongoing terrorism: The case of Jews and Arabs in Israel. *Journal of Consulting and Clinical Psychology, 77*(1), 138–148.https://doi.org/10.1037/a0014360

Hobfoll, S. E., Stevens, N. R., & Zalta, A. K. (2015). Expanding the science of resilience: Conserving resources in the aid of adaptation. *Psychological Inquiry*, *26*(2), 174–180. https://doi.org/10.1080/1047840x.2015.1002377

Jackson, D., Firtko, A., & Edenborough, M. (2007). Personal resilience as a strategy for surviving and thriving in the face of workplace adversity: a literature review. *Journal of Advanced Nursing*, *60*(1), 1–9. https://doi.org/10.1111/j.1365-2648.2007.04412.x

Kang, H., Na, P. J., Fischer, I. C., Tsai, J., Tedeschi, R. G., & Pietrzak, R. H. (2023). Pandemic-related posttraumatic psychological growth in U.S. military veterans: A 3-year, nationally representative, longitudinal study. *Psychiatry Research*, *326*, 1–9. https://doi.org/10.1016/j.psychres.2023.115370

Kelada, L., Schiff, M., Gilbar, O., Pat-Horenczyk, R., & Benbenishty, R. (2023). University students' psychological distress during the COVID-19 pandemic: A structural equation model of the role of resource loss and gain. *Journal of Community Psychology*, *51*(7), 3012–3028. https://doi.org/10.1002/jcop.23076

Kennedy, F., & Pearson, D. (2021). *Integrating CBT and third wave therapies: Distinctive features*. Routledge/Taylor & Francis Group.

Lahad, M., Shacham, M., & Ayalon, O. (2013). *The "BASIC Ph" model of coping and resiliency: Theory, research and cross-cultural application*. Jessica Kingsley Publishers.

Layne, C. M., Warren, J. S., Watson, P. J., & Shalev, A. Y. (2007). Risk, vulnerability, resistance, and resilience: Toward an integrative conceptualization of posttraumatic adaptation. In *Handbook of PTSD: Science and practice* (pp. 497–520). The Guilford Press.

Lazarus, P. S., & Folkman, S. (1984). *Stress, appraisal, and coping*. Springer Publishing Company.

Li, T., Dong, Y., & Liu, Z. (2020). A review of social-ecological system resilience: Mechanism, assessment and management. *Science of The Total Environment*, *723*, 138113. https://doi.org/10.1016/j.scitotenv.2020.138113

Lunansky, G., Bonanno, G. A., Blanken, T. F., van Borkulo, C. D., Cramer, A. O. J., & Borsboom, D. (2024). Bouncing back from life's perturbations: Formalizing psychological resilience from a complex systems perspective. *Psychological Review*. https://doi.org/10.1037/rev0000497

Maddi, S. R. (1999). The personality construct of hardiness: I. Effects on experiencing, coping, and strain. *Consulting Psychology Journal: Practice and Research*, *51*(2), 83–94. https://doi.org/10.1037/1061-4087.51.2.83

Maddi, S. R. (2002). The story of hardiness: Twenty years of theorizing, research, and practice. *Consulting Psychology Journal: Practice and Research*, *54*(3), 173–185. https://doi.org/10.1037/1061-4087.54.3.173

Maddi, S. R., & Kobasa, S. C. (1991). The development of hardiness. In A. Monat & R. S. Lazarus (Eds.), *Stress and coping. An anthology* (3rd ed., pp. 246–257). Columbia University Press.

Mak, V. W. M., Ho, S. M. Y., Kwong, R. W. Y., & Li, W. L. (2018). A gender-responsive treatment facility in correctional services: The development of psychological gymnasium for women offenders. *International Journal of Offender Therapy and Comparative Criminology* 62(4), 1062–1079. https://doi.org/10.1177/0306624x16667572

Matthews, G., Lin, J., & Wohleber, R. (2017). Personality, stress and resilience: A multifactorial cognitive science perspective. *Psihologijske Teme, 26*(1), 139–162. https://doi.org/10.31820/pt.26.1.6

Meraj, N., Arbeau, K., Fadiya, B., Ketelaars, T., St. Pierre, J., Swart, G. T., & Zayed, R. (2023). Introducing the Adverse Life Events Inventory for Children (ALEIC): An examination of adverse experiences and related impacts in a large clinical sample of children and youth. *Traumatology: An International Journal, 29*(2), 137–148. https://doi.org/10.1037/trm0000385

Moorey, S., & Greer, S. (2012). *Oxford guide to CBT for people with cancer.* Oxford University Press.

Morales, A. S. (2012). *Trait anxiety.* Nova Science Publishers.

Muris, P., de Jong, P. J., & Engelen, S. (2004). Relationships between neuroticism, attentional control, and anxiety disorders symptoms in non-clinical children. *Personality and Individual Differences, 37*(4), 789–797. https://doi.org/10.1016/j.paid.2003.10.007

Nolan, S. A., Roberts, J. E., & Gotlib, I. H. (1998). Neuroticism and ruminative response style as predictors of change in depressive symptomatology. *Cognitive Therapy and Research, 22*(5), 445–455. https://doi.org/10.1023/A:101876 9531641

Norris, F. H. (1992). Epidemiology of trauma: frequency and impact of different potentially traumatic events on different demographic groups. *Journal of Consulting and Clinical Psychology, 60*(3), 409–418. https://doi.org/10.1037//0022-006x.60.3.409

Park, C. L., & Folkman, S. (1997). Meaning in the context of stress and coping. *Review of General Psychology, 1*(2), 115–144. https://doi.org/10.1037/1089-2680.1.2.115

Park, C. L., Folkman, S., & Bostrom, A. (2001). Appraisals of controllability and coping in caregivers and HIV+ men: Testing the goodness-of-fit hypothesis. *Journal of Consulting and Clinical Psychology, 69*(3), 481–488. https://doi.org/10.1037/0022-006X.69.3.481

Peterson, C., & Seligman, M. E. P. (2004). *Character strengths and virtues: A handbook and classification.* American Psychological Association.

Quick, J. C., Wright, T. A., Adkins, J. A., Nelson, D. L., & Quick, J. D. (2013). Primary prevention for individuals: Managing and coping with stressors (2nd ed., pp. 147–163, 247 Pages). American Psychological Association. https://doi.org/10.1037/13942-010

Raugh, I. M., & Strauss, G. P. (2023). Integrating mindfulness into the extended process model of emotion regulation: The dual-mode model of mindful emotion regulation. *Emotion.* https://doi.org/10.1037/emo0001308

Reisig, V., & Wildner, M. (2008). Prevention, primary. In W. Kirch (Ed.), *Encyclopedia of public health* (pp. 1141–1143). Springer Netherlands. https://doi.org/10.1007/978-1-4020-5614-7_2759

Russo, S. J., Murrough, J. W., Han, M.-H., Charney, D. S., & Nestler, E. J. (2012). Neurobiology of resilience. *Nature Neuroscience*, 15(11), 1475–1484. https://doi.org/10.1038/nn.3234

Scheier, M. F., & Carver, C. S. (1985). Optimism, coping, and health: Assessment and implications of generalized outcome expectancies. *Health Psychology*, 4, 219–247. https://doi.org/10.1037/0278-6133.4.3.219

Scheier, M. F., & Carver, C. S. (1988). Dispositional optimism and physical well-being: The influence of outcome expectancies on health. *Journal of Personality*, 55, 169–210. https://doi.org/10.1111/j.1467-6494.1987.tb00434.x

Scheier, M. F., Carver, C. S., & Bridges, M. W. (1994). Distinguishing optimism from neuroticism (and trait anxiety, self-mastery, and self-esteem): A reevaluation of the life orientation test. *Journal of Personality and Social Psychology*, 67(6), 1063. https://doi.org/10.1037/0022-3514.67.6.1063

Seligman, M. E. P. (1990). *Learned optimism.* Random House Australia.

Seligman, M. E. P., & Csikszentmihalyi, M. (2000). Positive psychology. An introduction. *American Psychologist*, 55(1), 5–14. https://doi.org/10.1037/0003-066X.55.1.5

Shakespeare-Finch, J., & Obst, P. L. (2011). The development of the 2-way social support scale: A measure of giving and receiving emotional and instrumental support. *Journal of Personality Assessment*, 93(5), 483–490. https://doi.org/10.1080/00223891.2011.594124

Shoychet, G., Kimber, M., Weiss, J., Honest, O., & Prime, H. (2023). Empirical support for a model of risk and resilience in children and families during covid-19: A systematic review & narrative synthesis. *Development and Psychopathology.* https://doi.org/10.1017/S0954579423000767

Sin, N. L., & Lyubomirsky, S. (2009). Enhancing well-being and alleviating depressive symptoms with positive psychology interventions: A practice-friendly meta-analysis. *Journal of Clinical Psychology*, 65(5), 467–487. https://doi.org/10.1002/jclp.20593

Sinclair, R. R., & Tetrick, L. E. (2000). Implications of item wording for hardiness structure, relation with neuroticism, and stress buffering. *Journal of Research in Personality*, 34(1), 1–25. https://doi.org/10.1006/jrpe.1999.2265

Sisto, A., Vicinanza, F., Campanozzi, L. L., Ricci, G., Tartaglini, D., & Tambone, V. (2019). Towards a transversal definition of psychological resilience: A literature review. *Medicina (Kaunas)*, 55(11). https://doi.org/10.3390/medicina55110745

Snook, D. W., Kaczkowski, W., & Fodeman, A. D. (2023). Mask on, mask off: Risk perceptions for COVID-19 and compliance with COVID-19 safety measures. *Behavioral Medicine*, 49(3), 246–257. https://doi.org/10.1080/08964289.2021.2021384

Southwick, S. M., & Charney, D. S. (2022). *Resilience: The science of mastering life's greatest challenges*. Cambridge University Press. http://ebookcentral.proquest.com/lib/cityuhk/detail.action?docID=1024995

Southwick, S. M., Charney, D. S., & DePierro, J. M. (2023). *Resilience: The science of mastering life's greatest challenges* (3rd ed.). Cambridge University Press.

Snyder, C. R., Cheavens, J. S., & Michael, S. T. (2005). Hope Theory: History and elaborated model. In J. Eliott (Ed.), *Interdisciplinary perspective on hope* (pp. 101-118). Nova Science Publishers.

Teasdale, J. D. (1983). Negative thinking in depression: Cause, effect, or reciprocal relationship. *Advances in Behaviour Research & Therapy*, 5(1), 3–25. https://doi.org/10.1016/0146-6402(83)90013-9

Teasdale, J. D., & Dent, J. (1987). Cognitive vulnerability to depression: An investigation of two hypotheses. *British Journal of Clinical Psychology*, 26(2), 113–126. https://doi.org/10.1111/j.2044-8260.1987.tb00737.x

Tedeschi, R. G., & Calhoun, L. G. (2004). TARGET ARTICLE: "Posttraumatic Growth: Conceptual Foundations and Empirical Evidence." *Psychological Inquiry*, 15(1), 1–18. https://doi.org/10.1207/s15327965pli1501_01

Tedeschi, R. G., Park, C. L., & Calhoun, L. G. (1998a). Posttraumatic growth: Conceptual issues. In R. G. Tedeschi, C. L. Park, & L. G. Calhoun (Eds.), *Posttraumatic growth: Positive changes in the aftermath of crisis* (pp. 1–22). Lawrence Erlbaum Associates.

Tedeschi, R. G., Park, C. L., & Calhoun, L. G. (Eds.). (1998b). *Posttraumatic growth: Positive changes in the aftermath of crisis*. Lawrence Erlbaum Associates.

Watson, M., Greer, S., Young, J., Inayat, Q., Burgess, C., & Robertson, B. (1988). Development of a questionnaire measure of adjustment to cancer: The MAC scale. *Psychological Medicine*, 18, 203–209. https://doi.org/10.1017/S0033291700002026

Watson, M., Law, M., dos Santos, M., Greer, S., Baruch, J., & Bliss, J. (1994). The Mini-MAC: Further development of the mental adjustment to cancer scale. *Journal of Psychosocial Oncology*, 12(3), 33–46. https://doi.org/10.1300/J077V12N03_03

World Health Organization. (2023b). WHO Director-General's opening remarks at the media briefing – 5 May 2023. Retrieved Janurary 2, 2024, from https://www.who.int/director-general/speeches/detail/who-director-general-s-opening-remarks-at-the-media-briefing---5-may-2023

World Health Organization. (2024). *Health promotion and disease prevention through population-based interventions, including action to address social determinants and health inequity* https://www.emro.who.int/about-who/public-health-functions/health-promotion-disease-prevention.html

Zhang, L., Rakesh, D., Cropley, V., & Whittle, S. (2023b). Neurobiological correlates of resilience during childhood and adolescence – A systematic review. *Clinical Psychology Review, 105,* 1–12. https://doi.org/10.1016/j.cpr.2023.102333

Zinbarg, R. E., Schmidt, M., Feinstein, B., Williams, A. L., Murillo, A., Echiverri-Cohen, A. M., Enders, C., Craske, M., & Nusslock, R. (2023). Personality predicts pre-COVID-19 to COVID-19 trajectories of transdiagnostic anxiety and depression symptoms. *Journal of Psychopathology and Clinical Science, 132*(6), 645–656. https://doi.org/10.1037/abn0000803

CHAPTER 2

Distress and Psychopathology in the Context of Adversity and Resilience

Abstract Because the lack of psychopathology is often an indicator of positive adaptation, it is important to be familiar with the trauma- and stressor-related disorders in the Diagnostic and Statistical Manual of Mental Disorders to understand resilience. This chapter highlights the prevalence of traumatic events and their association with distress and psychopathological conditions, including acute stress disorder, posttraumatic stress disorder, and adjustment disorder. The SHINE resilience framework offers practical strategies for maintaining psychological well-being and fostering personal growth in the face of adversity. The key components of resilience include managing depressive and anxiety symptoms, embracing change, and focusing on positive experiences. The chapter concludes by setting the stage for a deeper exploration of each component of the SHINE framework in the subsequent chapters.

Keywords Psychopathology · Acute stress disorder · Posttraumatic stress disorder · Adjustment disorder · Depression · Anxiety · Prolonged grief disorder · Rumination · Cognitive triad of depression

© The Author(s), under exclusive license to Springer Nature Switzerland AG 2025
S. M. Y. Ho, *The SHINE Framework*,
https://doi.org/10.1007/978-3-031-89106-9_2

30 S. M. Y. HO

2.1 DISTRESS AND PSYCHOPATHOLOGY

Traumatic and stressful events are common sources of adversity, which can cause individuals to experience significant distress and even psychiatric disorders. As you will see later in this book, psychological research has often used (the absence of) psychopathology to indicate resilience. Hence, knowing these negative consequences is important to understand how to achieve resilience and growth in the face of adversity. However, you can skip this chapter if you are familiar with psychiatric disorders or are not interested in information about these disorders.

The Diagnostic and Statistical Manual of Mental Disorders, Fifth Edition, Text Revision (DSM-5-TR)[1] groups psychiatric disorders developed after a traumatic experience into the trauma and stressor-related disorders category (American Psychiatric Association, 2022). Disorders in this category include adjustment disorders, characterised by persistent anxiety and depression following a major life event, as well as reactions to trauma, including posttraumatic stress disorder and acute stress disorder. The DSM-5-TR added a new item called "prolonged grief disorder" to this category to identify the persistent sadness exhibited by individuals following the loss of a loved one. We discuss these disorders below. The other two disorders in the trauma and stress-related disorders category, namely reactive adjustment disorder and disinhibited social engagement disorder, are diagnosed only in children and are not covered here.

2.1.1 *Acute Stress Disorder and Posttraumatic Stress Disorder*

Acute stress disorder and posttraumatic stress disorder share similar features, but their temporal patterns differ. Acute stress disorder typically appears immediately after a traumatic event, with symptoms lasting for 3 days to a month. In contrast, posttraumatic stress disorder can manifest either as a continuation of acute stress disorder or as a distinct episode that begins 1 month or more after the trauma. Additionally, posttraumatic

---

[1] This book uses the DSM-5-TR, a manual published by the American Psychiatric Association, to guide the discussion. The DSM-5-TR is adopted by many professional psychology associations such as the American Psychological Association, the British Psychological Association, and the Hong Kong Psychological Association for the assessment and diagnosis of mental disorders. The International Classification of Diseases (ICD-11) (World Health Organization, 2022) published by the WHO is another major classification system that serves similar functions to the DSM-5-TR.

stress disorder may appear with delayed expression, occurring 6 months or more after the traumatic experience (Barnhill & Zimmerman, 2023b).

According to the DSM-5-TR, for the diagnosis of acute stress disorder and posttraumatic stress disorder, the traumatic events must be directly experienced or witnessed in person by the individual. Exposure through electronic media, television, movies, or images does not apply unless it is work-related (American Psychiatric Association, 2022). This criterion avoids overdiagnosis and provides a more accurate estimate of the prevalence rate of posttraumatic stress disorder (Pai et al., 2017).

Furthermore, the DSM-5-TR (American Psychiatric Association, 2022) requires that only events that involve the actual or potential occurrence of death, severe physical harm, or sexual violence be considered traumatic events. Accordingly, unemployment, divorce, and other psychosocial stressors do not meet this requirement, and a diagnosis of acute stress disorder or posttraumatic stress disorder is not appropriate in this case. Furthermore, medical conditions, including the diagnosis of life-threatening illnesses such as cancer, do not qualify as trauma and therefore preclude the diagnosis of acute stress disorder or posttraumatic stress disorder (Pai et al., 2017). COVID-19 infection is not a traumatic event according to the above definition, and therefore, it is not appropriate to investigate posttraumatic stress disorder in patients with COVID-19. The above criteria limit the scope of trauma research. As an example, a meta-analysis reported that the prevalence of posttraumatic stress disorder diagnosis among cancer survivors was higher than in the general population (Swartzman et al., 2017). This study would not be appropriate today, because a cancer diagnosis should not be regarded as a traumatic event.

However, many stressful events not classified as trauma in the DSM system can still cause psychiatric symptoms similar to acute stress disorder and posttraumatic stress disorder. However, the diagnosis of acute stress disorder or posttraumatic stress disorder does not apply because individuals have not experienced a traumatic encounter in the first place. As readers will see later in this book, many studies of resilience (Chan et al., 2013; Cordova et al., 2017; Ho et al., 2011; Ma et al., 2023) have used *trauma-like symptoms or posttraumatic symptomatology* instead of the diagnosis of posttraumatic stress disorder to indicate adjustment.

There are four categories of posttraumatic stress symptoms (American Psychiatric Association, 2022; Barlow et al., 2023; Barnhill & Zimmerman, 2023c):

1. *Intrusion.* Recurring, involuntary, and distressing memories and dreams. The intrusion may take the form of flashbacks, and individuals may feel or act as if the event(s) is/are happening again.
2. *Avoidance.* Persistent avoidance of stimuli such as places and activities associated with the traumatic event(s).
3. *Negative alterations in cognition and mood.* Inability to remember salient aspects of the traumatic event(s), self-blame, anhedonia (i.e. the inability to experience joy or pleasure), and inability to experience positive emotions.
4. *Alterations in arousal and reactivity.* Excessive arousal, such as irritability, hypervigilance, angry outbursts, sleep disturbances, and self-destructive behaviour.

Not everyone who experiences trauma will develop acute stress disorder or posttraumatic stress disorder. The prevalence of posttraumatic stress disorder varies depending on many factors, including the type and severity of the trauma. Kramper et al. (2023) used DSM-5-TR criteria to identify trauma exposure in 359 veterinary professionals and reported that 3.6% to 13.9% of the participants may have posttraumatic stress disorder. My study of survivors of the massive earthquake that occurred on 12 May 2008 in Wenchuan County, Sichuan province, southwest China, showed a prevalence rate of posttraumatic stress disorder of 84.4% 1–2 months after the earthquake (Zhang & Ho, 2011). Another research team reported a prevalence rate of posttraumatic stress disorder of 62.8% and 37.8% one to three months, respectively, after the earthquake (Wang et al., 2011; Wang et al., 2009; Wang et al., 2009). The percentage of people who suffer from posttraumatic stress disorder varies, but many people do not suffer from posttraumatic stress disorder even after a major traumatic encounter; that is, they exhibit resilience in the face of adversity.

2.1.2 Adjustment Disorder

Acute stress disorder and posttraumatic stress disorder represent the reactions of people who experience trauma firsthand according to the DSM-5-TR (American Psychiatric Association, 2000). How do people respond to more common stressful events, such as unemployment, chronic illness, divorce, and traffic accidents? The symptoms related to adjustment disorder in the DSM-5-TR answer this question. Adjustment disorder describes people's prototypical psychological responses to an identifiable stressor, which can fall into four main types (Barnhill & Zimmerman, 2023a):

1. *Singular, discrete events*, referring to individual occurrences with distinct starting and ending points (e.g. losing a job).
2. *Multiple events*, which are interconnected over time (e.g. financial problems, marital conflicts).
3. *Common developmental milestones*, referring to important moments in a person's life that mark a transition or achievement (e.g. parenthood, study–work transition).
4. *Ongoing challenges*, which are difficulties that persist over an extended period (e.g. chronic illnesses, disabilities).

Unlike trauma in acute stress disorder and posttraumatic stress disorder, the DSM-5-TR does not specify any requirements for what can be considered a stressor in adjustment disorder. This is partly why the prevalence rate of adjustment disorder varies according to the type of stressor (O'Donnell et al., 2019): namely approximately 2% of the general population (Glaesmer et al., 2015), 27% of recently unemployed people (Perkonigg et al., 2018), and 15%–19% of cancer patients (Mitchell et al., 2011).

Symptoms of adjustment disorder present as depressed mood, anxiety, misconduct, or a combination of these (Barnhill & Zimmerman, 2023a). These symptoms may appear shortly after the stressful event and should subside within six months after the stressors have disappeared. However, multiple stressful events can occur in chronic adversity, perpetuating symptoms.

As many components of the SHINE framework aim to address depressed mood and anxiety in the face of adversity, these two elements are introduced below to facilitate discussion in later chapters.

a. Depression

Major depressive disorder and persistent depressive disorder in the DSM-5-TR (American Psychiatric Association, 2000) capture the clinical features of depressed mood. Both disorders have similar symptoms characterised by loss of interest or pleasure in daily activities (anhedonia), physical fatigue, hopelessness, feelings of guilt and worthlessness, and disturbances in sleep, appetite, and cognitive functioning (e.g. concentration). As illustrated in Figure 2.1, people in depressed mood may exhibit negative views of themselves, the world, and the future, often referred to as Beck's cognitive triad of depression (Beck et al., 1979). Recent studies have shown that this model provides a valid explanation of depression. For example, Sacco et al. (2023) surveyed 243 technical and community college students in the US and reported that negative views of themselves and the world mediated the relationship between their perceptions of daily discrimination and depression. Using a meta-analytic commonality analysis approach, Marchetti and Pössel (2023) showed that all three components of the triad had significant associations with depressive symptoms in adolescents, although their effects overlapped.

Other theorists have proposed that the mere presence of negative thinking styles, such as Beck's cognitive triad, is insufficient to produce depressed mood; instead, an activating agent must be present to trigger

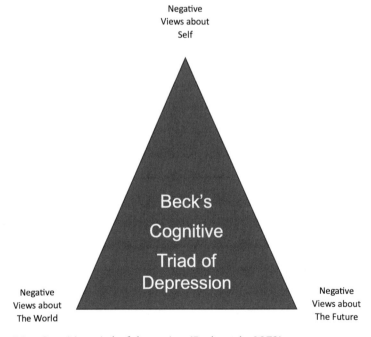

Fig. 2.1 Cognitive triad of depression (Beck et al., 1979)

the depressive schemas (Scher et al., 2005). For instance, Watkins and Teasdale (2001) suggested that rumination is an important activating agent of depression. Rumination is repetitive, passive thinking related to the symptoms, causes, and consequences of depression (Michl et al., 2013). Accordingly, people with a negative cognitive style are more likely than others to exhibit maladaptive rumination related to their adversity, leading to the onset and persistence of depressed mood. My research revealed that the brooding style of rumination, a form of evaluative moody pondering, was a significant mediator of the relationship between negative cognitive style and the severity of depressive symptoms (Lo et al., 2008) (Figure 2.2). In other words, individuals with a negative cognitive style (negative view of self, the world, and the future) are prone to exhibit brooding rumination when confronted with negative events. Such a maladaptive style of rumination will trigger the underlying depressive schemas, leading to and intensifying their depressive mood. These depressive symptoms will prolong their adversity, leading to a vicious circle. More recently, Segerberg et al. (2024) reported that rumination was positively (although not significantly) related to the severity of depression prior to pharmaceutical treatment, and that a decrease in depression severity due to medication was associated with lower rumination.

The above findings suggest that there are at least two ways to reduce depressive symptoms caused by adversity. The first method is to help the person become less broody by cultivating another attitude to view the adverse situation. In an experimental study, Lo et al. (2014) primed

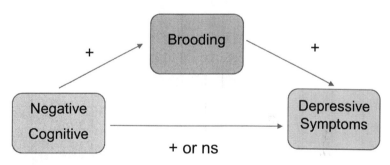

Fig. 2.2 Relationship between brooding, negative cognitive style, and depressive symptoms. "+" = significant positive relationship, ns = non-significant relationship. Adapted from Lo et al. (2008)

participants for a decentring mode of rumination (Bennett et al., 2021), defined as the ability to adopt a present-focus and non-judgemental stance to observe thoughts and feelings as temporary and objective events in the mind, and found that it reduced negative cognition related to depression. The second method is to help people shift their focus on negative events by increasing their memories and rumination of positive events. I discuss rumination on attentional bias in Chapter 6 and suggest strategies to increase positive attention and rumination.

Due to depressive symptoms, people in depressed mood may exhibit avoidance behaviour, leading to a loss of positive reinforcement (Hoevenaars & van Son, 1990). Behavioural activation, a psychological intervention aimed at increasing behavioural outcomes in depressed individuals, has been shown to be effective in reducing depressive symptoms (Dobson, 2024; Quigley & Dobson, 2017). Setting realistic, future-oriented goals and motivating oneself to implement ways to achieve them can activate behavioural outcomes to combat adversity. The hope-oriented cognitive thinking style introduced in Chapter 4 explains how to achieve this.

b. Anxiety

Anxiety has a high comorbidity with depression, meaning that many individuals have concurrent diagnoses of anxiety and depression. A recent study of 4,951 working adults in Australia reported a 16% comorbidity of depression and anxiety (Deady et al., 2021). Hopwood (2023) reported that around 60%–70% of individuals with both anxiety and depression initially experience symptoms of anxiety, although it is usually the onset of depression that prompts them to seek medical help. Despite their high comorbidity, anxiety differs from depression both in symptom presentation and aetiology.

The DSM-5-TR (American Psychiatric Association, 2022) describes several subtypes of anxiety disorders, such as generalised anxiety disorder, panic disorder, social anxiety disorder, specific phobia, and agoraphobia. In general, all anxiety disorders share a common feature: their symptoms are due to an anticipation of future threats (American Psychiatric Association, 2022; Barlow et al., 2023). In the face of adversity, people are confronted to difficulties and threats on a daily basis, which leads to anxiety. Gradually, they interpret many events or activities as potential threats through generalisation. As a result, they develop excessive worry (apprehensive expectation) and exhibit physical symptoms of restlessness, fatigue, difficulty concentrating, irritability, muscle tension, and sleep problems about many things in life (American Psychiatric Association, 2022). Finally, their anxiety symptoms cause additional anxiety about the symptoms themselves, a phenomenon called "fear of fear" (Zalta, 2023), leading to avoidance and perpetuating their anxiety.

There are bio-neurological, psychological, and socioenvironmental factors leading to anxiety (see Olatunji, 2019, for a review). The cognitive processing factors described in the integrated cognitive model (Mogg & Bradley, 1998) are most relevant to the resilience framework in this book. According to this model, anxiety is related to a bottom-up threat detection system and a top-down cognitive control system. The bottom-up system is the automatic detection of threatening stimuli, facilitating reactive attention to the threats and interrupting task performance. The top-down process is associated with the ability to shift or focus attention effortfully, which requires people to control their attention voluntarily. Threats are first detected by the bottom-up detection system, which automatically shifts attention to negative stimuli; subsequently, the top-down cognitive control system can regulate the bottom-up detection system, which voluntarily shifts attention away from threats and helps refocus attention on tasks. The bottom-up system is more likely to be activated in anxious individuals than in non-anxious individuals, turning their attention towards threats. Attentional bias is one of the most frequently studied cognitive factors related to the bottom-up system of the integrated cognitive model of anxiety (Grafton & MacLeod, 2024; Quigley et al., 2024; Taylor et al., 2010, 2011a; Van Bockstaele et al., 2014; Yuan et al., 2024). As we will see in Chapters 5 and 6, learning to disengage from negative stimuli and increase attention to and memory of positive events can facilitate resilience.

2.1.3 Prolonged Grief Disorder

Extreme adjustments and adversity can occur after the loss of a loved one. For example, the deceased's spouse may need to learn how to manage financial matters, perform household chores, and seek new social support and emotional companionship. People's psychological reactions to the loss of a loved one are so unique that the American Psychiatric Association added a new disorder, prolonged grief disorder, to the DSM-5-TR (American Psychiatric Association, 2022), a decision made after more than 20 years of research and discussion. Prolonged grief disorder is a timely new diagnosis to raise awareness of complicated grief, with COVID-19 having claimed more than 7 million lives as of December 2023 (World Health Organization, 2023a).

Prolonged grief disorder differs from depression and posttraumatic stress disorder, both in terms of underlying neurological mechanisms and clinical presentation (Aoun et al., 2021; Jordan & Litz, 2014; Khosravi & Kasaeiyan, 2023). The core clinical feature of prolonged grief disorder is an intense longing for the deceased and cognitive preoccupation with the loved one, leading to symptoms such as difficulty reintegrating into the community and social network, disbelief that the deceased is permanently gone, intense loneliness, and feeling that life is meaningless. In psychology, bereavement is related to three concepts: loss, grief, and mourning (Cheung & Ho, 2004, 2006). The *loss* of a loved one stimulates a powerful emotional reaction of *grief* in a person, and the socially constructed ways of grieving (e.g. crying next to the body of the deceased) are called *mourning*. The three concepts of loss, grief, and mourning are depicted in the single ancient Chinese oracle word for death, which represents a person mourning next to the remains of a loved one (Figure 2.3).

Most people, regardless of age and culture, want to continue their relationships with deceased loved ones (Klass et al., 1996). In some cultures, such as Chinese culture, giving up the relationship with the deceased is regarded as "abandoning" the loved one, which can lead to guilt and remorse (Ho et al., 2002). Hence, most grieving people maintain an ongoing inner relationship with the deceased, sometimes referred to in psychology as "continuing bonds" (CBs) (Field & Filanosky, 2010; Field et al., 2003). CBs with the deceased can interfere with normal grieving and recovery by reducing a grieving person's emotional energy to invest in new relationships. For instance, the dual process theory proposed by Strobe et al. (Stroebe & Schut, 2005; Stroebe et al., 2001; Stroebe et al., 2010) posits that grieving individuals must complete loss-focused tasks related to the deceased and that restoration-focused tasks arise from secondary stressors due to the death of the loved one (such as establishing new social networks). Strong CBs with the deceased can cause a grieving individual to focus too much on loss-focused tasks and to lack the energy to deal with restoration-focused tasks.

Stroebe et al. (2010) acknowledged that there are healthy and unhealthy types of CBs, which may affect grief outcomes differently. My

Fig. 2.3 The Chinese oracle character for "death" depicts a person crying next to the body of the deceased: The person has lost a loved one, leading to the emotional reactions of grief and mourning, which are the socially constructed ways of expressing grief (Cheung & Ho, 2004).

research identified two types of CBs: externalised and internalised (Ho & Chan, 2018; Ho et al., 2013). Internalised CBs represent the feeling of the loving presence of the deceased as well as the use of the deceased as an autonomy-promoting secure base by the grieving person. A person exhibiting internalised CBs may maintain these bonds by thinking about how the deceased would have enjoyed something the person sees daily or by trying to carry out the deceased's wishes. Externalised CBs, in contrast, are represented by the grieving individual's refusal to acknowledge that the deceased is gone forever and their attempts to dwell on the deceased's physical presence. People with externalised CBs may mistake sounds for the voice, footsteps, or movements of the deceased. Some may feel that the deceased is haunting them. My research revealed that externalised CBs are related to a prolonged grief reaction, while internalised CBs are related to adaptive adjustment after bereavement (Ho et al., 2013). A recent systematic review of 79 CB studies echoed the above proposition by showing that CBs provide comfort and distress to the bereaved,

40 S. M. Y. HO

who oscillates between the comforting presence and the uncomfortable absence of the deceased (Hewson et al., 2023).

My research findings and clinical experience in grief research reveal that accepting changes as an indispensable part of life is essential to resilience after adversity. Hence, an important component of the resilience model in this book, called Embracing Change, will be discussed in Chapter 7.

2.2 SUMMARY

This chapter introduces adversity and its associated psychopathology, using the trauma and stressor-related disorders discussed in the DSM-5-TR (American Psychiatric Association, 2022) as a key reference to inform the discussion. It illustrates why the five components of the SHINE framework are relevant in helping us maintain normal functioning and even experience true personal growth during and after adversity.

In summary, depression and anxiety are two common psychological issues experienced by people facing adversity. Learning to generate enjoyable activities by exercising our strengths (Chapter 3), developing realistic future goals and implementing strategies to achieve them (Chapter 4), and increasing attention to positive stimuli and events (Chapters 5 and 6) will increase our resilience during and after adversity. Finally, learning that change is an inevitable part of life and cultivating an attitude to embrace it is essential to resilience (Chapter 7).

In the next chapter, we turn to something more positive by first addressing definitions of resilience and then introducing different models of resilience in psychology. The SHINE framework is introduced and compared with other models of resilience in the literature.

REFERENCES

American Psychiatric Association. (2000). *Diagnostic and statistical manual of mental disorders (4th ed., text rev.) (DSM-IV-TR)*. Author.

American Psychiatric Association. (2022). *Diagnostic and statistical manual of mental disorders (5th ed., text rev.)*. American Psychiatric Association. https://doi.org/10.1176/appi.books.9780890425787

Aoun, E. G., Brent, D. A., Melhem, N. M., & Porta, G. (2021). Prospective evaluation of the DSM-5 persistent complex bereavement disorder criteria in adults: dimensional and diagnostic approaches. *Psychological Medicine, 51*(5), 825–834. https://doi.org/10.1017/S0033291719003829

Barlow, D. H., Durand, M. V., & Hofmann, S. G. (2023). *Psychopathology: An integrative approach to mental disorders* (9th ed.). Cengage.

Barnhill, J. W. & Zimmerman, M. (2023a). Adjustment Disorders. In *MSD Manual. Professional Version.* Merck & Co., Inc. https://www.msdmanuals.com/professional/psychiatric-disorders/anxiety-and-stressor-related-disorders/adjustment-disorders#:~:text=Symptoms%20and%20Signs%20of%20Adjustment,%2C%20anxiety%2C%20and%20conduct%20disturbance

Barnhill, J. W. & Zimmerman, M. (2023b). Overview of trauma- and stressor-related disorders. In *MSD Manual. Professional Version.* Merck & Co., Inc. https://www.msdmanuals.com/professional/psychiatric-disorders/anxiety-and-stressor-related-disorders/overview-of-trauma-and-stressor-related-disorders

Barnhill, J. W. & Zimmerman, M. (2023c). Posttraumatic disorder (PTSD). In *MSD Manual. Professional Version.* Merck & Co., Inc. https://www.msdmanuals.com/professional/psychiatric-disorders/anxiety-and-stressor-related-disorders/posttraumatic-stress-disorder-ptsd?query=ptsd#top

Beck, A. T., Rush, A. J., Shaw, B. F., & Emery, G. (1979). *Cognitive therapy of depression.* Guildford Press.

Bennett, M. P., Knight, R., Patel, S., So, T., Dunning, D., Barnhofer, T., Smith, P., Kuyken, W., Ford, T., & Dalgleish, T. (2021). Decentering as a core component in the psychological treatment and prevention of youth anxiety and depression: A narrative review and insight report. *Translational Psychiatry, 11*(1), 288. https://doi.org/10.1038/s41398-021-01397-5

Chan, M. W. C., Ho, S. M. Y., Law, L. S. C., & Pau, B. K. Y. (2013). A visual dot-probe task as a measurement of attentional bias and its relationship with the symptoms of posttraumatic stress disorder among women with breast cancer. *Advances in Cancer: Research and Treatment, 2013 (2013)*(Article ID 813339). https://doi.org/10.5171/2013.813339

Cheung, W.-S., & Ho, S. M. Y. (2004). The use of death metaphors to understand personal meaning of death among Hong Kong Chinese undergraduates. *Death Studies, 28,* 47–62. https://doi.org/10.1080/07481180490249265

Cheung, W. S., & Ho, S. M. Y. (2006). Death metaphors in Chinese. In C. L. W. Chan & A. Y. M. Chow (Eds.), *Death, dying and bereavement. A Hong Kong Chinese experience* (pp. 117–126). Hong Kong University Press.

Cordova, M. J., Riba, M. B., & Spiegel, D. (2017). Post-traumatic stress disorder and cancer. *Lancet Psychiatry, 4*(4), 330–338. https://doi.org/10.1016/s2215-0366(17)30014-7

Deady, M., Collins, D. A. J., Johnston, D. A., Glozier, N., Calvo, R. A., Christensen, H., & Harvey, S. B. (2021). The impact of depression, anxiety and comorbidity on occupational outcomes. *Occupational Medicine, 72*(1), 17–24. https://doi.org/10.1093/occmed/kqab142

Dobson, K. S. (2024). Behavioral activation: Addressing risk factors for depression. In *Clinical depression: An individualized, biopsychosocial approach to assessment and treatment* (pp. 121–148, 291 Pages). American Psychological Association. https://doi.org/10.1037/0000398-008

Field, N. P., & Filanosky, C. (2010). Continuing bonds, risk factors for complicated grief, and adjustment to bereavement. *Death Studies, 34*(1), 1–29. https://doi.org/10.1080/07481180903372269

Field, N. P., Gal-Oz, E., & Bonanno, G. A. (2003). Continuing bonds and adjustment at 5 years after the death of a spouse. *Journal of Consulting & Clinical Psychology, 71*(1), 110–117. https://doi.org/10.1037/0022-006X.71.1.110

Glaesmer, H., Romppel, M., Brähler, E., Hinz, A., & Maercker, A. (2015). Adjustment disorder as proposed for ICD-11: Dimensionality and symptom differentiation. *Psychiatry Research, 229*(3), 940–948. https://doi.org/10.1016/j.psychres.2015.07.010

Grafton, B., & MacLeod, C. (2024). Regulation of anxious emotion through the modification of attentional bias. In J. J. Gross & B. Q. Ford (Eds.), *Handbook of emotion regulation* (3rd ed., pp. 417). The Guilford Press.

Hewson, H., Galbraith, N., Jones, C., & Heath, G. (2023). The impact of continuing bonds following bereavement: A systematic review. *Death Studies.* https://doi.org/10.1080/07481187.2023.2223593

Ho, S. M. Y., & Chan, I. S. F. (2018). Externalized and internalized continuing bonds in understanding of grief. In K. Dennis & E. Steffen (Eds.), *Continuing bonds in bereavement. New directions for research and practice* (pp. 129–138). Routledge.

Ho, S. M. Y., Chan, I. S., Ma, E. P., & Field, N. P. (2013). Continuing bonds, attachment style, and adjustment in the conjugal bereavement among Hong Kong Chinese. *Death Studies, 37*(3), 248–268. https://doi.org/10.1080/07481187.2011.634086

Ho, S. M. Y., Chan, M. W. Y., Yau, T. K., & Yeung, R. M. W. (2011). Relationships between explanatory style, posttraumatic growth and posttraumatic stress disorder symptoms among Chinese breast cancer patients. *Psychology & Health, 26*(3), 269–285. https://doi.org/10.1080/08870440903287926

Ho, S. M. Y., Chow, A. Y. M., Chan, C. L.-W., & Tsui, Y. K. Y. (2002). The assessment of grief among Hong Kong Chinese: A preliminary report. *Death Studies, 26*, 91–98. https://doi.org/10.1080/074811802753455226

Hoevenaars, J., & van Son, M. J. M. (1990). New chances for Lewinsohn's social reinforcement theory of depression. In H.-G. Zapotoczky & T. Wenzel (Eds.), *The scientific dialogue: From basic research to clinical intervention* (pp. 65–70, 313 Pages). Swets & Zeitlinger Publishers.

2 DISTRESS AND PSYCHOPATHOLOGY IN THE CONTEXT ... 43

Hopwood, M. (2023). Anxiety symptoms in patients with major depressive disorder: Commentary on prevalence and clinical implications. *Neurology and Therapy*, *12*(Suppl 1), 5–12.https://doi.org/10.1007/s40120-023-00469-6

Jordan, A. H., & Litz, B. T. (2014). Prolonged grief disorder: Diagnostic, assessment, and treatment considerations. *Professional Psychology: Research and Practice*, *45*(3), 180–187. https://doi.org/10.1037/a0036836

Khosravi, M., & Kasaeiyan, R. (2023). A current challenge in classification and treatment of DSM-5-TR prolonged grief disorder. *Psychological Trauma: Theory, Research, Practice, and Policy*. https://doi.org/10.1037/tra0001510

Klass, D., Silverman, P., & Nickman, S. L. (Eds.). (1996). *Continuing bonds: New understandings of grief*. Taylor & Francis.

Kramper, S., Crosby, E. S., Waitz-Kudla, S. N., Weathers, F., & Witte, T. K. (2023). Highly stressful events and posttraumatic stress disorder symptoms among veterinary professionals: Prevalence and associations with mental health and job-related outcomes. *Psychological Trauma: Theory, Research, Practice, and Policy*, *15*(Suppl 2), S275–S285. https://doi.org/10.1037/tra0001432

Lo, C. S. L., Ho, S. M. Y., & Hollon, S. D. (2008). The effects of rumination and negative cognitive styles on depression: A mediation analysis. *Behaviour Research and Therapy*, *46*(4), 487–495. https://doi.org/10.1016/j.brat.2008.01.013

Lo, C. S. L., Ho, S. M. Y., Yu, N. K. K., & Siu, B. P. Y. (2014). Decentering mediates the effect of ruminative and experiential self-focus on negative thinking in depression. *Cognitive Therapy and Research*, *38*(4), 389–396. https://doi.org/10.1007/s10608-014-9603-2

Ma, W., Koenig, H. G., Wen, J., Liu, J., Shi, X., & Wang, Z. (2023). The moral injury, posttraumatic stress disorder, and suicidal behaviors in health professionals 1 year after the COVID-19 pandemic peak in China. *Psychological Trauma: Theory, Research, Practice, and Policy*, *15*(Suppl 2), S352–S356. https://doi.org/10.1037/tra0001483

Marchetti, I., & Pössel, P. (2023). Cognitive triad and depressive symptoms in adolescence: Specificity and overlap. *Child Psychiatry and Human Development*, *54*(4), 1209–1217. https://doi.org/10.1007/s10578-022-01323-w

Michl, L. C., McLaughlin, K. A., Shepherd, K., & Nolen-Hoeksema, S. (2013). Rumination as a mechanism linking stressful life events to symptoms of depression and anxiety: Longitudinal evidence in early adolescents and adults. *Journal of Abnormal Psychology*, *122*(2), 339–352. https://doi.org/10.1037/a0031994

Mitchell, A. J., Chan, M., Bhatti, H., Halton, M., Grassi, L., Johansen, C., & Meader, N. (2011). Prevalence of depression, anxiety, and adjustment disorder in oncological, haematological, and palliative-care settings: A meta-analysis of

94 interview-based studies. *The Lancet Oncology*, *12*(2), 160–174. https://doi.org/10.1016/S1470-2045(11)70002-X

Mogg, K., & Bradley, B. P. (1998). A cognitive-motivational analysis of anxiety. *Behaviour Research and Therapy*, *36*(9), 809–848. https://doi.org/10.1016/s0005-7967(98)00063-1

O'Donnell, M. L., Agathos, J. A., Metcalf, O., Gibson, K., & Lau, W. (2019). Adjustment disorder: Current developments and future directions. *International Journal of Environmental Research and Public Health*, *16*(14). https://doi.org/10.3390/ijerph16142537

Olatunji, B. O. (Ed.). (2019). *The Cambridge handbook of anxiety and related disorders*. Cambridge University Press. https://doi.org/10.1017/9781108140416

Pai, A., Suris, A. M., & North, C. S. (2017). Posttraumatic stress disorder in the DSM-5: Controversy, change, and conceptual considerations. *Behavioral Sciences (Basel)*, *7*(1). https://doi.org/10.3390/bs7010007

Perkonigg, A., Lorenz, L., & Maercker, A. (2018). Prevalence and correlates of ICD-11 adjustment disorder: Findings from the Zurich adjustment disorder study. *International Journal of Clinical and Health Psychology*, *18*(3), 209–217. https://doi.org/10.1016/j.ijchp.2018.05.001

Quigley, L., & Dobson, K. S. (2017). Behavioral activation treatments for depression. In S. G. Hofmann & G. J. G. Asmundson (Eds.), *The science of cognitive behavioral therapy* (pp. 291–318, 610 Pages). Elsevier Academic Press. https://doi.org/10.1016/B978-0-12-803457-6.00012-X

Quigley, L., Russell, K., Yung, C., Dobson, K. S., & Sears, C. R. (2024). Associations between attentional biases for emotional images and rumination in depression. *Cognition and Emotion*. https://doi.org/10.1080/02699931.2024.2434158

Sacco, A., Pössel, P., & Roane, S. J. (2023). Perceived discrimination and depressive symptoms: What role does the cognitive triad play? *Journal of Clinical Psychology*, *79*(4), 985–1001. https://doi.org/10.1002/jclp.23452

Scher, C. D., Ingram, R. E., & Segal, Z. V. (2005). Cognitive reactivity and vulnerability: empirical evaluation of construct activation and cognitive diatheses in unipolar depression. *Clinical Psychology Review*, *25*(4), 487–510. https://doi.org/10.1016/j.cpr.2005.01.005

Segerberg, T. S. S., Ozenne, B., Dam, V. H., Köhler-Forsberg, K., Jørgensen, M. B., Frokjaer, V. G., Knudsen, G. M., & Stenbæk, D. S. (2024). Rumination in patients with major depressive disorder before and after antidepressant treatment. *Journal of Affective Disorders*, *360*, 322–325. https://doi.org/10.1016/j.jad.2024.05.135

Stroebe, M. S., Hansson, R. O., & Stroebe, W. (Eds.). (2001). *Handbook of bereavement research: Consequences, coping, and care* (1st ed.). American Psychological Association.

Stroebe, M., & Schut, H. (2005). To continue or relinquish bonds: A review of consequences for the bereaved. *Death Studies*, *29*, 477–494. https://doi.org/10.1080/07481180590962659

Stroebe, M., Schut, H., & Boerner, K. (2010). Continuing bonds in adaptation to bereavement: Toward theoretical integration. *Clinical Psychology Review*, *30*(2), 259–268. https://doi.org/10.1016/j.cpr.2009.11.007

Swartzman, S., Booth, J. N., Munro, A., & Sani, F. (2017). Posttraumatic stress disorder after cancer diagnosis in adults: A meta-analysis. *Depress Anxiety*, *34*(4), 327–339. https://doi.org/10.1002/da.22542

Taylor, C. T., Bomyea, J., & Amir, N. (2010). Attentional bias away from positive social information mediates the link between social anxiety and anxiety vulnerability to a social stressor. *Journal of Anxiety Disorders*, *24*(4), 403–408. https://doi.org/10.1016/j.janxdis.2010.02.004

Taylor, C. T., Bomyea, J., & Amir, N. (2011a). Malleability of attentional bias for positive emotional information and anxiety vulnerability. *Emotion*, *11*(1), 127–138. https://doi.org/10.1037/a0021301

Van Bockstaele, B., Verschuere, B., Tibboel, H., De Houwer, J., Crombez, G., & Koster, E. H. W. (2014). A review of current evidence for the causal impact of attentional bias on fear and anxiety. *Psychological Bulletin*, *140*(3), 682–724. https://doi.org/10.1037/a0034834

Wang, B., Ni, C., Chen, J., Liu, X., Wang, A., Shao, Z., Xiao, D., Cheng, H., Jiang, J., & Yan, Y. (2011). Posttraumatic stress disorder 1 month after 2008 earthquake in China: Wenchuan earthquake survey. *Psychiatry Reearch*, *187*(3), 392–396. https://doi.org/10.1016/j.psychres.2009.07.001

Wang, L., Zhang, Y., Shi, Z., & Wang, W. (2009). Symptoms of posttraumatic stress disorder among adult survivors two months after the Wenchuan earthquake. *Psychological Reports*, *105*(3 Pt 1), 879–885.https://doi.org/10.2466/pr0.105.3.879-885

Wang, L., Zhang, Y., Wang, W., Shi, Z., Shen, J., Li, M., & Xin, Y. (2009). Symptoms of posttraumatic stress disorder among adult survivors three months after the Sichuan earthquake in China. *Journal of Traumatic Stress*, *22*(5), 444–450. https://doi.org/10.1002/jts.20439

Watkins, E., & Teasdale, J. D. (2001). Rumination and overgeneral memory in depression: Effects of self-focus and analytic thinking. *Journal of Abnormal Psychology*, *110*(2), 353–357. https://doi.org/10.1037/0021-843X.110.2.333

World Health Organization. (2022). *ICD-11: International classification of diseases (11th revision)*. https://icd.who.int/. .

World Health Organization. (2023a). *Number of COVID-19 deaths reported to WHO (cumulative total)*. Retrieved January 16, 2024, from https://data.who.int/dashboards/covid19/deaths?n=c

Yuan, J., Shi, G., Zhang, Q., & Cui, L. (2024). Visual search attentional bias modification reduced the attentional bias in socially anxious individuals. *Psychophysiology*, 11. https://doi.org/10.1111/psyp.14724

Zalta, A. K. (2023). Dianne L. Chambless (1948–2023). *American Psychologist*. https://doi.org/10.1037/amp0001291

Zhang, Y., & Ho, S. M. Y. (2011). Risk factors of posttraumatic stress disorder among survivors after the 512 Wenchuan earthquake in China. *PLoS ONE*, 6(7), e22371. https://doi.org/10.1371/journal.pone.0022371

CHAPTER 3

Strength-Based Habit-Building

Abstract The strength-based habit-building component of SHINE emphasises the importance of character strengths as foundational resources for resilience. Based on the virtues in action model, the SHINE framework focuses on three core strengths: interpersonal, temperamental, and intellectual. It emphasises the significance of vital engagement—activities that combine flow and meaning—in enhancing well-being and resilience. Adaptive habit-building strategies are also discussed, providing a structured approach to cultivating resilience by establishing positive habits. The chapter introduces the Brief Strengths Scale (BSS-12) as a practical tool for assessing these strengths. Systematic activities are introduced to identify and exercise personal strengths, integrate them into meaningful activities, and develop them into established habits.

Keywords Character strengths · Habit-building · Virtues in action · Interpersonal strengths · Temperance · Intellectual strengths · Vital engagement · Flow

© The Author(s), under exclusive license to Springer Nature 47
Switzerland AG 2025
S. M. Y. Ho, *The SHINE Framework*,
https://doi.org/10.1007/978-3-031-89106-9_3

3.1 Virtue and Character Strengths

Character strengths are positive traits valued by society that are manifested in an individual's thoughts, emotions, and behaviours (Peterson & Seligman, 2004). The most popular and systematic theory of virtue and character strengths in psychology is the virtues in action (VIA) model proposed by Peterson and Seligman (2004). These researchers identified 24 universal positive traits, called "character strengths," across cultures and grouped them into six ubiquitous virtues: wisdom and knowledge, courage, humanity, justice, temperance, and transcendence (Peterson & Seligman, 2004; Steger et al., 2007). Table 3.1 shows the 24 character strengths grouped under the six virtues in the VIA model of Peterson and Seligman (2004). Peterson and Seligman (2004) also developed the Values in Action Inventory of Strengths (VIA-IS) to measure adults' character strengths based on their taxonomy. The VIA-IS consists of 24 character strength subscales, with 10 items per subscale (240 items in total).

The study of character strengths has garnered considerable interest from researchers and practitioners around the world, largely driven by the momentum gained by the positive psychology movement (Brdar & Kashdan, 2010; Duan & Ho, 2018; Duan et al., 2014; Lavy & Benish-Weisman, 2021; Linley et al., 2007; Park et al., 2004; Peterson et al., 2010; Wagner et al., 2020). Some studies have administered the VIA-IS (Peterson & Seligman, 2004) to their participants and have discovered, mainly using factor analysis and principal component analysis, different dimensions and classifications of virtues and character strengths (Cawley et al., 2000; Duan & Ho, 2017; McGrath, 2014, 2015; Peterson et al., 2008; Shryack et al., 2010; van Eeden et al., 2008). Most relevant to the SHINE framework are the three-dimensional models proposed by various researchers (Duan & Ho, 2017; McGrath, 2015; Shryack et al., 2010). First, Shryack et al. (2010) administered the VIA-IS (Peterson & Seligman, 2004) to 332 individuals in the US and reported a three-dimensional model of character strengths, including *agency/self-assuredness*, *sociability*, and *conscientiousness*. Subsequently, McGrath (2015) conducted two studies to analyse data from individuals who completed the VIA-IS on the VIA Institute on Character website (https://www.viacharacter.org/) and another independent study (Study 3) of 1135 individuals residing in Oregon, US. All three studies consistently found a three-factor model of virtue: caring, self-control, and

Table 3.1 The six virtues and 24 character strengths in positive psychology (Peterson & Seligman, 2004)

Virtue	Character strength	Virtue	Character strength
1. Wisdom: strengths of acquiring and using knowledge	**1. Creativity**: thinking of new ways and concepts **2. Curiosity**: interest in things, exploration **3. Perspective**: understanding the world, wise advice **4. Open-mindedness**: evaluating all evidence fairly **5. Love of learning**: systematically adding knowledge	**2. Courage**: strengths of exercising willpower to achieve goals despite opposing forces	**6. Persistence**: completing tasks started **7. Bravery**: not backing down in the face of threats or difficulties **8. Integrity**: presenting oneself in a genuine way **9. Vitality**: feeling alive and excited
3. Humanity: interpersonal strengths, cultivating relationships	**10. Social intelligence**: understanding the social world **11. Kindness**: helping and taking care of others **12. Love**: valuing close relationships	**4. Justice**: civic strengths underlying healthy community life	**13. Leadership**: organising group activities **14. Fairness**: treating everyone fairly and justly **15. Citizenship**: being a good team member
5. Temperance: protective forces against excess	**16. Forgiveness/mercy**: forgiving others **17. Self-regulation**: regulating feelings and actions **18. Prudence**: choosing actions carefully **19. Humility/modesty**: not overestimating oneself	**6. Transcendence**: strengths that give meaning, connections to the universe	**20. Spirituality**: beliefs about purpose and meaning **21. Appreciation of beauty**: awareness of excellence **22. Hope**: hoping/working for a better future **23. Gratitude**: being grateful for good things **24. Humour**: seeing the bright side of life, loving to laugh

inquisitiveness. My research team examined the factor structure of the VIA-IS among Chinese people and also found that a three-dimensional model of virtue best fit our data (Duan et al., 2012; Duan et al., 2013), based on the following three virtues:

1. Interpersonal, which includes kindness, teamwork, fairness, love, authenticity, leadership, forgiveness, and gratitude in the VIA model. It represents a person's love, concern, and gratitude towards others in the VIA-IS.
2. Vitality, which consists of curiosity, zest, creativity, hope, perspective, bravery, beliefs, social intelligence, beauty, and humour in the VIA-IS. It reflects a person's qualities to seek new knowledge and apply it to achieve goals even in difficult circumstances.
3. Cautiousness, which includes judgment, prudence, regulation, perseverance, learning, and modesty in the VIA-IS. It represents a person's persistence in achieving goals and exhibiting self-control.

Due to the need to develop a short and user-friendly strength questionnaire to help individuals build resilience and alleviate mental health issues, I developed the 12-item Brief Strength Scale (BSS-12) to measure the three virtues established in my previous studies (Ho et al., 2016). Because virtue is a higher-order and more abstract concept than character strengths in the original 24-strength VIA model (McGrath, 2015; Peterson & Seligman, 2004), I changed the labels from virtue to strength in the BSS-12 to increase understanding and compliance. In other words, using strength instead of virtue is more practical. The SHINE framework uses strength (i.e. Strength-based Habit-building) instead of virtue to represent our intention to treat it as a pragmatic rather than theoretical resilience framework. The three strengths in our BSS model are as follows (see Fig. 3.1):

1. Temperance strength, which describes people who persist in achieving their goals and exhibit self-control.
2. Interpersonal strength, which describes a person's love, concern, and gratitude towards others.
3. Intellectual strength, which represents a person's curiosity and zest for creativity.

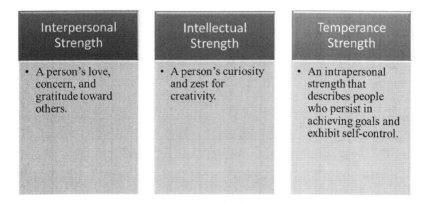

Fig. 3.1 The three core strengths of the BSS model (Ho et al., 2016)

The SHINE framework uses the labels above to conceptualise strengths and the BSS-12 to assess the three core strengths (see below).

3.1.1 Different Names, Same Three Strengths

Although researchers have used different names in the three-dimensional model, these names describe the same strengths. For example, McGrath (2015) mentioned that his three virtues are similar to those proposed by Duan et al. (2012), who also acknowledged that their three factors are similar to those proposed by Shryack et al. (2010). Table 3.2 compares the three strengths of the BSS model to other three-dimensional models.

3.1.2 Assessment of Strengths in the SHINE Framework

The SHINE framework assesses strengths using the BSS-12. Duan and Ho (2017) administered the simplified Chinese version of the BSS-12 to a community sample in mainland China (n = 375) to examine the three-factor structure of the BSS using multi-group confirmatory factor analysis. Their results showed measurement invariance across cultures, gender, and age groups. Furthermore, Lim (2023) examined the psychometric properties, including factor structure, of the BSS-12 among 288 college students in Korea and reported that the three-dimensional model of the original BSS-12, including interpersonal, temperance, and intellectual strengths,

52   S. M. Y. HO

Table 3.2 The three strengths of the SHINE framework and their corresponding strengths in other three-dimensional models

SHINE framework based on the BSS model (Ho et al., 2016)	Duan et al. (2012) model	Shryack et al. (2010) model	McGrath (2015) model
Temperance. Persistence in achieving goals and exercising self-control	Cautiousness	Conscientiousness	Self-control
Interpersonal. Love, concern, and gratitude towards others	Interpersonal	Sociability	Caring
Intellectual. Curiosity and zest for creativity	Vitality	Agency/ self-assuredness	Inquisitiveness

fit their data better than other competing models. Research has shown that the three strengths measured by the BSS-12 are appropriate for people from different cultural and demographic backgrounds.

3.1.3   Character Strengths and Resilience

Some of you may be wondering why bother with character strengths. Before continuing, it is important to discuss the relationship, if any, between character strengths and resilience.

First, the COR model (Hobfoll, 1989; Hobfoll et al., 2018) introduced in Chapter 1 emphasises the negative impact of resource loss in the event of adversity. Resilience during and after adversity relies on maintaining existing valued resources despite losses resulting from adversity. Character strengths are positive personal characteristics and resources. Knowing and developing our strengths can increase our resources to combat the impact of resources lost in adversity. The 3-PR model (de Terte et al., 2014) introduced in Chapter 1 proposes that regular self-care practice can foster personal resources (such as improved physical and emotional well-being, increased social connections) to navigate difficult circumstances, ultimately enhancing resilience. Hence, habitual use of character strengths can increase our resources to facilitate resilience.

Research has confirmed the important role of character strengths in resilience. For example, Hutchinson et al. (2011) administered the Resilience Scale (Wagnild & Young, 1993) and the VIA-IS (Peterson & Seligman, 2004) to measure resilience and virtues, respectively, in 620 young adults aged 17 to 30. Their results revealed a significant positive correlation between resilience and virtues, with higher virtues being associated with higher resilience among the participants. Duan et al. (2015) administered a battery of scales to measure stress levels, psychological symptoms, and the three virtues of cautiousness, interpersonal, and vitality in their model to 235 undergraduate students in Chongqing, China. They reported that all three virtues were negatively correlated with stress and psychological symptoms. They also found that vitality (similar to intellectual strength in the SHINE framework) mediated stress levels and the severity of psychological symptoms. In other words, when faced with adversity, people who exhibit higher intellectual strengths (curiosity, zest, creativity) may feel less stressed, which, in turn, may lead to fewer psychological problems (i.e. higher resilience). Lapierre et al. (2023) conducted a survey of 92 people aged 72 or older during the COVID-19 pandemic. They reported that courage and transcendence were significant predictors of resilience among the participants.

Although character strengths have been shown to be positively associated with resilience, it is necessary to examine whether people who practise their character strengths, compared with those who do not, achieve better outcomes. In a randomised controlled trial, Zhu et al. (2024) reported that developing knowledge and practice of character strengths could increase psychological well-being. Research conducted by my team confirmed these findings. Duan et al. (2014) conducted an intervention study on the outcome of strengths among 285 undergraduate students in China to investigate the above question. Students were asked to complete the VIA-IS (Peterson & Seligman, 2004) to learn more about their character strengths and were then assigned to either a strength training group or a life experiencer group. Those in the strength training group used their core strengths and reported when, where, and how they used them to the researchers each week. Those in the life experiencer group were asked to be mindful and calm in their daily lives and to describe 10 things they had done to the researchers each week. The researchers found that both groups reported significant increases in satisfaction with life after their respective interventions. However, only the students in the strength training group maintained their life

54 S. M. Y. HO

satisfaction levels for at least 10 weeks after the intervention. The life satisfaction levels of the students in the life experiencer group decreased to the pre-intervention level at the 10-week post-intervention assessment. The participants in the strength training group may have continued to use their strengths after the intervention, leading to sustained intervention effects. In other words, creating regular activities to exercise your strengths can cultivate resilience, and I use Strength-based Habit-building in the SHINE framework to capture this.

There are two important requirements for using the Strength-based Habit-building component of the SHINE framework: vital engagement and adaptive habit-building. I describe them below.

3.2 Vital Engagement = Flow + Meaning

Activities that involve both flow and meaning (Nakamura & Csikszentmihalyi, 2003; Wellman, 2022) can create a state of vital engagement (Nakamura & Csikszentmihalyi, 2003; Wellman, 2022). According to Csikszentmihalyi and colleagues (Csikszentmihalyi, 1975, 1994; Csikszentmihalyi et al., 2005; Nakamura & Csikszentmihalyi, 2003; Tse et al., 2022), when a person is fully absorbed in an autogenic (intrinsically rewarding) activity that represents a balance between the perceived challenges of the situation and the ability to handle it, the person enters a state of flow. In other words, flow can occur in an activity that is

1. Autogenic: the person does it solely because the process is rewarding, not for other reasons such as financial gain or friendship.
2. Challenging: it requires skills.
3. Manageable: the person can handle it even if it requires expanding existing skills or acquiring new skills.

For example, running faster is a challenge for runners. Often, they have to use their full abilities to break records. If running is an autogenic activity for them, they may enter a state of flow while running when they achieve a balance between challenge and skill. Figure 3.2 illustrates different flow conditions, called "the quadrant model of flow" (Mao et al., 2020). According to this model, highly challenging situations beyond our capabilities lead to anxiety. A combination of low challenge and low skill situations leads to apathy. Relaxation or boredom can occur when

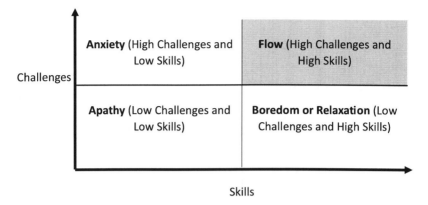

Fig. 3.2 The quadrant model of flow shows the flow state occurring in high challenge and high skill situations

the challenges posed by activities are below our capabilities. Finally, flow occurs in situations that balance high challenge and high skill.

Flow activities include work-related or leisure activities (e.g. sports, arts, writing). Cultivating flow has been shown to lead to a fulfilling life and reduced psychological symptoms (Csikszentmihalyi, 1994; Csikszentmihalyi & Asakawa, 2016; Mao et al., 2020; Tse et al., 2022). People in a flow state will exhibit the following characteristics (Csikszentmihalyi, 1975; Nakamura & Csikszentmihalyi, 2003; Tse et al., 2022):

- Complete and effortless concentration on the here and now.
- A distorted perception of time, meaning that time has passed faster or slower than reality.
- A feeling of control and mastery because they know how to handle the situation.
- An experience of intrinsic reward, regardless of the results.

Vital engagement is more than a flow activity: it requires that meaning emerge from the activities that produce flow (also called emergent meaning) (Nakamura & Csikszentmihalyi, 2003). In other words, having a meaningful experience alongside flow experiences contributes to vital engagement (Csikszentmihalyi, 1994). This meaning can arise because of the pleasure that flow activities provide, called "pull factors." In addition, meaning can arise from existing flow activities due to adversity, called "push factors." (Nakamura & Csikszentmihalyi, 2003; Wellman, 2022). For example, marathon runners experience flow while running. The simple pleasure of running motivates them to run again (pull factors). When adversity arises, such as unemployment, marathon running can provide a refuge from the financial crisis (push factors), thereby strengthening runners' relationship with marathon running.

However, some people may stop their existing flow activities in times of adversity when the external environment becomes increasingly challenging. The adaptive habit-building strategy aims to reduce this situation.

3.3   Adaptive Habit-Building

Habits are automatic actions triggered by contextual prompts associated with their performance (Gardner et al., 2012). Habits are basically dispositions to repeat a familiar behaviour (Neal et al., 2012). Once a habit is formed, people may feel uncomfortable not doing it. A good example is brushing your teeth. Most people feel uncomfortable if they do not brush their teeth after waking up in the morning. An activity becomes automatic and easier to maintain when it becomes a habit. More importantly, adaptive habits can increase resilience in the face of adversity (Sajquim de Torres & Dura, 2019). Many of us may have continued to practise regular habits (e.g. yoga, piano) at home during the COVID-19 lockdown, which helped us navigate many challenges during the pandemic.

Gardner et al. (2012) suggested the following steps to create habits:

1. Start with an activity that interests you and motivates you enough to do it. A flow activity using your strengths is a good way to identify such activities.
2. Find an appropriate context to trigger your intention to perform the activity. It can be an event (when I go to work) or a moment (after work).
3. During the learning phase, continue to practise the activity regularly (reading on the bus to work).
4. Set goals related to the activity (read one book per month). We will discuss goal setting in the next SHINE strategy (i.e. Hopeful Thinking) in Chapter 4.

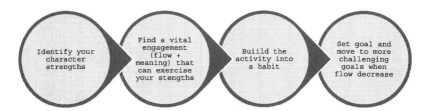

Fig. 3.3 Steps of the strength-based adaptive habit-building strategy of the SHINE framework

5. Repeat the activity in the same context until it becomes automatic and effortless.

3.4 Summary

Overall, the Strength-based Adaptive Habit-building strategy of the SHINE framework recommends that people

1. Identify their strengths.
2. Find a vital engagement activity (i.e. a meaningful activity with flow experiences).
3. Exercise their strengths in the vital engagement activity.
4. Turn the activity into a habit so that it eventually becomes effortless and automatic.
5. When the activity lacks challenges due to improved skills and reduced flow, set new goals (a higher level) to maintain the habit.

Figure 3.3 illustrates the above steps.

3.5 Practical Applications

3.5.1 Identify Your Character Strengths

A common way to identify your character strengths is to complete assessment questionnaires. There are many free online surveys on character strengths. Probably the most popular survey is the VIA survey, which measures the 24 character strengths proposed by Peterson and Seligman (2004) (https://www.viacharacter.org/).

58 S. M. Y. HO

Table 3.3 Brief Strength Scale (BSS-12) result

Temperance (Item 1, Item 2, Item 9, Item 11) Score: _____	This factor represents intrapersonal strengths, including persistence in achieving goals and exhibiting self-control
Interpersonal (Item 4, Item 5, Item 8, Item 10) Score: _____	This factor reflects positive behaviour toward other people, including love, concern, and gratitude
Intellectual (Item 3, Item 6, Item 7, Item 12) Score: _____	This factor reflects positive qualities in the world /society, such as curiosity and zest for creativity

As mentioned, the SHINE framework uses a three-dimensional strength model that includes temperance, interpersonal, and intellectual strengths. To measure these strengths, I developed the BSS-12 (Ho et al., 2016), provided below. You can find the scoring key below before the scale. However, I strongly recommend completing *the scale without looking at the scoring key*. Next, calculate the score for each strength by adding the scores for the relevant items and entering them in Table 3.3.

Brief Strengths Scale 12 (BSS -12)

Please read the following statements carefully and rate the extent to which each statement described you and your thoughts, feelings, and behaviours according to a score from 1 to 7. Please circle your response.

	Totally disagree (1)	*Disagree* (2)	*Somewhat disagree* (3)	*Neutral* (4)	*Somewhat agree* (5)	*Agree* (6)	*Totally agree* (7)
1. I am a persistent person.	1	2	3	4	5	6	7
2. I am a hard-working person.	1	2	3	4	5	6	7
3. I think there are a lot of interesting things in this world to be explored.	1	2	3	4	5	6	7

(continued)

3 STRENGTH-BASED HABIT-BUILDING **59**

(continued)

	Totally disagree (1)	Disagree (2)	Somewhat disagree (3)	Neutral (4)	Somewhat agree (5)	Agree (6)	Totally agree (7)
4. I appreciate people's gratitude to me.	1	2	3	4	5	6	7
5. I feel happy for other people's happiness	1	2	3	4	5	6	7
6. I am excited when I can think of the possibility of producing a new creation	1	2	3	4	5	6	7
7. I always revel in some interesting things.	1	2	3	4	5	6	7
8. I am a person with compassion.	1	2	3	4	5	6	7
9. I ask myself to persist in the face of difficulty.	1	2	3	4	5	6	7
10. I strongly treasure my relationships with the people around me.	1	2	3	4	5	6	7
11. I am a person with strong self-control.	1	2	3	4	5	6	7

(continued)

60 S. M. Y. HO

(continued)

	Totally disagree (1)	Disagree (2)	Somewhat disagree (3)	Neutral (4)	Somewhat agree (5)	Agree (6)	Totally agree (7)
12. I am a person who likes to find new things.	1	2	3	4	5	6	7

3.5.2 My Strengths for Overcoming Adversity

Describe a time when you exhibited the (single) strength with the highest score in Table 3.3 (temperance, interpersonal, or intellectual) to overcome a difficult situation. Choose one strength if you have equal scores. It would be better if other people could easily identify your strengths by listening to your experience sharing. Then answer the following questions:

I was in (describe the situation) _____

_____

_____

I used _____ (strength) to overcome adversity by (describe how you used the focal strength to meet challenges) _____

The outcome (s) was/were _____

_____

3.5.3 Using Your Strengths in Daily Life

Use your strengths in your daily activities. Some examples are given in Table 3.4.

3 STRENGTH-BASED HABIT-BUILDING 61

Table 3.4 Examples of using your strengths in daily life

Temperance	– When facing the next challenge, imagine the best and worst-case scenarios and decide on the most realistic course of action (Judgment)
	– Take control of at least one new situation at home or at work, a situation that you can handle. If you fail, revise your plan, but don't give up until you're done (Perseverance)
	– Make important decisions when you are relaxed, not anxious or depressed (Prudence)
	– Clarify your values by reflecting on how they have served you best in difficult situations (Bravery)
Interpersonal	– Explore and appreciate the strengths of your loved ones (Love)
	– Greet others with a smile (Kindness)
	– Ask your neighbours, especially older people, if they need anything from the supermarket (Teamwork)
	– Remember times when you have offended someone and been forgiven, then extend that gift to others (Forgiveness)
	– List three blessings (good things that have happened to you) before you go to bed each day (Gratitude)
Intellectual	– Do a physical activity of your choice, one that you don't "have to do" or that you're told to do (Vitality/Zest)
	– List all the bad things that have happened to you, then find at least two positive things for each one (Hope)
	– Identify three past accomplishments in detail and let them inspire your future (Hope)
	– Propose at least one creative solution to challenges faced by a sibling or friend (Creativity)

3.5.4 Using Your Strength(s) in a Vital Engagement Activity to Create Habits

Identify a vital engagement activity (flow + meaning) and try to exercise your strength(s) when doing it. Next, plan to turn this vital engagement activity into a habit. Complete Table 3.5 each time you perform your vital activity if you wish to keep a record of it.

1. Create a designated time in your schedule, at least once a week, to do the vital engagement activity, such as every Saturday after breakfast or when coming home from work.
2. Continue to perform the activity on your schedule until it becomes a habit (automatic; you feel uncomfortable if you don't do it).
3. When the activity becomes boring, set new goals, repeat Steps 1 and 2.

62 S. M. Y. HO

Table 3.5 Use your strength(s) in a vital engagement activity to create habits

Date:_____
Time: From _____ to _____
Mood Before the Activity: _____
My Strength(s):

My Vital Engagement Activity:

Mood During the Activity: _____
Mood After the Activity: _____
The activity is challenging/easy
I was aware that time was passing slowly/quickly during the activity

REFERENCES

Brdar, I., & Kashdan, T. B. (2010). Character strengths and well-being in Croatia: An empirical investigation of structure and correlates. *Journal of Research in Personality*, *44*(1), 151–154.https://doi.org/10.1016/j.jrp. 2009.12.001

Cawley, M. J., Martin, J. E., & Johnson, J. A. (2000). A virtues approach to personality. *Personality and Individual Differences*, *28*(5), 997–1013. https://doi.org/10.1016/S0191-8869(99)00207-X

Csikszentmihalyi, M. (1994). *Flow and the foundations of positive psychology. The collected works of mihaly csikszentmihalyi.* Springer. https://doi.org/10.1007/978-94-017-9088-8

Csikszentmihalyi, M. (1975). *Beyond boredom and anxiety: Experiencing flow in work and play.* Jossey-Bass Publishers.

Csikszentmihalyi, M., & Asakawa, K. (2016). Universal and cultural dimensions of optimal experiences. *Japanese Psychological Research*, *58*(1), 4–13. https://doi.org/10.1111/jpr.12104

Csikszentmihalyi, M., Abuhamdeh, S., & Nakamura, J. (2005). Flow. In A. J. Elliot & C. S. Dweck (Eds.), *Handbook of competence and motivation* (pp. 598–608, 704 Pages). Guilford Publications.

Duan, W., & Ho, S. M. Y. (2017). Three-dimensional model of strengths: examination of invariance across gender, age, education levels, and marriage status. *Community Mental Health Journal*, *53*(1), 233–240. https://doi.org/10. 1007/s10597-016-0038-y

Duan, W., & Ho, S. M. Y. (2018). Does being mindful of your character strengths enhance psychological wellbeing? A longitudinal mediation analysis. *Journal of Happiness Studies*, *19*(4), 1045–1066. https://doi.org/10.1007/s10902-017-9864-z

Duan, W., Ho, S. M. Y., Bai, Y., & Tang, X. (2013). Psychometric evaluation of the Chinese Virtues Questionnaire. *Research on Social Work Practice*, 23(3), 336–345. https://doi.org/10.1177/1049731513477214

Duan, W., Ho, S. M. Y., Siu, B. P. Y., Li, T., & Zhang, Y. (2015). Role of virtues and perceived life stress in affecting psychological symptoms among Chinese college students. *Journal of American College Health*, 63(1), 32–39. https://doi.org/10.1080/07448481.2014.963109

Duan, W., Ho, S. M. Y., Tang, X., Li, T., & Zhang, Y. (2014). Character strength-based intervention to promote satisfaction with life in the Chinese university context. *Journal of Happiness Studies*, 15(6), 1347–1361. https://doi.org/10.1007/s10902-013-9479-y

Duan, W., Ho, S. M. Y., Yu, B., Tang, X., Zhang, Y., Li, T., & Yuen, T. (2012). Factor structure of the Chinese virtues questionnaire. *Research on Social Work Practice*, 22(6), 680–688. https://doi.org/10.1177/1049731512450074

van Eeden, C., Wissing, M. P., Dreyer, J., Park, N., & Peterson, C. (2008). Validation of the Values in Action Inventory of Strengths for Youth (VIA-Youth) among South African learners. *Journal of Psychology in Africa*, 18(1), 143–154.

Gardner, B., Lally, P., & Wardle, J. (2012). Making health habitual: the psychology of 'habit-formation' and general practice. *British Journal of General Practice*, 62(605), 664–666. https://doi.org/10.3399/bjgp12X659466

Ho, S. M. Y., Li, W. L., Duan, W., Siu, B. P. Y., Yau, S., Yeung, G., & Wong, K. (2016). A brief strengths scale for individuals with mental health issues. *Psychological Assessment*, 28(1), 147–157. https://doi.org/10.1037/pas0000164

Hobfoll, S. E. (1989). Conservation of resources: A new attempt at conceptualizing stress. *American Psychologist*, 44(3), 513–524. https://doi.org/10.1037/0003-066X.44.3.513

Hobfoll, S. E., Halbesleben, J., Neveu, J.-P., & Westman, M. (2018). Conservation of resources in the organizational context: The reality of resources and their consequences. *Annual Review of Organizational Psychology and Organizational Behavior*, 5(1), 103–128. https://doi.org/10.1146/annurev-orgpsych-032117-104640

Hutchinson, A.-M. K., Stuart, A. D., & Pretorius, H. G. (2011). The relationships between temperament, character strengths, and resilience. In I. Brdar (Ed.), *The human pursuit of well-being: A cultural approach* (pp. 133–144). Springer Netherlands. https://doi.org/10.1007/978-94-007-1375-8_12

Lapierre, S., Chauvette, S., Bolduc, L., Adams-Lemieux, M., Boller, B., & Desjardins, S. (2023). Character strengths and resilience in older adults during the COVID-19 pandemic. *Canadian Journal on Aging*, 42(3), 455–465. https://doi.org/10.1017/S0714980823000089

64 S. M. Y. HO

Lavy, S., & Benish-Weisman, M. (2021). Character strengths as "values in action": Linking character strengths with values theory – An exploratory study of the case of gratitude and self-transcendence. *Frontiers in Psychology*, *12*, 9. https://doi.org/10.3389/fpsyg.2021.576189

Lim, Y.-J. (2023). Psychometric properties of the brief strengths scale-12 in Korean population. *Sage Open*, *13*(4), 21582440231210045. https://doi.org/10.1177/21582440231210045

Linley, P. A., Maltby, J., Wood, A. M., Joseph, S., Harrington, S., Peterson, C., Park, N., & Seligman, M. E. P. (2007). Character strengths in the United Kingdom: The VIA inventory of strengths. *Personality and Individual Differences*, *43*(2), 341–351. https://doi.org/10.1016/j.paid.2006.12.004

Mao, Y., Yang, R., Bonaiuto, M., Ma, J., & Harmat, L. (2020). Can flow alleviate anxiety? The roles of academic self-efficacy and self-esteem in building psychological sustainability and resilience. *Sustainability*, *12*(7), 2987. https://doi.org/10.3390/su12072987

McGrath, R. E. (2014). Scale- and item-level factor analyses of the VIA inventory of strengths. *Assessment*, *21*(1), 4–14. https://doi.org/10.1177/1073191112450612

McGrath, R. E. (2015). Integrating psychological and cultural perspectives on virtue: The hierarchical structure of character strengths. *The Journal of Positive Psychology*, *10*(5), 407–424. https://doi.org/10.1080/17439760.2014.994222

Nakamura, J., & Csikszentmihalyi, m. (2003). The construction of meaning through vital engagement. In C. L. M. Keyes & J. Haidt (Eds.), *Flourishing: Positive psychology and the life well-lived*. (pp. 83–104, 335 Pages). American Psychological Association. https://doi.org/10.1037/10594-004

Neal, D. T., Wood, W., Labrecque, J. S., & Lally, P. (2012). How do habits guide behavior? Perceived and actual triggers of habits in daily life. *Journal of Experimental Social Psychology*, *48*(2), 492–498. https://doi.org/10.1016/j.jesp.2011.10.011

Park, N., Peterson, C., & Seligman, M. E. P. (2004). Strengths of character and well-being: A closer look at hope and modesty. *Journal of Social and Clinical Psychology*, *23*(5), 628–634. https://doi.org/10.1521/jscp.23.5.628.50749

Peterson, C., & Seligman, M. E. P. (2004). *Character strengths and virtues: A handbook and classification*. American Psychological Association.

Peterson, C., Park, N., Pole, N., D'Andrea, W., & Seligman, M. E. (2008). Strengths of character and posttraumatic growth. *Journal of Traumatic Stress*, *21*(2), 214–217. https://doi.org/10.1002/jts.20332

Peterson, C., Stephens, J. P., Park, N., Lee, F., & Seligman, M. E. P. (2010). Strengths of character and work. In P. A. Linley, S. Harrington, & N. Garcea (Eds.), *Oxford handbook of positive psychology and work*. Oxford University Press.

Sajquim de Torres, M., & Dura, L. (2019). Habits as building blocks for the resilience of vulnerable populations: Two positive deviance case studies from the U.S.–Mexico Border Region. *Health Promotion Practice*, *20*(6), 793–797. https://doi.org/10.1177/1524839919855392

Shryack, J., Steger, M. F., Krueger, R. F., & Kallie, C. S. (2010). The structure of virtue: An empirical investigation of the dimensionality of the virtues in action inventory of strengths. *Personality and Individual Differences*, *48*(6), 714–719. https://doi.org/10.1016/j.paid.2010.01.007

Steger, M. F., Hicks, B. M., Kashdan, T. B., Krueger, R. F., & Bouchard Jr, T. J. (2007). Genetic and environmental influences on the positive traits of the values in action classification, and biometric covariance with normal personality. *Journal of Research in Personality*, *41*(3), 524–539. https://doi.org/10.1016/j.jrp.2006.06.002

de Terte, I., Stephens, C., & Huddleston, L. (2014). The development of a three part model of psychological resilience. *Stress and Health*, *30*(5), 416–424. https://doi.org/10.1002/smi.2625

Tse, D. C. K., Nakamura, J., & Csikszentmihalyi, M. (2022). Flow experiences across adulthood: Preliminary findings on the continuity hypothesis. *Journal of Happiness Studies*, *23*(6), 2517–2540. https://doi.org/10.1007/s10902-022-00514-5

Wagner, L., Gander, F., Proyer, R. T., & Ruch, W. (2020). Character strengths and PERMA: Investigating the relationships of character strengths with a multidimensional framework of well-being. *Applied Research in Quality of Life*, *15*(2), 307–328. https://doi.org/10.1007/s11482-018-9695-z

Wagnild, G. M., & Young, H. M. (1993). Development and psychometric evaluation of the resilience scale. *Journal of Nursing Measurement*, *1*(2), 165–178.

Wellman, J. (2022). Living in vivid color with "vital engagement". *Psychology Today*. https://www.psychologytoday.com/intl/blog/4000-mon days/202212/living-in-vivid-color-with-vital-engagement

Zhu, Q., Wang, Q., & Yang, S. (2024). Does mindfulness matter in the development of character strengths? A RCT study comparing mindfulness-based strengths practice and character strengths-based intervention. *The Journal of Positive Psychology*, *19*(5), 900. https://doi.org/10.1080/17439760.2023.2257678

CHAPTER 4

Hopeful Thinking

Abstract The original cognitive theory posits that hope has three core components: goal, agency, and pathway thinking. Based on this theory, the SHINE framework adopts an expanded model of hope that incorporates goal disengagement, goal reengagement, and sub-goaling, illustrating how high-hope individuals adaptively adjust their goals in response to adversity. The distinction between hope and optimism is clarified, highlighting the focus in hope on goal-directed cognition and its relevance to resilience. Research findings underscore the significant role of hope in psychological adjustment during challenging circumstances, including its protective effects against distress and its capacity to foster positive outcomes in high-risk populations. The chapter concludes that cultivating a hopeful mindset is crucial for navigating adversity, enabling individuals to identify new goals, and maintaining resilience in the face of setbacks. Practical exercises to cultivate hope are introduced.

Keywords Hope · Goal · Agency · Pathway · Willpower · Waypower · Goal disengagement · Goal reengagement · Regoaling · Goal-directed cognition

© The Author(s), under exclusive license to Springer Nature
Switzerland AG 2025
S. M. Y. Ho, *The SHINE Framework*,
https://doi.org/10.1007/978-3-031-89106-9_4

4.1 The Story of a High-Hope Person

Jane was a 17-year-old girl who aspired to study medicine at university. She studied hard and was always the top student at her high school. One month before the public university entrance exam, Jane suffered a stroke in her left brain, requiring neurosurgery. As a result, Jane was unable to attend the public exam. The brain operation affected her intellectual and physical functioning. She needed crutches to walk and suffered from mild short-term memory loss. Jane knew full well that it would be very difficult, if not impossible, for her to achieve her goal of entering medical school.

Many would feel frustrated if they were in Jane's situation and see no hope for the future. Jane reacted differently. She decided to use her experience to help others. Jane eventually took the public exam and applied for a social work diploma offered by a private university. She learnt to use technological devices to compensate for her memory problems, exercised regularly, and maintained a good diet to stay healthy. She used positive, energising self-talk (e.g. "This is hard, but I'll keep trying.") to stay motivated. Jane is an example of a high-hope person within the SHINE framework, which conceptualises hope as a type of adaptive cognition.

4.2 The Adaptive Cognitive Triad of Hope

The cognitive theory of hope emphasises the cognitive processes involved in hope, namely the interconnections between goal, agency, and pathway thinking (Snyder, 2000, 2002). Hopeful thinking is based on the assumption that people's daily behaviour is goal-oriented. Goals are desired mental targets that can vary in many ways, such as short-term or long-term, specific or non-specific, conscious or non-conscious, approaching or avoiding in nature, or represented as verbal self-statements or visual images (Lopez & Snyder, 2011). High-hope individuals tend to set more goals than their counterparts, have more ambitious goals than their past achievements, and incorporate some uncertainty into their highly attainable goals (Cheavens et al., 2006).

The other two essential components of the cognitive model of hope are pathway thinking and agency thinking (Snyder et al., 1991). Pathway, also known as "waypower," is the perceived ability to generate plausible routes and strategies to achieve one's goals (Snyder, 2002). For goal pursuit to occur, individuals must believe that they can formulate multiple strategies.

Fig. 4.1 The three cognitive components of hope proposed by Snyder (2000)

When one route is blocked, they can consider alternative ways to reach the desired outcome. Research has shown that high-hope individuals can generate more pathways and alternatives when faced with obstacles than their counterparts (Snyder et al., 1991).

Agency, also known as "willpower," is the perceived ability to use and sustain strategies along the path towards goal pursuit (Snyder, 2002). Agency thinking is the motivational component often evident in positive self-talk, such as "I am capable of doing this" and "I will never give up" (Lopez & Snyder, 2011). When faced with obstacles, agency is particularly important in channelling positive energy to encourage individuals to use alternative strategies instead of giving up (Lopez & Snyder, 2011). Figure 4.1 illustrates the three components of hope.

4.3 The Expanded Model of Hope

In the face of adversity, initial goals may no longer be achievable due to changes in oneself or external circumstances. I added the components of "upward regoaling," "downward regoaling," and "sub-goaling" to Snyder's (2000) model to create the expanded model of hope (Ho, 2016) in the *World Book of Hope* (Bormans, 2016).

> *Goal Disengagement*: High-hope individuals do not cling to their previous goals, but rather tend to let go of them when circumstances change. For example, Jane disengaged from her goal of entering medical school after her operation.
> *Goal Reengagement*: After disengaging from their previous goals, high-hope individuals reengage in new goals that are more appropriate for their new situation. Depending on the circumstances, people can set higher goals (upward regoaling) or lower goals (downward regoaling). Jane set herself a new goal: to become a social worker and use her experience to help others.
> *Sub-goaling*: High-hope individuals divide their final goals into smaller, more manageable sub-goals. Furthermore, they can continue to make efforts to overcome current difficulties and pursue their higher-level goals. Jane learnt to use technology to overcome her memory problems, gained a professional qualification, and eventually became a social worker.

Overall, the above concepts highlight how high-hope people are future-oriented and flexible in letting go of old goals and adeptly reengaging in more fitting goals when their situation changes due to adversity. They also break down larger goals into smaller steps and work persistently to achieve their long-term aspirations despite challenges. Figure 4.2 illustrates the expanded model of hope.

4.4   WHAT HOPE IS AND IS NOT?

First, hope is a character strength related to expecting/working towards a better future in the VIA model (Peterson & Seligman, 2004) (see Chapter 3, Table 3.1). It is also a component of temperance in the three-dimensional strength model proposed by our research team (Ho et al., 2016). Hence, cultivating hope may help improve your character strengths profile. In the SHINE framework, hope is a type of learnable cognition (i.e. your ways of thinking), which differs from the religious and philosophical meaning of hope.

Another concept in psychology is optimism, which is similar to hope. Optimism is believing that good things will happen in the future despite external circumstances (Scheier & Carver, 1988). Optimism concerns the agency (willpower) of goal-directed thinking, while hope involves pathway thinking and agency related to goal achievement (Snyder et al.,

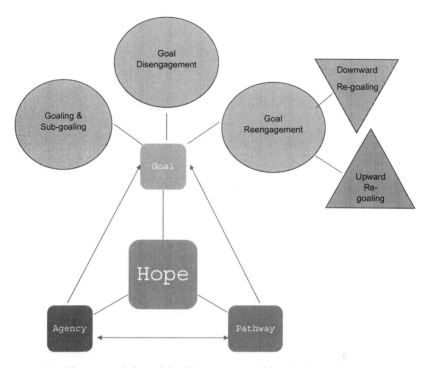

Fig. 4.2 The expanded model of hope proposed by Ho (2016)

2000). Research has also shown that hope and optimism are different constructs with different effects on stress outcomes. For instance, Rand (2009) measured hope and optimism among 345 students in a university psychology course and reported that hope, but not optimism, influenced students' grade expectations, which, in turn, affected their grade performance.

However, in a study of 334 secondary school students in Singapore, Wong and Lim (2009) reported that hope and optimism were strongly correlated; that is, high-hope students also reported high optimism, and vice versa. In addition, both hope and optimism could predict depression, with the latter being a better predictor. Long et al. (2024) assessed 788 American adults over three periods in 2020 during the COVID-19 pandemic. They reported that hope and optimism were associated with lower initial COVID-19-related stress and higher levels of well-being.

72   S. M. Y. HO

Considering their combined effects, both factors were significant predictors of well-being, although optimism had a stronger correlation with health-related distress.

In summary, both optimism and hope are important constructs related to resilience. Hope emphasises goal, pathway, and agency thinking in goal achievement, while optimism focuses on agency thinking. The SHINE framework focuses on hopeful thinking because, as mentioned, goal-related cognition, especially goal disengagement and reengagement, is particularly relevant to resilience in the face of adversity. However, the development of optimism is included as an Embracing Change strategy in the context of developing a self-serving explanatory style (Chapter 7).

In my previous workshops (Ho et al., 2012), some of the participants were confused about hope-based resilience and problem-solving skills (Davidson & Sternberg, 2003). As mentioned, hope is a type of future-oriented cognition related to goal setting and goal achievement. In contrast, problems are current difficulties, and problem-solving skills involve developing and choosing the best solution(s) to solve current problems. The steps related to achieving hope-based goals and problem-solving skills are described in Table 4.1. I discuss hope-based skills in more detail later in this chapter.

Table 4.1   Hope-based versus problem-focused strategies

Hope-based strategies	Problem-solving strategies
Step 1: Set goal(s)	Step 1: Define problems
Step 2: Generate and learn ways to achieve these goals	Step 2: Generate alternative solutions
Step 3: Engage in sub-goaling, if necessary	Step 3: Review and select an alternative
Step 4: Increase and maintain willpower	Step 4: Implement and monitor the solution
Step 5: Evaluate effectiveness in achieving goals	Step 5: Evaluate the effectiveness of problem-solving
Step 6: Engage in regoaling (goal disengagement and reengagement), if necessary	Step 6: Choose and implement another solution, if necessary

4.5 HOPE AND RESILIENCE

In my previous research on resilience (Ho & Lo, 2011; Ho et al., 2010; Ho et al., 2012; Ho et al., 2011a, b; Ho et al., 2013d; Huen et al., 2015; Mak et al., 2021; Or et al., 2021; Rajandram et al., 2011; Yuen et al., 2013), hope was consistently one of the most important factors related to positive adjustment to adversity. Other researchers have also reported that hope is a buffer against academic distress (Gilman et al., 2006; Lagace-Seguin & d'Entremont, 2010; Onwuegbuzie, 1998; Snyder et al., 2002; Worrell & Hale, 2001), health-related psychological distress among children/adolescents (Barnum et al., 1998; Berg et al., 2007; Eche et al., 2022; Fearnow-Kenney & Kliewer, 2000; Lewis & Kliewer, 1996; Lloyd & Hastings, 2009), adults patients (Chang, 1998; Chang & DeSimone, 2001; Elliott et al., 1991; Herth, 1989; Irving et al., 1997; Irving et al., 1998; Miao et al., 2024; Stanton et al., 2000), and their carers (Kashdan et al., 2002; Mednick et al., 2007; Ogston et al., 2011; Truitt et al., 2012). The above studies are described elsewhere (Ho et al., 2013d). Below, I highlight some lessons learnt from my research on hope.

4.5.1 High-Hope Individuals Are Better Prepared to Face the Unknown

Many years ago, I received a telephone call from a surgeon, Dr Judy Ho, who asked me an interesting question: her department was offering free genetic colon cancer screening to people at risk of hereditary colorectal cancer (HCRC) for early intervention, and yet many people rejected their offer. "You are a psychologist. Why do people refuse to undergo this free and potentially life-saving procedure?" At the time, I did not know much about this relatively new medical procedure in Hong Kong, so I said, "This is a good clinical question. I don't know the exact answer, but let's do some research to find out." Judy accepted my suggestion, which began a 10 + year collaboration between Judy and me on psychological research related to HCRC screening.

First, consistent with the literature, we found that people view HCRC screening as a procedure with potential benefits and harms (Ho et al., 2003a). They may feel relief if the result is negative (i.e. they do not carry the mutant gene). In addition, carriers can reduce their risk of

74   S. M. Y. HO

cancer by using available prevention options. However, those with positive results may face psychological burdens, including long-term fears of developing cancer, as well as concerns about passing the altered gene to their children. Hence, people will evaluate the pros and cons of HCRC screening for themselves and their loved ones before making a decision. Next, we conducted a longitudinal study to investigate the psychological factors that affect HCRC adjustment among recipients (Ho et al., 2010). Four outcome trajectories, namely chronic dysfunction, recovery, delayed dysfunction, and resilience, were created. More importantly, baseline hope significantly predicted a resilience outcome trajectory among HCRC recipients.

Finally, we conducted an outcome study to investigate the effect of a hope-based intervention on the psychological adjustments of HCRC genetic screening recipients (Ho et al., 2012). The results showed that those who received the intervention had increased levels of hope and decreased levels of anxiety from pre- to post-intervention.

HCRC screening recipients face many uncertainties during and after the procedures: test results, how their loved ones will react, and decisions related to marriage and parenthood. High-hope individuals are better prepared to face such uncertainty than their counterparts because they can set new goals, practise goal disengagement and reengagement, and exercise agency and pathway strategies to update their goals when circumstances change.

4.5.2   *High-Hope Individuals Exhibit Resilience Even in Life-Threatening Situations*

Prof Lim Cheung, Chair Professor at a dental hospital in Hong Kong, ringed me one day and asked, "We have patients with severe dentofacial deformities. We can treat them with surgery, but some of our patients suffered psychological breakdowns during and after the operation. They then exhibited symptoms related to personality change, depression, and anxiety. Could you tell us how to identify the patients who may not have the psychological strength to undergo the intrusive medical procedure early enough before treatment begins so that they can be referred for psychological support?" This is an unusual but important question from a dentist, and I did not have the answer. As a result, I offered my usual response: "This is an important clinical question. Let's do some research together to find the answer." Prof Cheung and I then started a long and fruitful research journey. Throughout the years, we conducted studies on a variety of topics in patients with dentofacial deformities, especially cleft lip and palate deformities (Cheung et al., 2006, 2007; Chua et al., 2012; Leung et al., 2013; Suen et al., 2018; Tam et al., 2014). More relevant to our current topic, we found that hope is an important resilience factor affecting the psychological outcomes of patients with oral cancer (Rajandram et al., 2011).

In another study supported by the Children's Cancer Foundation, my research team found that high-hope children with cancer were more resilient (lower levels of depression and anxiety) than their counterparts, and that negative cancer-related rumination was an important mediator of this relationship (Yuen et al., 2013). In other words, high-hope children tend to have fewer repetitive negative thoughts related to cancer, leading to greater resilience. Individuals with adaptive hope cognition may think more about goal setting/resetting and how to exercise agency and pathway strategies to achieve their goals in the face of adversity, which may replace negative thoughts related to their adversity.

4.5.3 High-Hope Individuals Are Sensitive to Both Positive and Negative Information in the Environment

Dr Vivian Mak, a senior clinical psychologist at the Hong Kong Correctional Services Department, contacted me one day to explore a collaborative project to develop a new gender-responsive rehabilitation facility within one of the correctional institutions for female offenders. The proposed project seemed interesting to me, so I agreed to collaborate with Vivian almost without hesitation. Another exciting venture that would last more than 10 years had just begun!

The characteristics of female offenders differ from the usual (stigmatised) image of criminal offenders in the media. Many of them had been victims of abuse and had, to some extent, suffered from traumatic experiences and mental health problems prior to their incarceration (Salisbury & Van Voorhis, 2009). Female offenders may have had more childcare responsibilities than their male counterparts prior to their incarceration (Loper et al., 2009). Accordingly, they should have a gender-responsive rehabilitation facility that is not based on the conventional male-oriented approach.

We developed a facility combining traditional cognitive-behavioural approaches and positive psychology interventions for female offenders within a correctional institution of the Hong Kong Correctional Services Department (Mak et al., 2018). We named this gender-responsive correctional facility the Psychological Gymnasium (PSY GYM) to convey the idea that many of us go to the gym to regularly train our body muscles to maintain our physical well-being. We should create a place where people can periodically train their mental strengths for psychological wellness. A hope-based intervention is a core component of the PSY GYM rehabilitation programme, and we found that increasing hope could lead to better psychological adjustment for female offenders. More importantly, in a subsequent study (Mak et al., 2021), we found that high-hope female offenders were more inclined than their counterparts to pay attention to positive information and less to negative information, leading to better psychological resilience (lower levels of depression and anxiety).

In summary, I believe that high-hope individuals are sensitive to positive and negative information in their environment to facilitate goal setting and the implementation of agency and pathway strategies. In contrast, low-hope individuals are inclined to pay attention to negative information and stimuli in a challenging environment. As Chapter 6 will show, balanced attention to positive and negative adversity stimuli is important for resilience.

4.5.4   High-Hope Individuals See Hope in Hopeless Situations

Hope theory does not specify that the goals set by high-hope individuals are always positive and prosocial (Snyder, 1994, 2000). When high-hope individuals set undesirable goals that may harm themselves and others, are they more likely to achieve them? For example, if high-hope individuals set a goal to die, are they more likely to achieve their goal of committing suicide than their counterparts? Even Snyder (2002) mentioned that when the situation is unbearable and there are no achievable goals (i.e. under conditions of extreme adversity), suicide might become the only attainable goal. This question has puzzled me for years. This is one of the most common questions I received during my hope-based resilience training workshops and seminars.

I had the opportunity to address the above question as part of a collaborative research project with Prof Paul Yip, a scholar in suicide research and prevention, and his team. As part of a larger project, we measured hope, hopelessness, and suicidal ideation (i.e. thoughts of engaging in suicide-related behaviour) in a community sample of 2106 participants using a population-based household survey (Huen et al., 2015). Some people may conceptualise hope and hopelessness as opposite poles of the same continuum. In psychology, hopelessness is commonly conceptualised as the perceptual anticipation of undesirable situations or consequences that are largely beyond one's control (Beck et al., 1974). This definition differs from Snyder's cognitive model of hope, which involves goal, agency, and pathway thinking (Grewal & Porter, 2007). Our main research question was as follows: When subjective appraisals of hopelessness are high, would high-hope individuals exhibit more suicidal ideation than low-hope individuals?

In short, we found that high suicidal ideation only occurred in people with a combination of low hope and high hopelessness appraisals. Individuals with high levels of hope did not exhibit significantly more suicidal ideation, even when they had high self-rated hopelessness. Table 4.2 presents the findings.

Table 4.2 Interaction between hope and hopelessness on suicidal ideation, adapted from Huen et al. (2015)

Hope	High Hope	Low Suicidal Ideation	Low Suicidal Ideation
	Low Hope	Low Suicidal Ideation	High Suicidal Ideation
		Low Hopelessness	High Hopelessness

Hopelessness

I believe that in the face of adversity, high-hope individuals, when they fail to achieve their original life goals, can generate new goals by exercising goal disengagement, downward regoaling, and goal reengagement to maintain a meaningful life. They may feel frustrated, depressed, and anxious, but they will not think about ending their lives because they can identify new meanings and life goals in the face of adversity. However, it is important to note that suicide can become a viable option for high-hope people when the pain is truly unbearable.

4.6 Summary

Hopeful Thinking is perhaps the most important component of the SHINE framework. Adversity often leads to change. Cultivating a hopeful thinking style can help us cope with uncertainty and better adapt to unfamiliar situations. It can help us notice positive information in difficult conditions. When the external environment deteriorates, a hopeful thinking style enables us to disengage from existing goals and practise downward regoaling to set new goals so as not to give up easily. As we do not give up, we can reengage in new and more ambitious goals when circumstances improve.

4.7 Practical Applications

4.7.1 Measuring Hope

The first thing to do is to better understand your hope profile. Because hope is a conscious thinking style, it can be assessed using questionnaires, like other constructs in cognitive psychology.

The Trait Hope Scale (Babyak et al., 1993; Snyder et al., 1991), the State Hope Scale (Snyder et al., 1996), and the Children's Hope Scale (Snyder et al., 1997) are three psychometrically sound self-report scales developed by Snyder and colleagues. All three scales comprise two subscales, namely agency and pathway, with a total hope score generated by adding the scores from the two subscales. The Trait Hope Scale measures dispositional or trait-level hope, consisting of 12 items (4 each for pathways and agency, plus 4 distraction items) rated on an 8-point Likert scale (1 = definitely false to 8 = definitely true). The State Hope Scale assesses momentary or state-level hope, with eight items (3 each for pathways and agency). The Children's Hope Scale is designed for youth aged 8–16 and measures trait-level hope with six items (three each for agency and pathways).

The scales have demonstrated strong internal reliability, a clear two-factor structure differentiating agency and pathway components, and convergent and discriminant validity (Babyak et al., 1993; Snyder et al., 1991, 1996, 1997).

With Snyder's permission, I translated and adapted the Trait Hope Scale into Chinese and called it the Future Scale for my research and training. This scale has shown good psychometric properties (Ho et al., 2010; Ho et al., 2012; Ho et al., 2011a, b; Huen et al., 2015; Mak et al., 2021; Rajandram et al., 2011; Yuen et al., 2013).

The Future Scale is provided below. I encourage you to read all items carefully and circle the numbers that best describe you. I strongly advise you to complete all items before reading the scoring key provided below the scale.

The future scale	1 (Definitely false)	2 (Mostly false)	3 (Mostly true)	4 (Definitely true)
1. I energetically pursue my goals	1	2	3	4
2. I can think of many ways to get out of a jam	1	2	3	4
3. My past experiences have prepared me well for my future	1	2	3	4
4. There are lots of ways around any problems	1	2	3	4
5. I've been pretty successful in life	1	2	3	4
6. I can think of many ways to get the things in life that are important to me	1	2	3	4
7. I meet the goals that I set for myself	1	2	3	4
8. Even when others get discouraged, I know I can find a way to solve the problem	1	2	3	4

Scoring: Total Hope Score: add the scores of all items. Pathway Score: add the four even-numbered items. Agency Score: add the four odd-numbered items.

Your score: Total Hope _____; Pathway _____; Agency ___

80 S. M. Y. HO

Table 4.3 Hope profile by McDermott and Snyder (1999)

Agency		Mixed-Low Pathway	
	High (> 12)		Full High
	Low (<12)	Full Low	Mixed-Low Agency
		Low (< 12)	High (> 12)
		Pathway	

It is important to note that the Future Scale (like the other scales in this book) is not a tool for assessing psychological disorders. Regardless of your scores, you do not have psychological disorders. However, the scores can help you decide whether you want to develop your agency or pathway thinking (or both) to increase resilience. I understand that it can be helpful to have some guidelines for interpreting the scores. McDermott and Snyder (1999) proposed a cut-off score of 12 for agency and pathway scores and created four profiles of hope cognition. Accordingly, those with agency and pathway scores above 12 are fully high-hope people. People in the full low-hope group have agency and pathway scores below 12. There are also two mixed groups: low agency–high pathway and high agency–low pathway. These people have either high agency but low pathways, or vice versa (Table 4.3).

4.7.2 Goal Setting

People can set goals in different domains of their lives so that when the goals in one domain crumble due to adversity, there are goals in other domains to maintain hope. The following worksheet, adapted from a hope-based intervention manual I developed for people receiving heredi-tary colorectal cancer screening (Ho et al., 2012), helps you explore goals in different domains of your life.

The Goal Worksheet

The goal I want to work towards is _____

_____

_____
_____
_____

Below are some guidelines that can inspire you to set goals in different domains of life.

The Academic Domain

Are you satisfied with your current level of education? Does your education allow you to do the type of work you want? Do you feel knowledgeable about the subjects that interest you? Do you sometimes wish you had more formal education and training to feel more competent?

The Family Domain

How much time and energy do you devote to your family and loved ones? Are your relationships as fulfilling as you would like them to be? Are there any conflicts you need to resolve? Are you getting enough support?

The Leisure Domain

How will you spend your leisure time? Do you take the time to do the things you love and dream of? Do your other responsibilities always seem to absorb your time and energy?

The Personal Growth and Development Domain

How do you deal with problems? Do you consider yourself a work in progress? Do you want solutions you can implement to help you reach your next goal?

The Health and Physical Fitness Domain

Are you satisfied with your health habits? Do you exercise often enough? Do you eat junk food instead of nutritious meals? Do you smoke or drink more than you should? Are you satisfied with your habits?

The Romantic Domain

Is your relationship with your partner as intimate and fulfilling as you would like it to be? How much time and energy do you currently devote to your partner? Do you have conflicts you need to resolve? If you are attracted to someone, do you feel comfortable pursuing that person?

The Social Domain

Are you able to make friends whenever you want? Do you have as many friends as you want?

The Work Domain

Do you find your job fulfilling? Is your job challenging and interesting? Do you wake up every day dreading what is going to happen? How important is your job to you and how satisfied are you with it?

4.7.3 Pathways (Waypower)

Below are some tips to help you build pathway and agency thinking to achieve your goals.

a. Practise your problem-solving skills (see Table 4.1)

1. Identify obstacles to achieving your goals.
2. Generate alternative options to remove these obstacles and solve problems.
3. Evaluate the pros and cons of all alternatives to select the best option.
4. Implement the selected strategy.
5. Evaluate the effectiveness of this strategy in solving your problems.
6. Return to Step 2 or 3 if necessary.

b. Engage in sub-goaling

High-pathway people not only set ambitious goals but also identify effective strategies to achieve them. A key aspect of their approach is their ability to break larger, seemingly daunting objectives into smaller, more achievable steps. For instance, the ambitious goal of becoming a brilliant chef may initially seem insurmountable to many. However, those with high pathways can methodically break down this ambition into more manageable sub-goals. Rather than tackling the entire journey to culinary mastery at once, they might start by

1. Visiting local markets to identify fresh, high-quality ingredients.
2. Learning proper techniques for chopping, slicing, and using different knives and utensils.
3. Studying the use and combination of herbs, spices, and seasonings.
4. Practising preparing relatively simple dishes like salads and soups.

The path to becoming a skilled chef seems much less daunting by breaking the larger objective into these incremental steps. Individuals can easily track their progress and gain confidence by methodically achieving each milestone.

This ability to perceive and pursue goals in a measured and step-by-step manner is a characteristic of those with high waypower. This allows them to stay motivated and overcome obstacles that might otherwise discourage those trying to tackle a monumental goal in one go. Through this strategic and modular approach, ambitious goals become more achievable.

c. Learn new skills

High-pathway people identify the skills needed to achieve their goals and are willing to acquire them if they do not have them. If you need a new skill or qualification to achieve your goal, get it!

d. Engage in goal disengagement and reengagement

Even the most confident and capable individuals can face situations in which their initial goals become unachievable or untenable. Perhaps your financial situation has changed due to unemployment, key collaborators are no longer available, or your physical health has deteriorated, making your initial strategies unfeasible.

In such cases, it is crucial to disengage from these initial goals and set new goals that are more suited to your current reality. It is important to recognise that this change does not equate to failure; rather, it reflects the valuable learning experience of examining the viability of a previous goal and making necessary adjustments.

Abandoning an initial goal is not a sign of weakness but rather an act of wisdom and adaptability. In the face of great adversity, stubbornly clinging to unattainable goals can be counterproductive and demoralising. The ability to objectively reevaluate the feasibility of a plan and then move on to new, more viable goals is a hallmark of resilience and strong self-awareness.

This process of disengagement and redirection should be seen as an opportunity for growth, not a failure. Reflect on what you learnt from the initial goal-setting experience. Consider how your priorities or circumstances have changed and use these insights to chart a new path forward. With flexibility and an open mind, you can turn apparent setbacks into opportunities to refine your goals and develop strategies that are better suited to your current reality.

By embracing this adaptive approach, you demonstrate qualities, such as self-awareness, pragmatism, and resilience, that will serve you well as you pursue your new goals. The ability to change goals in the face of adversity is a characteristic of those who ultimately achieve lasting success.

  e. Cultivate relationships where you can receive and give productive advice

Many believe that success is minimised or reduced if a goal is not achieved alone. This belief is FALSE! High-waypower people are willing to ask for help or seek advice from experienced people on strategies to achieve their goals. Do not take asking for help as a sign of weakness. Actively cultivate friendships that can provide you with instrumental support.

4.7.4 Agency (Willpower)

The key to increasing willpower is to develop greater awareness and control over one's thoughts and behaviours. Below are some tips:

a. Build your energy base through healthy eating, exercise, and rest.

Although good physical health can enhance willpower, it is important to recognise that individuals can still demonstrate strong willpower even when faced with physical limitations or illness. Nevertheless, establishing the foundation for good physical health can significantly boost well-being and willpower. The strategies outlined below can help cultivate this important connection:

1. Good nutrition and healthy habits

Maintaining a nutrient-rich diet and other healthy lifestyle habits is not about following a strict "diet." Rather, these fundamental principles

4 HOPEFUL THINKING **85**

help lay the foundation for lasting willpower and motivation. A healthcare professional can provide you with personalised advice on optimal nutrition based on your needs and activity level. At a minimum, aim for a substance-free lifestyle, low in caffeine and alcohol.

2. Stay active, not sedentary

Regular physical exercise can do wonders for building stamina and willpower. People who exercise regularly often find it easier to stay motivated and achieve their goals. The specific activities do not matter as much as finding exercises you enjoy.

3. Prioritise quality rest

High-willpower individuals understand the importance of rejuvenation. Everyone needs adequate time to recover from daily stress, clear their minds, and restore their energy. Rest is especially crucial in situations of high stress. Like an overstretched rubber band, the body and mind require periodic breaks to avoid fatigue and burnout.

b. Practise positive self-talk: Be your own cheerleader

It is important to cultivate tools for thinking and talking positively to combat and counteract negative energy. One effective technique is the practice of positive self-talk.

Starting today, make a conscious effort to familiarise yourself with positive self-talk and let go of those negative, harmful thought patterns. From now on, be a cheerleader for yourself and those around you. Fill your mind with uplifting ideas and affirmations.

Positive self-talk is a great way to build morale, confidence, and resilience. Replacing negative self-talk with constructive self-talk can reshape your mindset and bring more positivity into your life. Begin this shift now and experience the transformative effects of thinking and speaking kindly to yourself. Below are some examples of positive self-talk.

1. I can do it!
2. I will handle this!

86   S. M. Y. HO

3. I can manage it.
4. I can be whatever I want to be!
5. How should I handle this new challenge?

4.7.5   Cultivate Relationships Where You Can Get Functional and Emotional Support

Social support can provide instrumental help with pathways and emotional support to maintain our goal-related agency thinking. Social support plays an important role in resilience. The third component of the SHINE framework, Interpersonal Communication and Support, focuses on social support (Chapter 5).

REFERENCES

Babyak, M. A., Snyder, C. R., & Yoshinobu, L. (1993). Psychometric properties of the hope scale: A confirmatory factor analysis. *Journal of Research in Personality, 27*, 154–169. https://doi.org/10.1006/jrpe.1993.1011

Barnum, D. D., Snyder, C. R., Rapoff, M. A., Mani, M. M., & Thompson, R. (1998). Hope and social support in psychological adjustment of children who have survived burn injuries and their matched controls. *Children's Health Care, 27*, 15–30. https://doi.org/10.1207/s15326888chc2701_2

Beck, A. T., Weissman, A., Lester, D., & Trexler, L. (1974). The measurement of pessimism: The hopelessness scale. *Journal of Consulting and Clinical Psychology, 42*(6), 861–865. https://doi.org/10.1037/h0037562

Berg, C. J., Rapoff, M. A., Snyder, C. R., & Balmont, J. M. (2007). The relationship of children's hope to pediatric asthma treatment adherence. *Journal of Positive Psychology, 2*, 176–184. https://doi.org/10.1080/174397607014 09629

Bormans, L. (2016). *The world book of hope: The source of success, strength and happiness.* Lannoo.

Chang, E. C. (1998). Hope, problem-solving ability, and coping in a college student population: Some implications for theory and practice. *Journal of Clinical Psychology, 54*, 953–962. https://doi.org/10.1002/(SICI)1097-467 9(199811)54:73.0.CO;2-F

Chang, E. C., & DeSimone, S. L. (2001). The influence of hope on appraisals, coping, and dysphoria: A test of hope theory. *Journal of Social and Clinical Psychology, 20*, 117–129. https://doi.org/10.1521/jscp.20.2.117.22262

Cheavens, J. S., Feldman, D. B., Woodward, J. T., & Snyder, C. R. (2006). Hope in cognitive psychotherapies: On working with client strengths. *Journal of Cognitive Psychotherapy: An International Quarterly, 20*, 135–145. https://doi.org/10.1891/jcop.20.2.135

Cheung, L. K., Loh, J. S. P., & Ho, S. M. Y. (2006). The early psychological adjustment of cleft patients after maxillary distraction osteogenesis and conventional orthognathic surgery: A preliminary study. *Journal of Oral and Maxillofacial Surgery, 64*, 1743–1750. https://doi.org/10.1016/j.joms.2005.12.060

Cheung, L. K., Loh, J. S. P., & Ho, S. M. Y. (2007). Psychological profile of Chinese with cleft lip and palate deformities. *Cleft Palate-Craniofacial Journal, 44*(1), 79–86. https://doi.org/10.1597/05-053

Chua, H. D. P., Ho, S. M. Y., & Cheung, L. K. (2012). The comparison of psychological adjustment of patients with cleft lip and palate after maxillary distraction osteogenesis and conventional orthognathic surgery. *Oral Surgery, Oral Medicine, Oral Pathology and Oral Radiology, 114*(5), S5–S10. https://doi.org/10.1016/j.tripleo.2011.07.047

Eche, I. J., Eche, I. M., Pires, C., Isibor, C., Achibiri, A., & Aronowitz, T. (2022). A systematic mixed-studies review of hope experiences in parents of children with cancer. *Cancer Nursing, 45*(1), E43–E58. https://doi.org/10.1097/NCC.0000000000000841

Elliott, T. R., Witty, T. E., Herrick, S., & Hoffman, J. T. (1991). Negotiating reality after physical loss: Hope, depression, and disability. *Journal of Personality and Social Psychology, 61*(4), 608–613. https://doi.org/10.1037/0022-3514.61.4.608

Fearnow-Kenney, M., & Kliewer, W. (2000). Threat appraisal and adjustment among children with cancer. *Journal of Psychosocial Oncology, 18*, 1–17. https://doi.org/10.1300/J077v18n03_01

Gilman, R., Dooley, J., & Florell, D. (2006). Relative levels of hope and their relationship with academic and psychological indicators among adolescents. *Journal of Social and Clinical Psychology, 25*, 166–178. https://doi.org/10.1521/jscp.2006.25.2.166

Grewal, P. K., & Porter, J. E. (2007). Hope theory: A framework for understanding suicidal action. *Death Studies, 31*(2), 131–154. https://doi.org/10.1080/07481180601100491

Herth K. A. (1989). The relationship between level of hope and level of coping response and other variables in patients with cancer. *Oncology nursing forum, 16*(1), 67–72.

Ho, S. M. Y. (2016). Adapting goals. In L. Bormans (Ed.), *The world book of hope: The source of success, strength and happiness* (pp. 355–358). Lannoo.

Ho, S. M. Y., Chan, M. W. Y., Yau, T. K., & Yeung, R. M. W. (2011a). Relationships between explanatory style, posttraumatic growth and posttraumatic

88   S. M. Y. HO

stress disorder symptoms among Chinese breast cancer patients. *Psychology &*
Health, 26(3), 269–285. https://doi.org/10.1080/08870440903287926

Ho, S. M. Y., Ho, J. W. C., Bonanno, G. A., Chu, A. T. W., & Chan, E. M.
S. (2010). Hopefulness predicts resilience after hereditary colorectal cancer
genetic testing: A prospective outcome trajectories study. *BMC Cancer, 10,*
279. https://doi.org/10.1186/1471-2407-10-279

Ho, S. M. Y., Ho, J. W. C., Chan, C. L. W., Kwan, K., & Tsui, Y. K. Y. (2003a).
Decisional consideration of hereditary colon cancer genetic test results among
Hong Kong Chinese adults. *Cancer Epidemiology, Biomarkers & Prevention,*
12(5), 426–432. http://cebp.aacrjournals.org/

Ho, S. M. Y., Ho, J. W. C., Pau, B. K.-Y., Hui, B. P.-H., Wong, R. S.-M., &
Chu, A. T.-W. (2012). Hope-based intervention for individuals susceptible to
colorectal cancer: A pilot study. *Familial Cancer, 11,* 545–551. https://doi.
org/10.1007/s10689-012-9545-3

Ho, S. M. Y., Li, W. L., Duan, W., Siu, B. P. Y., Yau, S., Yeung, G., & Wong,
K. (2016). A brief strengths scale for individuals with mental health issues.
Psychological Assessment, 28(1), 147–157. https://doi.org/10.1037/pas000
0164

Ho, S. M. Y., & Lo, R. S. Y. (2011). Dispositional hope as a protective
factor among medical emergency professionals: A preliminary investigation.
Traumatology, 17, 3–9. https://doi.org/10.1177/1534765611426786

Ho, S. M. Y., Rajandram, R. K., Chan, N., Samman, N., McGrath, C., &
Zwahlen, R. A. (2011). The roles of hope and optimism on posttraumatic
growth in oral cavity cancer patients. *Oral Oncology, 47,* 121–124. https://
doi.org/10.1016/j.oraloncology.2010.11.015

Ho, S. M. Y., Yuen, A. N. Y., & Siu, B. P. Y. (2013d). Hope as a positive cognition against adversity and beyond. In G. M. Katsaros (Ed.), *The psychology of*
hope (pp. 91–115). Nova Science Publisher.

Huen, J. M. Y., Ip, B. Y. T., Ho, S. M. Y., & Yip, P. S. F. (2015). Hope and
hopelessness: The role of hope in buffering the impact of hopelessness on
suicidal ideation. *PLoS ONE, 10*(6), e0130073. https://doi.org/10.1371/
journal.pone.0130073

Irving, L. M., Snyder, C. R., Gravel, L., Hanke, J., Hillberg, P., & Nelson,
N. (1997). *Hope and the effectiveness of a pre-therapy orientation group for*
community mental health center client. Western Psychological Association
Convention.

Irving, L. M., Snyder, C. K., & Crowson, J. J., Jr. (1998). Hope and coping with
cancer by college women. *Journal of Personality, 66*(2), 195–214. https://
doi.org/10.1111/1467-6494.00009

Kashdan, T. B., Pelham, W. E., Lang, A. R., Hoza, B., Jacob, R. G., J.R., J.,
Blumenthal, J. D., & Gnagy, E. M. (2002). Hope and optimism as human
strengths in parents of children with externalizing disorders: Stress in the

eye of the beholder. *Journal of Social & Clinical Psychology*, *21*, 441–468. https://doi.org/10.1521/jscp.21.4.441.22597

Lagacé-Séguin, D. G., & d'Entremont, M.-R. L. (2010). A scientific exploration of positive psychology in adolescence: The role of hope as a buffer against the influences of psychosocial negativities. *International Journal of Adolescence and Youth*, 16(1), 69–95. https://doi.org/10.1080/02673843.2010.9748046

Leung, Y. Y., Lee, T. C. P., Ho, S. M. Y., & Cheung, L. K. (2013). Trigeminal neurosensory deficit and patient reported outcome measures: The effect on life satisfaction and depression symptoms. *PLoS ONE*, *8*(8), e72891. https://doi.org/10.1371/journal.pone.0072891

Lewis, H. A., & Kliewer, W. (1996). Hope, coping, and adjustment among children with sickle cell disease: Tests of mediator and moderator models. *Journal of Pediatric Psychology*, *21*, 25–41. https://doi.org/10.1093/jpepsy/21.1.25

Lloyd, T. J., & Hastings, R. (2009). Hope as a psychological resilience factor in mothers and fathers of children with intellectual disabilities. *Journal of Intellectual Disability Research*, *53*, 957–968. https://doi.org/10.1111/j.1365-2788.2009.01206.x

Long, L. J., Viana, A. G., Zvolensky, M. J., Lu, Q., & Gallagher, M. W. (2024). The influence of hope and optimism on trajectories of covid-19 stress, health anxiety, and wellbeing during the covid-19 pandemic. *Journal of Clinical Psychology*. https://doi.org/10.1002/jclp.23746

Loper, A. B., Carlson, L. W., Levitt, L., & Scheffel, K. (2009). Parenting stress, alliance, child contact, and adjustment of imprisoned mothers and fathers. *Journal of Offender Rehabilitation*, *48*(6), 483–503. https://doi.org/10.1080/10509670903081300

Lopez, S. J., & Snyder, C. R. (2011). *The Oxford handbook of positive psychology*. Oxford University Press.

Mak, V. W. M., Ho, S. M. Y., Kwong, R. W. Y., & Li, W. L. (2018). A gender-responsive treatment facility in correctional services: The development of psychological gymnasium for women offenders. *International Journal of Offender Therapy and Comparative Criminology* 62(4), 1062–1079. https://doi.org/10.1177/0306624x16667572

Mak, V. W. M., Ho, S. M. Y., Li, W. L., & Pau, K.-Y. B. (2021). Relationships between hope and mental health among women in prison. *Criminal Behavior and Mental Health*, *31*(2), 96–108.https://doi.org/10.1002/cbm.2191

McDermott, D., & Snyder, C. R. (1999). *Making hope happen. A workbook for turning possibilities into reality*. New Harbinger.

Mednick, L., Cogen, F., Henderson, C., Rohrbeck, C. A., Kitessa, D., & Streisand, R. (2007). Hope more, worry less: Hope as a potential resilience factor in mothers of very young children with type 1 diabetes. *Children's Healthcare*, *36*, 385–396. https://doi.org/10.1080/02739610701601403

Miao, M., Zhou, Z., Qi, W., & Zheng, L. (2024). The mediating role of hope in the relationship between benefit finding and anxiety: Insights from the covid-19 pandemic. *Anxiety, Stress & Coping: An International Journal*. https://doi.org/10.1080/10615806.2024.2378864

Davidson, J. E., & Sternberg, R. J. (Eds.). (2003). The psychology of problem solving. Cambridge University Press. https://doi.org/10.1017/CBO978051 1615771.

Ogston, P. L., Mackintosh, V. H., & Myers, B. J. (2011). Hope and worry in mothers of children with an autism spectrum disorder or down syndrome. *Research in Autism Spectrum Disorders*, *5*, 1378–1384. https://doi.org/10.1016/j.rasd.2011.01.020

Onwuegbuzie, A. J. (1998). Role of hope in predicting anxiety about statistics. *Psychological Reports*, *82*, 1315–1320. https://doi.org/10.2466/pr0.1998.82.3c.1315

Or, D. Y. L., Lam, C. S., Chen, P. P., Wong, H. S. S., Lam, C. W. F., Fok, Y. Y., Chan, S. F. I., & Ho, S. M. Y. (2021). Hope in the context of chronic musculoskeletal pain: relationships of hope to pain and psychological distress. *Pain Reports*, *6*(4), e965. https://doi.org/10.1097/pr9.0000000000000965

Peterson, C., & Seligman, M. E. P. (2004). *Character strengths and virtues: A handbook and classification*. American Psychological Association.

Rajandram, R. K., Ho, S. M. Y., Samman, N., Chan, N., McGrath, C., & Zwahlen, R. A. (2011). Interaction of hope and optimism with anxiety and depression in a specific group of cancer survivors: A preliminary study. *BMC Research*, *4*, 519. https://doi.org/10.1186/1756-0500-4-519

Rand, K. L. (2009). Hope and optimism: Latent structures and influences on grade expectancy and academic performance. *Journal of Personality*, *77*(1), 231–260. https://doi.org/10.1111/j.1467-6494.2008.00544.x

Salisbury, E. J., & Van Voorhis, P. (2009). Gendered pathways: A quantitative investigation of women probationers' paths to incarceration. *Criminal Justice and Behavior*, *36*(6), 541–566. https://doi.org/10.1177/009385480 9334076

Scheier, M. F., & Carver, C. S. (1988). Dispositional optimism and physical well-being: The influence of outcome expectancies on health. *Journal of Personality*, *55*, 169–210. https://doi.org/10.1111/j.1467-6494.1987.tb00434.x

Snyder, C. R. (1994). *The psychology of hope: You can get there from here*. Free Press.

Snyder, C. R. (2000). *Handbook of hope: Theory, measures, and applications*. Access Online via Elsevier.

Snyder, C. R. (2002). Hope theory: Rainbows in the mind. *Psychological Inquiry*, *13*(4), 249–275. https://doi.org/10.1207/S15327965PLI1304_01

Snyder, C. R., Harris, C., Anderson, J. R., Holleran, S. A., Irving, L. M., Sigmon, S. T., Yoshinobu, L., Gibb, J., Langelle, C., & Harney, P. (1991). The will and the ways: Development and validation of an individual-differences measure of hope. *Journal of Personality and Social Psychology*, *60*(4), 570–585. https://doi.org/10.1037/0022-3514.60.4.570

Snyder, C. R., Hoza, B., Pelham, W. E., Rapoff, M., Ware, L., Danovsky, M., Highberger, L., Rubinstein, H., & Stahl, K. J. (1997). The development and validation of the children's hope scale. *Journal of Pediatric Psychology*, *22*, 399–421. https://doi.org/10.1093/jpepsy/22.3.399

Snyder, C. R., Sympson, S. C., Michael, S. T., & Cheavens, J. (2000). The optimism and hope constructs: Variants on a positive expectancy theme. In E. C. Chang (Ed.), *Optimism and Pessimism* (pp. 103–124). American Psychological Association.

Snyder, C. R., Sympson, S. C., Ybasco, F. C., Borders, T. F., Babyak, M. A., & Higgins, R. L. (1996). Development and validation of the state hope scale. *Journal of Personality and Social Psychology*, *70*, 321–335. https://doi.org/10.1037/0022-3514.70.2.321

Stanton, A. L., Danoff-Burg, S., Cameron, C. L., Bishop, M., Collins, C. A., Kirk, S. B., Sworowski, L. A., & Twillman, R. (2000). Emotionally expressive coping predicts psychological and physical adjustment to breast cancer. *Journal of Consulting and Clinical Psychology*, *68*, 875–882. https://doi.org/10.1037/0022-006X.68.5.875

Suen, K. S., Lai, Y., Ho, S. M. Y., Cheung, L. K., & Choi, W. S. (2018). A longitudinal evaluation of psychosocial changes throughout orthognathic surgery. *PLoS ONE*, *13*(9), e0203883. https://doi.org/10.1371/journal.pone.0203883

Tam, C. K., McGrath, C. P., Ho, S. M. Y., Pow, E. H. N., Luk, H. W. K., & Cheung, L. K. (2014). Psychosocial and quality of life outcomes of prosthetic auricular rehabilitation with CAD/CAM technology. *International Journal of Dentistry*, *2014*(Article ID 393571), 12. https://doi.org/ https://doi.org/10.1155/2014/393571

Truitt, M., Biesecker, B., Capone, G., Bailey, T., & Erby, L. (2012). The role of hope in adaptation to uncertainty: the experience of caregivers of children with down syndrome. *Patient Education and Counseling*, *87*, 233–238. https://doi.org/10.1016/j.pec.2011.08.015

Wong, S. S., & Lim, T. (2009). Hope versus optimism in Singaporean adolescents: Contributions to depression and life satisfaction. *Personality and Individual Differences*, *46*(5), 648–652. https://doi.org/10.1016/j.paid.2009.01.009

Worrell, F. C., & Hale, R. L. (2001). The relationship of hope in the future and perceived school climate to school completion. *School Psychology Quarterly, 16,* 370–388. https://doi.org/10.1521/scpq.16.4.370.19896

Yuen, A. N. Y., Ho, S. M. Y., Chan, C. K. Y., Chiang, A., Lee, V., Yuen, H. L., & Ling, S. C. (2013). The relationship between hope, rumination response styles, rumination content and psychological adjustment among childhood cancer patients and survivors. *Pediatric Blood & Cancer, 60*(S3), S180. Article P-0542. https://doi.org/10.1002/pbc.24719

CHAPTER 5

Interpersonal Support and Communication

Abstract According to many resilience models, such as social support resource theory, social support is a vital resource for coping with adversity. This chapter examines the critical role of social support in navigating adversity, highlighting how the breakdown of interpersonal relationships exacerbates stress and hinders resilience. Strategies for enhancing social support are introduced, including the psychological first aid framework and active constructive responding to foster positive interactions. The chapter concludes with practical guidelines for responding to negative and positive experiences, promoting a balanced approach to social support that bolsters resilience during challenging times.

Keywords Social support · Coping · Psychological first aid · Active constructive responding · Interpersonal relationships · Transactional model of stress

5.1 Social Support and Adversity

Adversity and disasters can destroy our existing interpersonal and social support. Lack of social support is one of the strongest predictors of post-traumatic stress disorder after a disaster (Feeny et al., 2014). Recently,

© The Author(s), under exclusive license to Springer Nature
Switzerland AG 2025
S. M. Y. Ho, *The SHINE Framework*,
https://doi.org/10.1007/978-3-031-89106-9_5

94   S. M. Y. HO

Ntontis et al. (2023) reported that high exposure to secondary stressors, such as disruption of social support due to quarantine measures, was related to low resilience after the COVID-19 pandemic.

Stress theories distinguish between primary and secondary stressors (Williams et al., 2021). Primary stressors are inherent or directly arise from adverse incidents, such as physical injury or witnessing a death. Secondary stressors are personal or structural factors that exist before or arise because of adverse events. Disruption of social networks is a common secondary stressor. Accordingly, social support is mentioned by many models of resilience (Hobfoll et al., 1990; Southwick & Watson, 2015). For instance, the researchers who developed the COR model (Hobfoll, 1989; Hobfoll et al., 2018) (see Chapter 1, Sect. 1.3.2) also developed a related theory, namely social support resource theory (SSRT) (Hobfoll et al., 1990), to emphasise the importance of interpersonal support in resilience to adversity. Hobfoll and Stokes (1988) defined social support as the "social interactions or relationships that provide individuals with actual assistance or with a feeling of attachment to a person or group perceived as caring or loving" (p. 499). Social support serves two main purposes, according to SSRT. First, it provides additional resources to help preserve existing resources. For example, people may borrow money from friends to pay their mortgage. Friends thus provide the financial resources needed to maintain people's existing homes. Second, social support can provide a social identity for people to maintain a sense of caring and self-worth during adversity and trauma. Two examples from my experience after the 512 Wenchuan Earthquake illustrate this point.

On 12 May 2008, a powerful earthquake (magnitude 8.0) struck Wenchuan County, Sichuan province, southwestern China. The 512 Wenchuan Earthquake was one of the most devastating natural disasters in modern Chinese history (Zhang & Ho, 2011). I met a woman in one of the villages in the earthquake zone a few months after the disaster. She lost her two children during the earthquake and her husband left home to work in the city after the disaster (as a way to escape family turmoil). The woman was in great distress when I met her. She told me that before the earthquake, people in the village saw her as a mother. This identity had disappeared and she no longer knew who she was! Helping this woman to build a new social identity in the village was important for her resilience.

Another example is that of a doctor who lost her only child and her husband during the earthquake. After the earthquake, she volunteered in the village, visiting families and providing them with medical and emotional support. This new role earned her enormous respect from the people of the village. "People see me as a member of their family. This new role helps me to overcome my grief," she told me.

Social support also plays a special role in Lazarus and Folkman's (1984) famous transactional model of stress (TMS). This model proposes two broad categories of coping based on their functions: problem-focused and emotion-focused (Folkman et al., 1986; Xanthopoulos & Daniel, 2013). Problem-focused coping aims to change the external environment to reduce stress, while emotion-focused coping aims to manage internal emotions to reduce the impact of stressors. Social support is the only coping strategy that addresses both problem-focused and emotion-focused functions in the TMS. In stressful situations, people may seek social support for instrumental purposes, such as for advice. They may also receive emotional care by seeking social support from friends who can offer them a listening ear in difficult times.

5.2 Social Support in the SHINE Framework

There are many strategies available to increase social support for different populations, including people with chronic illness (Grauf-Grounds, 2007), depression (Siegel et al., 2012; Wang & Pavelko, 2024), and children and adolescents (Grapin et al., 2016; Mumm et al., 2017). Ways to increase social support through online platforms have also been proposed (Wright, 2009). For example, Beard (2021) offered six tips for building social support, namely adopting a pet, taking up a hobby, joining a volunteer or religious organisation, getting out of the house and getting to know your community, reaching out to friends and people you know, and joining a support group. While recognising the importance and usefulness of the above ways, the SHINE framework does not seek to repeat them. These tips are widely available on the internet, and I encourage you to learn them.

Instead, the SHINE framework uses a communication framework to address social support in the face of adversity, considering both positive and negative social support. Many conceive social support as always positive. However, social support can be negative (Feeny et al., 2014; Hobfoll et al., 1990), and interpersonal communication is important in affecting both. Negative social support often occurs when people share negative experiences with others and receive inappropriate responses from them, such as criticism, blame, and doubt (Feeny et al., 2014) (see Table 5.1).

96   S. M. Y. HO

Table 5.1   Negative responses to negative experiences

Type	Description
Blame	You imply, directly or indirectly, that the person is responsible for the negative events
Criticism	You respond by directly or subtly suggesting that the situation is not as serious as the person perceives
Doubt	You question the accuracy of the experience described by the person
Indifference/ invalidation	You provide a neutral response (talk about other things, talk about personal issues), which does not validate/address the experience and emotion of the person sharing

Imagine that a person in great distress tells a friend that she has been diagnosed with stage III breast cancer and receives the following reactions:

- "As I have told you many times, you should stop eating too much junk food. Now you have cancer because you did not listening to me." [Blame]
- "This is not the time to worry. It would be better if you devoted all your energy to fighting cancer." [Criticism]
- "Are you sure the diagnosis is accurate? Maybe it is not as serious as you think." [Doubt]

Sometimes, because we do not know how to react, we adopt an indifferent attitude when people share their negative experiences with us, such as "Don't worry. It will be over very soon" or "I know someone worse than you." Such responses also result in negative social support (Feeny et al., 2014). It is not difficult to predict that people receiving the above inappropriate reactions will become more distressed and will avoid seeking support from that person. The SHINE framework uses the psychological first aid (PFA) framework (Southwick & Watson, 2015) to guide the development of appropriate responses to people sharing negative experiences with us (and beyond), which may, in turn, increase our social support from others.

One might think that positive experience is non-existent or rare in adverse situations. This is not the case. As you will see, Chapter 7 discusses PTG, that is, people who report positive changes during and after adversity. Sharing positive experiences is not uncommon in the face of adversity. The SHINE framework uses the ACR model (Gable et al., 2004) to help us understand adaptive responses to good news to cultivate positive social support.

5.3 Responding to Negative Experiences

In professional counselling and psychotherapy, there are systematic ways to foster rapport, mutual respect, and trust with a client, often referred to as micro-skills (Hall & Horvath, 2015; Joyce-Beaulieu & Zaboski, 2021). Learning professional micro-skills is a good thing, but it is not necessary to provide good responses to negative experiences shared by your friends and loved ones. Some generic principles described by the PFA approach (Southwick & Watson, 2015; World Health Organization et al., 2011) to crisis management enable us to provide positive social support to people facing adversity.

PFA was first developed to help first responders, military personnel, and civilian populations facilitate resilience in stressful situations (Southwick & Watson, 2015). Today, PFA has been expanded to help people from all walks of life cope with the immediate impact of a crisis and facilitate their longer-term recovery. The WHO and other organisations have published a guide for implementing PFA (World Health Organization et al., 2011), and its communication principles provide a user-friendly framework for communicating with people in difficult situations. The SHINE framework adapts the principles of PFA to facilitate positive social support, as outlined below.

5.3.1 *Prepare Yourself*

If you are anxious yourself, this may not be an appropriate time to listen to other people's struggles. Being calm and collected can help the person sharing feel safe. If possible, understand the problems faced by the person in distress and the sources of referral, called Learn and Link in the PFA model. For example, during the COVID-19 pandemic, learning how to prevent infection and how to get treatment after infection helped us to provide positive social support to people with a strong fear of infection. Finally, allow plenty of time for interaction. Do not rush.

5.3.2 Find an Appropriate Place

There is no hard and fast rule about where to talk about difficult experiences. It depends on the topic and the relationship between you and the person sharing. In general, a quiet space allows the person in distress to talk about their difficulties in private. A private space will enable them to express their emotions safely, without being distracted by other people.

5.3.3 During the Conversation

Listening is the most important principle during the conversation. Do not worry if you do not know what to say. A listening ear can be enough to provide positive social support. Listen with both your ears and eyes. That is, Listen to the story and Look for bodily signs of distress, such as shivering. Show that you are listening: nod or say "Umm," "I see what you mean." Your nonverbal behaviour, such as body posture, facial expression, and eye contact, can influence the interaction. Take into account social and cultural norms. For instance, some cultures do not value close physical contact (e.g. hug), while others view it as an expression of support.

Another important principle is not to force the person to tell you about their difficulties. Be patient. It may take several conversations to get to the root issues the person is facing. Finally, keep the information confidential. Disclosing a friend's private information to other people without their consent is very negative social support!

5.3.4 What You Can Offer

The above principles already enable you to offer your friends and loved ones facing adversity a supportive person, ready to listen and understand their situation. If you have this information, you may provide them with factual knowledge and links to resources.

5.3.5 Summary

The 4L key technique, including Listen, Learn, Look, and Link, enables you to provide positive social support to people who share their negative experiences with you, as shown in Fig. 5.1. The 4L communication technique does not apply only to adverse situations or people sharing negative

Fig. 5.1 Learn, Look, Listen, and Link: The 4L principles of good communications based on PFA (World Health Organization et al., 2011)

experiences with you. The above communication practices can provide you with positive social support to build your resilience in the face of adversity.

5.4 Responding to Positive Experiences

Some cultures do not place much emphasis on positive experiences. For example, in some Eastern cultures, it is more common for parents to ask their children whether they have been punished at school or if they have failed assignments or tests. These parents rarely care about the positive and happy moments their children experience at school. They do not know how to react when their children tell them about positive experiences. They may adopt an evasive attitude by quickly changing the subject or ignoring the interaction. Their children gradually learn that positive experiences are not important and pay more attention to negative experiences. Like their parents, they may not know how to respond when other people share positive experiences with them.

Appropriate responses to people's positive experiences play a particular role in adversity. It helps to increase our attention to and memory of positive experiences to combat stressful situations. Balanced attention to positive and negative experiences is the next SHINE strategy discussed in Chapter 6.

ACR is a form of positive communication proposed by Gable and colleagues (Gable et al., 2003; Gable et al., 2018; Gable & Strachman,

2006), who explored the effects of sharing good news with others and their responses. People typically respond in four ways when someone tells them good news, as shown in Table 5.2.

A genuine active constructive response to good news is especially important for creating supportive and positive relationships in the face of adversity. Giving an active constructive response when someone shares positive news and experiences with you facilitates positive emotional exchanges, nurtures close connections, and builds relationship resources (Gable & Haidt, 2005; Gable et al., 2018). Fredrickson's broaden-and-build theory of positive emotions (1998) proposes that positive emotions broaden the thought-action repertoire, expand attention, and build trust and personal resources.

When someone shares a good experience with you, we recommend that you respond actively and constructively, saying, "I am happy to hear this great news. Thanks for sharing it with me"; "I know that you worked hard, and now it's paying off"; "I can't wait to hear about your new job. Tell me more about it." Table 5.3 gives more examples.

Table 5.2 Active constructive communication matrix

	Constructive	Destructive
Active	– You provide enthusiastic support by elaborating on the experience. – The receiver feels validated and understood.	– You respond by dismissing the event and ending the conversation. – The receiver feels ashamed, embarrassed, guilty, or angry.
Passive	– You remain silent and offer discreet support, and the conversation dies down. – The receiver feels unimportant, misunderstood, embarrassed, and guilty.	– You respond by ignoring the event and the conversation never starts. – The receiver feels confused, guilty, or disappointed.

Table 5.3 Examples of active constructive responses

Example 1. Your partner says, "I finally got a job offer!"

Verbal: "That is great! I am so proud of you. I know how important that job was to us! Where did you get the offer? What did the employer say? How did you react? We should go out and celebrate!"
Nonverbal: Maintain eye contact and display positive emotions.

Example 2. Your colleague says, "I am happy. I got the day off I asked for, even if many people are willing to give up their annual leave to keep their jobs. I will have more time to accompany my kids this summer!"

Verbal: "I'm so happy for you. I know how important it is to you! Your kids will be very happy when they hear this good news. Are you planning to go on a trip with your family? Just let me know if you need help finding travel packages".
Nonverbal: Maintain eye contact, display positive emotions, smile, and nod. Keep an open body posture.

Example 3. Your subordinate says, "I received a letter of appreciation from a customer. What a surprise to me!"

Verbal: "That is excellent! I am so happy for you. What did the customer write? Your hard work deserves to be appreciated and praised. I am proud of you".
Nonverbal: Respond enthusiastically, maintain eye contact, smile, and display positive emotions.

5.5 SUMMARY

We propose the 4L (Learn, Look, Listen, Link) technique to respond to the sharing of negative experiences, and recommend the ACR approach for good news. There are overlaps between the 4Ls and ACR. For example, active and empathic listening applies to both good and bad news. It would be helpful if you practised the 4Ls and ACR daily, with or without adversity.

5.6 PRACTICAL APPLICATIONS

5.6.1 Your Response Styles to Positive and Negative Experiences

You can discover your response style to positive and negative experiences shared by your loved ones by answering the following questions.

1. Think of the factors that influence your response style (e.g. your mood, your energy level, your busy daily schedule, your family of origin) to
Bad news: _____

_____

Good news: _____

_____

2. Which of your positive psychological resources/strengths helps you stay in 4L mode for bad news and in ACR mode for good news?
Bad news: _____

_____

Good news: _____
_____;

5.6.2 Tips on Practising the 4Ls and ACR

As with all communication, you begin by listening to the experience of the person sharing it, using both your eyes and ears. Pay attention to your nonverbal responses (e.g. nodding, posture, eye contact) to show your empathic understanding of the story. Next, demonstrate the intention to ask questions to get more details about the story. For negative experiences, provide the person sharing them with appropriate resources after learning about the situation. For positive experiences, let the person sharing them relive and savour those positive experiences using ACR ("Tell me more about it"; "Your efforts are finally paying off"). Finally, express your appreciation to the person sharing and recognise their efforts to handle difficulties. Figure 5.2 illustrates the above tips (Ho et al., 2017).

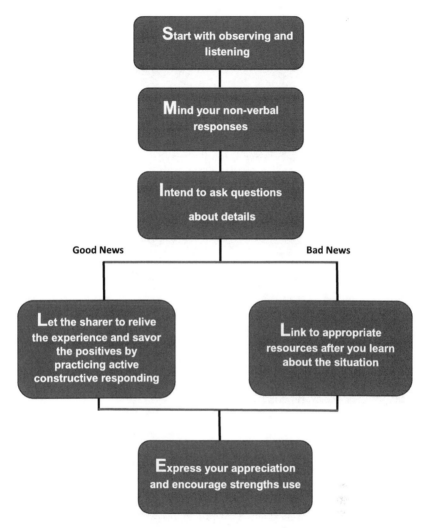

Fig. 5.2 Ways of responding to positive and negative experiences

104 S. M. Y. HO

REFERENCES

Beard, C. (2021, June). 6 Tips for Increasing Social Support. *Psychology Today*. https://www.psychologytoday.com/us/blog/lab-real-world/202106/6-tips-increasing-social-support

Feeny, N. C., Rytwinski, N. K., & Zoellner, L. A. (2014). The crucial role of social support. In *Facilitating resilience and recovery following trauma*. (pp. 291–321). The Guilford Press.

Folkman, S., Lazarus, R. S., Dunkel-Schetter, C., DeLongis, A., & Gruen, R. (1986). The dynamics of a stressful encounter: Cognitive appraisal, coping, and encounter outcomes. *Journal of Personality and Social Psychology, 50*, 992–1003. https://doi.org/10.1037/0022-3514.50.5.992

Fredrickson, B. L. (1998). What good are positive emotions? *Review of General Psychology, 2*, 300–319. https://doi.org/10.1037/1089-2680.2.3.300

Gable, S. L., & Haidt, J. (2005). What (and why) is positive psychology? *Review of General Psychology, 9*(2), 103–110. https://doi.org/10.1037/1089-2680.9.2.10

Gable, S. L., Reis, H. T., & Downey, G. (2003). HE SAID, SHE SAID: A quasi-signal detection analysis of daily interactions between close relationship partners. *Psychological Science, 14*(2), 100–105.

Gable, S. L., Reis, H. T., Impett, E. A., & Asher, E. R. (2004). What do you do when things go right? The intrapersonal and interpersonal benefits of sharing positive events. *Journal of Personality and Social Psychology, 87*(2), 228–245. https://doi.org/10.1037/0022-3514.87.2.228

Gable, S. L., Reis, H. T., Impett, E. A., & Asher, E. R. (2018). What do you do when things go right? The intrapersonal and interpersonal benefits of sharing positive events. In H. Reis (Ed.), *Relationships, well-being and behaviour: Selected works of Harry Reis* (1st ed., pp. 39). Routledge. https://doi.org/10.4324/9780203732496

Grapin, S. L., Sulkowski, M. L., & Lazarus, P. J. (2016). A multilevel framework for increasing social support in schools. *Contemporary School Psychology, 20*(2), 93–106. https://doi.org/10.1007/s40688-015-0051-0

Grauf-Grounds, C. (2007). Increasing social support to manage chronic illness. In D. Linville & K. M. Hertlein (Eds.), *The therapist's notebook for family health care: Homework, handouts, and activities for individuals, couples, and families coping with illness, loss, and disability* (pp. 19–23, 245 Pages). Haworth Press.

Hall, M. F., & Horvath, S. F. (2015). Micro-skills: Daily practice for mental health providers. In R. H. Witte & G. S. Mosley-Howard (Eds.), *Mental health practice in today's schools: Issues and interventions* (pp. 125–143, 450 Pages). Springer Publishing Company.

Ho, S. M. Y., Mak, C. W. Y., Ching, R., & Lo, E. T. T. (2017). An approach to motivation and empowerment: The Application of Positive Psychology. In

I. H. Amzat & N. P. Valdez (Eds.), *Teacher empowerment towards professional development and practices. Perspectives across borders* (pp. 167–182). Springer. https://doi.org/10.1007/978-981-10-4151-8

Hobfoll, S. E., Freedy, J., Lane, C., & Geller, P. (1990). Conservation of social resources: Social support resource theory. *Journal of Social and Personal Relationships, 7*(4), 465–478. https://doi.org/10.1177/0265407590074004

Hobfoll, S. E., Halbesleben, J., Neveu, J.-P., & Westman, M. (2018). Conservation of Resources in the Organizational Context: The Reality of Resources and Their Consequences *Annual Review of Organizational Psychology and Organizational Behavior, 5*(1), 103–128. https://doi.org/10.1146/annurev-org psych-032117-104640

Hobfoll, S. E., & Stokes, J. P. (1988). The process and mechanics of social support. In *Handbook of personal relationships: Theory, research and interventions* (pp. 497–517). Wiley.

Joyce-Beaulieu, D., & Zaboski, B. A. (2021). Counseling preparation. In D. Joyce-Beaulieu & B. A. Zaboski (Eds.), *Applied cognitive behavioral therapy in schools* (pp. 47–63, 211 Pages). Oxford University Press. https://doi.org/10.1093/med-psych/9780197581384.003.0003

Lazarus, P. S., & Folkman, S. (1984). *Stress, appraisal, and coping.* Springer Publishing Company.

Mumm, J., Hearst, M. O., Shanafelt, A., Wang, Q., Leduc, R., & Nanney, M. S. (2017). Increasing social support for breakfast: Project BreakFAST. *Health Promotion Practice, 18*(6), 862–868. https://doi.org/10.1177/152483991 7711123

Ntontis, E., Blackburn, A. M., Han, H., Stöckli, S., Milfont, T. L., Tuominen, J., Griffin, S. M., Ikizer, G., Jeftic, A., Chrona, S., Nasheedha, A., Liutsko, L., & Vestergren, S. (2023). The effects of secondary stressors, social identity, and social support on perceived stress and resilience: Findings from the COVID-19 pandemic. *Journal of Environmental Psychology, 88*, 1–11. https://doi.org/10.1016/j.jenvp.2023.102007

Siegel, J. T., Alvaro, E. M., Crano, W. D., Lienemann, B. A., Hohman, Z. P., & O'Brien, E. (2012). Increasing social support for depressed individuals: A cross-cultural assessment of an affect-expectancy approach. *Journal of Health Communication, 17*(6), 713–732. https://doi.org/10.1080/108 10730.2011.635775

Southwick, S., & Watson, P. (2015). The emerging scientific and clinical literature on resilience and psychological first aid. In N. C. Bernardy & M. J. Friedman (Eds.), *A practical guide to PTSD treatment: Pharmacological and psychotherapeutic approaches* (pp. 21–33, 194 Pages). American Psychological Association. https://doi.org/10.1037/14522-003

106 S. M. Y. HO

Wang, T., & Pavelko, R. (2024). Increasing social support for women via humanizing postpartum depression. *Health Communication.* https://doi.org/10.1080/10410236.2024.2361582

Williams, R., Ntontis, E., Alfadhli, K., Drury, J., & Amlôt, R. (2021). A social model of secondary stressors in relation to disasters, major incidents and conflict: Implications for practice. *International Journal of Disaster Risk Reduction, 63*, 102436. https://doi.org/10.1016/j.ijdrr.2021.102436

World Health Organization, War Trauma Foundation, & World Vision International. (2011). *Psychological first aid: Guide for field workers.* Geneva. https://iris.who.int/bitstream/handle/10665/44615/9789241548205_eng.pdf?sequence=1#:~:text=Suggested%20citation%3A%20World%20Health%20Organization,WHO%3A%20Geneva

Wright, K. B. (2009). Increasing computer-mediated social support. In J. C. Parker & E. Thorson (Eds.), *Health communication in the new media landscape* (pp. 243–265, Chapter xxxiii, 460 Pages). Springer Publishing Company.

Xanthopoulos, M. S., & Daniel, L. C. (2013). Coping and social support. In A. M. Nezu, C. M. Nezu, P. A. Geller, & I. B. Weiner (Eds.), *Handbook of psychology: Health psychology* (Vol. 9, 2nd ed., pp. 57–78, 686 Pages). Wiley

Zhang, Y., & Ho, S. M. Y. (2011). Risk factors of posttraumatic stress disorder among survivors after the 512 Wenchuan earthquake in China. *PLoS ONE, 6*(7), Article e22371. https://doi.org/10.1371/journal.pone.0022371

CHAPTER 6

Noticing Both Positives and Negatives

Abstract Attentional bias plays an important role in the onset and continuation of psychological problems, particularly anxiety and depression. This chapter focuses on the importance of balanced attention in the face of adversity, emphasising the need to notice both positive and negative environmental stimuli. There are four categories of attention deployment: full positive, full negative, total neglect, and balanced attention. Recognising threats and negative stimuli in the environment is important for survival during crises. However, positive attentional bias, i.e. noticing positive events and stimuli during crises, enhances resilience. The SHINE framework cultivates a balanced attention style during adversity. The practical guidelines offered by the framework include strategies for cultivating positive attention through personal strength recognition, goal setting, and actively recording positive experiences. The SHINE framework advocates for developing habits that promote positive attention to mitigate the adverse effects of negative stimuli, thereby fostering resilience.

Keywords Information processing · Positive attentional bias · Negative attentional bias · Attention deployment · Balanced attention · Anxiety

© The Author(s), under exclusive license to Springer Nature
Switzerland AG 2025
S. M. Y. Ho, *The SHINE Framework*,
https://doi.org/10.1007/978-3-031-89106-9_6

6.1 THE FOUR CATEGORIES OF ATTENTION DEPLOYMENT

In the face of adversity and trauma, the environment is full of threats and negative stimuli. It is, therefore, essential to pay attention to these threatening stimuli and apply timely strategies to handle them. For example, survivors of leukaemia (a blood cancer) pay special attention to any bruising on the skin, which can be a sign of relapse. As a result, they may spend a lot of effort each day looking for potential signs and symptoms related to their illness. Gradually, they may devote most of their capacity to focusing on negative information and ignoring positive environmental stimuli.

The above example can apply to people facing different challenges. When faced with adversity, people tend to pay more attention to negative environmental stimuli and ignore the positive stimuli around them. They become anxious and depressed because their subjective world is filled with nothing but threats and dangers, as explained below.

The integrated cognitive model (Mogg & Bradley, 2016) suggests that anxiety is related to a bottom-up threat detection system and a top-down cognitive control system. The bottom-up system is the automatic detection of threatening stimuli, facilitating reactive attention to threats and interrupting task performance. The top-down process is associated with the ability to shift or focus attention effortfully, which requires people to control their attention voluntarily. Threats are first detected by the bottom-up detection system, which automatically shifts attention to negative stimuli; subsequently, the top-down cognitive control system can regulate the bottom-up detection system, which voluntarily shifts attention away from threats and helps refocus attention on tasks. The bottom-up system is more likely to be activated in anxious individuals than in healthy individuals, directing their attention towards threats. It is important to understand that negative stimuli play an important role in resilience and survival in the face of adversity. Regarding the leukaemia survivors mentioned above, if they ignore the early signs and symptoms of relapse, they risk missing the best time for treatment, which can have serious consequences for their recovery and survival. In other words, negative information should not be ignored, especially in difficult situations. Therefore, the fourth element of the SHINE framework emphasises that we need to pay attention to both positive and negative environmental stimuli in the face of adversity, hence the name "Noticing both Positives and Negatives."

Four quadrants of attention deployment are described below (Fig. 6.1).

Full Positive. People with a full positive attentional bias pay attention only to positive stimuli and ignore threats and negative information. They may not see the signs of risk and danger in adversity. Therefore, they miss the opportunity to prepare for potential dangers and may suffer greatly when negative events occur.

Full Negative. People with a full negative attentional bias only see threats and dangers. Moreover, they are unable to shift their attention away from the negatives. Hence, threats and dangers fully occupy their subjective worlds. These people are very anxious and depressed, which hampers their resilience.

Total Neglect. People in this category tend to ignore both positive and negative environmental stimuli. This does not mean that they are visually blind, but rather that due to a strong avoidance tendency in the face of adversity, they withdraw and ignore everything around them. Of course, they are not resilient in the face of adversity.

Balanced Attention. The final group of people pay equal attention to positive and negative environmental stimuli. Due to this tendency, they

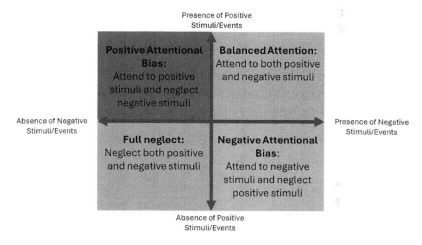

Fig. 6.1 The four categories of attention deployment

can shift their attention from negative stimuli to positive stimuli and vice versa. They can see and prepare for current and potential threats from adversity. They even see and seek out positive information in the face of adversity to maintain their well-being. They are expected to have higher resilience than the other three groups of people.

In summary, the SHINE framework proposes to pay balanced attention to both positive and negative stimuli to increase resilience. Before discussing the strategies for achieving this, let us briefly review how negative and positive attentional biases affect psychopathology and resilience.

6.2 Attentional Bias and Psychological Problems

According to cognitive models of anxiety, negative attentional bias may be a pivotal bias in information processing, contributing to the development and maintenance of anxiety symptoms (Bar-Haim et al., 2007; Mogg & Bradley, 1999; Williams et al., 1988). Compared with non-anxious individuals, anxious individuals frequently attend to negative stimuli and are less likely to move away from them, leading to affective, behavioural, and cognitive symptoms of anxiety disorders. Research has identified the relationship between negative attentional bias and anxiety symptoms in children and adults; individuals with higher anxiety symptoms exhibit greater negative attentional bias (Dong et al., 2017; Dudeney et al., 2015; Kelly et al., 2016). For youth, Abend et al. (2018) recruited 1,291 young people aged 6–18 (mean age = 13.5 years) from around the world and assessed their negative attentional bias using behavioural tasks. Their results revealed a significant positive association between negative attentional bias and anxiety symptoms.

Few theories and empirical studies have focused on positive attentional bias compared with negative attentional bias. Healthy individuals are more likely to engage with positive than neutral stimuli (Liang et al., 2017). Recently, Siegel and Peterson (2024) suggested that bypassing conscious awareness of threatening stimuli can reduce fear and anxiety. Increasing positive attentional bias may be one way to achieve this. Anxious individuals exhibit lower positive attentional bias than normal individuals (Chen et al., 2012; Chen et al., 2014; Chen et al., 2016).

High positive attentional bias also increases resilience against the development of anxiety disorders in children (Vrijen et al., 2019). Another study that measured positive attentional bias in children aged 7–17 using the eye-tracking technique found that compared with non-anxious children (N = 49), anxious children (N = 43) paid less attention to positive information (Gamble & Rapee, 2009). Other studies, however, have yielded inconsistent results. For example, in three studies, Waters and colleagues used visual dot-probe tasks to investigate attentional bias in children with varying levels of anxiety (Waters et al., 2004; Waters et al., 2008; Waters et al., 2010). Overall, their results showed that the participants had similar attentional biases towards positive and negative stimuli (e.g. happy vs. angry faces), regardless of their levels of anxiety. As pointed out by Taylor et al. (2011), it is (still) unclear whether anxious individuals are more, less, or equally likely to direct their attention to positive stimuli, especially when considering both positive and negative attentional biases simultaneously.

In a study of 712 teenagers in Hong Kong, my research team found that positive but not negative attentional bias mediated the relationship between hope (the second component of the SHINE framework) and anxiety/depressive symptoms (Yeung et al., 2015). In other words, high-hope teenagers tend to pay more attention to positive stimuli, which leads to reduced distress. Later, I used the directed forgetting paradigm to assess memory bias in 155 grade 7–10 students and reported that among teenagers with high levels of depression, greater anxiety was associated with less positive memory bias (Ho et al., 2018). As a follow-up study, we reassessed the same cohort of students and found that (the absence of) positive attentional bias was more important than negative attentional bias in predicting anxiety and depression one year later (Ho et al., 2018). Recently, we conducted a study among women with breast cancer in Taiwan and reported that self-perceived positive changes, even if illusory (i.e. positive attentional bias), can facilitate better resilience after a cancer diagnosis within seven years (Ho & Cheng, 2023).

In summary, in the context of resilience, my research findings are consistent with those of previous studies that negative attentional bias plays an important role in resilience. Less negative attentional bias is associated with better resilience. In general, my findings on positive attentional bias, consistent with previous studies, are mixed, with positive attentional bias having a positive, negative, or no relationship with psychopathology and resilience, particularly when negative attentional bias is considered simultaneously. As people are more inclined to focus on negative stimuli when faced with adversity, the SHINE framework proposes to develop our attention to positive information and stimuli in daily life to maintain a balanced attention style in times of difficulty.

6.3 Practical Applications

6.3.1 A Starting Point

First, it should be noted that personal strength in the first strategy of the SHINE framework (i.e. Strength-based habit-building) constitutes positive information about oneself. If you have followed the practices suggested in Chapter 3 to notice and apply your character strengths, you have taken a step towards tackling something positive! Furthermore, personal goals are positive things that we want to pursue. Goal setting is an important element of Hopeful Thinking in the second strategy of the SHINE framework. Practising the activities mentioned in Chapter 4 will enable you to increase your positive attention bias. The tendency to notice positive information serves two purposes: it dilutes the harmful effect of negative information and helps us shift our attention from negative events to positive events.

6.3.2 Building a Bank Account of Good Things

Establish an ongoing practice of observing the good things that happen to you. Write down three things that went well that day every night before you go to bed. These events can be trivial. By putting your positive experiences into words, you increase appreciation and memory of your blessings. Similar to other exercises in the SHINE framework, persistence is key. Do this regularly until it becomes a habit. You can either write it down or describe it verbally and record it.

1. _____
2. _____
3. _____

Note: You can write down your positive experiences on a small piece of paper, fold it into a star shape, and store it in a beautiful jar. Do this every day until the jar is full. Then start again with another jar. This trick works especially well for kids

6.3.3 Savour Positive Experiences to Enhance Positive Attention

You may practise the strategy below to prolong the effect of positive experiences and combat negative experiences during adversity.

1. Slow down and pay attention to the positive experience.
2. Share the experience in detail, including the different senses.
3. Amplify or prolong the duration of positive feelings.
4. Remember current positive events or anticipate future positive events.
5. Express gratitude to yourself or to the person who gave you this good experience.

References

Abend, R., de Voogd, L., Salemink, E., Wiers, R. W., Pérez-Edgar, K., Fitzgerald, A., White, L. K., Salum, G. A., He, J., Silverman, W. K., Pettit, J. W., Pine, D. S., & Bar-Haim, Y. (2018). Association between attention bias to threat and anxiety symptoms in children and adolescents. *Depression and Anxiety*, 35(3), 229–238. https://doi.org/10.1002/da.22706

Bar-Haim, Y., Lamy, D., Pergamin, L., Bakermans-Kranenburg, M. J., & van Ijzendoorn, M. H. (2007). Threat-related attentional bias in anxious and nonanxious individuals: A meta-analytic study. *Psychological Bulletin*, 133(1), 1–24. https://doi.org/10.1037/0033-2909.133.1.1

Chen, N. T. M., Clarke, P. J. F., MacLeod, C., & Guastella, A. J. (2012). Biased attentional processing of positive stimuli in social anxiety disorder: An eye movement study. *Cognitive Behaviour Therapy*, 41(2), 96–107. https://doi.org/10.1080/16506073.2012.666562

Chen, N. T., Clarke, P. J., Watson, T. L., Macleod, C., & Guastella, A. J. (2014). Biased saccadic responses to emotional stimuli in anxiety: An antisaccade study. *PLoS ONE*, 9(2), Article e86474. https://doi.org/10.1371/journal.pone.0086474

Chen, N. T. M., Clarke, P. J. F., MacLeod, C., Hickie, I. B., & Guastella, A. J. (2016). Aberrant gaze patterns in social anxiety disorder: An eye movement assessment during public speaking. *Journal of Experimental Psychopathology*, 7(1), 1–17. https://doi.org/10.5127/jep.040313

Dong, Y., De Beuckelaer, A., Yu, L., & Zhou, R. (2017). Eye-movement evidence of the time-course of attentional bias for threatening pictures in test-anxious students. *Cognition and Emotion*, 31(4), 781–790. https://doi.org/10.1080/02699931.2016.1152953

Dudeney, J., Sharpe, L., & Hunt, C. (2015). Attentional bias towards threatening stimuli in children with anxiety: A meta-analysis. *Clinical Psychology Review*, 40, 66–75. https://doi.org/10.1016/j.cpr.2015.05.007

Gamble, A. L., & Rapee, R. M. (2009). The time-course of attentional bias in anxious children and adolescents. *Journal of Anxiety Disorders*, 23(7), 841–847. https://doi.org/10.1016/j.janxdis.2009.04.001

Ho, S. M. Y., & Cheng, C.-T. (2023). Illusory versus constructive posttraumatic growth in cancer. In R. Berger (Ed.), *The Routledge international handbook of posttraumatic growth* (pp. 21–28). Routledge. https://doi.org/10.4324/9781032208688-4

Ho, S. M. Y., Cheng, J. C. K., Dai, D. W. T., Tam, T., & Hui, O. (2018). The effect of positive and negative memory biases on anxiety and depression symptoms among adolescents *Journal of Clinical Psychology*, Advance online publication. https://doi.org/10.1002/jclp.22597

Ho, S. M. Y., Dai, D. W. T., Mak, C., & Liu, K. W. K. (2018). Cognitive factors associated with depression and anxiety in adolescents: A two-year longitudinal study. *International Journal of Clinical and Health Psychology. Advanced online publication.* https://doi.org/10.1016/j.ijchp.2018.04.001

Kelly, L. C., Maratos, F. A., Lipka, S., & Croker, S. (2016). Attentional bias towards threatening and neutral facial expressions in high trait anxious children. *Journal of Experimental Psychopathology, 7*(3), 343–359. https://doi.org/10.5127/jep.052915

Liang, C.-W., Tsai, J.-L., & Hsu, W.-Y. (2017). Sustained visual attention for competing emotional stimuli in social anxiety: An eye tracking study. *Journal of Behavior Therapy and Experimental Psychiatry, 54*, 178–185. https://doi.org/10.1016/j.jbtep.2016.08.009

Mogg, K., & Bradley, B. P. (1999). Selective attention and anxiety: A cognitive–motivational perspective. In T. Dalgleish & M. J. Power (Eds.), *Handbook of cognition and emotion* (pp. 145–170, Chapter xxi, 843 Pages). Wiley.

Mogg, K., & Bradley, B. P. (2016). Anxiety and attention to threat: Cognitive mechanisms and treatment with attention bias modification. *Behaviour Research and Therapy, 87*, 76–108. https://doi.org/10.1016/j.brat.2016.08.001

Siegel, P., & Peterson, B. S. (2024). "All we have to fear is fear itself": Paradigms for reducing fear by preventing awareness of it. *Psychological Bulletin, 150*(9), 1118–1154. https://doi.org/10.1037/bul0000437

Taylor, C. T., Bomyea, J., & Amir, N. (2011). Malleability of attentional bias for positive emotional information and anxiety vulnerability. *Emotion, 11*, 127–138. https://doi.org/10.1037/a0021301

Vrijen, C., Hartman, C. A., & Oldehinkel, A. J. (2019). Reward-related attentional bias at age 16 predicts onset of depression during 9 years of follow-up. *Journal of the American Academy of Child and Adolescent Psychiatry, 58*(3), 329–338. https://doi.org/10.1016/j.jaac.2018.06.009

Waters, A. M., Henry, J., Mogg, K., Bradley, B. P., & Pine, D. S. (2010). Attentional bias towards angry faces in childhood anxiety disorders. *Journal of Behavior Therapy and Experimental Psychiatry, 41*(2), 158–164. https://doi.org/10.1016/j.jbtep.2009.12.001

Waters, A. M., Lipp, O. V., & Spence, S. H. (2004). Attentional bias toward fear-related stimuli: An investigation with nonselected children and adults and children with anxiety disorders. *Journal of Experimental Child Psychology, 89*(4), 320–337. https://doi.org/10.1016/j.jecp.2004.06.003

Waters, A. M., Mogg, K., Bradley, B., & Pine, D. (2008). Attentional bias for emotional faces in children with generalized anxiety disorder. *Journal of the American Academy of Child and Adolescent Psychiatry, 47*(4), 435–442. https://doi.org/10.1097/CHI.0b013e3181642992

Williams, J. M. G., Watts, F. N., MacLeod, C., & Mathews, A. (1988). *Cognitive psychology and emotional disorders*. Wiley.

Yeung, D. Y., Ho, S. M. Y., & Mak, C. W. Y. (2015). Attention to positive information mediates the relationship between hope and psychosocial well-being of adolescents. *Journal of Adolescence, 42*, 98–102. https://doi.org/10.1016/j.adolescence.2015.04.004

CHAPTER 7

Embracing Change

Abstract The embracing change component of SHINE contains strategies to help individuals navigate prolonged adversity, such as severe disabilities and poverty. It emphasises that although adversity may appear endless, resilience can be cultivated through optimism, explanatory styles, avoiding rumination, and recognising constructive positive changes such as posttraumatic growth (PTG). When facing prolonged adversity, people should seek valid and optimistic explanations for the causes of negative events, avoid brooding and pessimistic rumination, and differentiate between constructive and illusory PTG. Practical exercises are provided to foster a self-serving explanatory style and promote psychological resilience, urging individuals to be open to genuine positive changes that may arise from adversity. Through a comprehensive analysis of the interplay between psychological responses and adversity, the chapter underscores the potential for personal growth despite challenges.

Keywords Prolonged adversity · Optimism · Explanatory styles · Rumination · Brooding · Illusory growth · Constructive growth · Posttraumatic growth · Posttraumatic depreciation

© The Author(s), under exclusive license to Springer Nature
Switzerland AG 2025
S. M. Y. Ho, *The SHINE Framework*,
https://doi.org/10.1007/978-3-031-89106-9_7

117

7.1 When Adversity Seems Never-Ending

Adversity will not last forever. However, there are situations, particularly those related to severe disabilities and poverty, where the suffering seems endless. For example, persistent exposure to poverty can be considered a type of collective trauma leading to the development of "trauma-based behaviours" (Shamai, 2018). Sometimes we cannot see the end of an arduous journey, and our future seems hopeless. People have told us that even after implementing all of the SHINE strategies mentioned so far, namely building a habit of using one's character strengths, engaging in downward regoaling and finding ways to achieve these goals, looking for positive things around oneself, and developing constructive relationships, their difficulties persist.

The last component of the SHINE framework, *Embracing Change*, specifically targets such situations. It contains three strategies: optimism, rumination, and benefit finding (i.e., finding positive changes in the face of adversity). The following sections describe each of them.

7.2 Optimism

When discussing the hopeful thinking style, I mentioned that optimism is similar to hope (see Chapter 4). To recap, optimism is believing that good things will happen despite external circumstances (Scheier & Carver, 1988). Research has linked optimism to higher levels of well-being and better resilience (Peterson & Steen, 2021). In a recent study, Palacios-Delgado et al. (2024) showed that low optimism is a significant factor related to the onset of depression. In addition, optimism mediates the relationship between problem-focused coping and depression. In other words, people with higher optimism tend to use more problem-focused coping strategies (see Chapter 1 for a discussion of coping strategies), which leads to less depression (Palacios-Delgado et al., 2024). Another study found that higher optimism was associated with less distress during the COVID-19 pandemic (Shiloh et al., 2022).

7.3 Explanatory Style

The idea most relevant to the SHINE framework is that optimistic and pessimistic people have different ways of explaining positive and negative events that happen to them (Peterson & Steen, 2021). Peterson and

Buchanan (1995) used the term "explanatory style" to describe the above proposition. Explanatory style (or attributional style) refers to people's tendency to offer similar explanations for the causes of bad or good events that happen to them. This style consists of three key dimensions:

1. *Internal versus External*: This dimension reflects whether people attribute events to themselves ("It's me") or to others ("It's someone else").
2. *Global versus Specific*: This aspect considers whether people believe that an event affects many areas of their life ("It affects many aspects of my life") or is limited to a single domain ("It affects only this aspect of my life").
3. *Stable versus Unstable*: This dimension relates to whether people view the causes of events as lasting ("It's long-lasting") or temporary ("It's only passing").

A pessimistic explanatory style for negative events involves attributing their causes to internal, global, and stable factors. In contrast, an optimistic explanatory style for negative events attributes them to external, specific, and unstable factors. An optimistic explanatory style explains the causes of positive events as internal, global, and stable, while a pessimistic explanatory style views positive events as external, specific, and unstable (Fig. 7.1).

Research has indicated that individuals with a pessimistic explanatory style for negative events tend to show lower resilience, often experiencing more depressive symptoms and posttraumatic stress during difficult times (Joseph et al., 1993). Conversely, those with a self-serving bias (who perceive the causes of positive events as internal, global, and stable and the causes of negative events as external, specific, and unstable) tend to exhibit greater resilience (Jolley et al., 2006). Interestingly, an early meta-analysis reported that self-serving attributional bias is pervasive in the general population, but that there are significant age- and culture-related differences (Mezulis et al., 2004). For example, Asian people show much less self-serving attributional bias than people from the US or Western countries.

The original model of explanatory style focuses primarily on how individuals respond to negative events, leaving the role of explanatory style for positive events less defined (Seligman et al., 1984). Empirical research

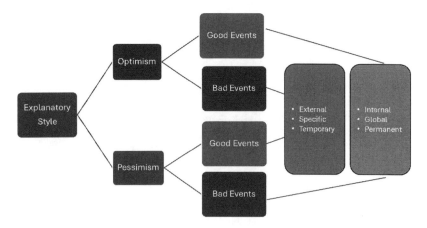

Fig. 7.1 Optimistic versus pessimistic explanatory style

has indicated that the connections between explanatory style for positive events and psychopathology are less consistent than those for negative events (Reivich, 1995).

In summary, evidence strongly suggests that people's explanatory style for negative events is more influential in predicting psychopathology than their explanatory style for positive events. Because empirical evidence shows that the explanatory style for negative events has a more persistent effect on resilience and that people are more likely to encounter negative events in situations of perpetual adversity, the SHINE framework prioritises the development of an optimistic explanatory style for negative events. In prolonged adverse situations, people should cultivate a habit of seeking valid and optimistic explanations for the causes of their adversity. They should also avoid focusing solely on blaming themselves for the bad things that happen to them. The Practical Applications section introduces ways to cultivate an optimistic explanatory style for negative events.

7.4 Rumination

A pessimistic explanatory style may intensify depressive moods through the process of rumination, which is a mode of thinking that involves repetitively and passively focusing on upsetting events, including depressive symptoms and the consequences of adversity (Lo et al., 2008,

2010, 2014; Nolen-Hoeksema, 1991). In a study involving both college students and psychiatric outpatients with depression (Lo et al., 2008), I discovered that people showing higher levels of pessimistic explanatory style (i.e. attribute negative events to internal, global, and stable factors) tend to engage in a form of brooding rumination, which in turn leads to more depressive symptoms. Brooding represents a tendency towards moody pondering and a passive recycling characteristic of rumination that does not provide insight into coping with adverse situations (Treynor et al., 2003). For example, people may think emotionally and repeatedly about the idea of being diagnosed with cancer ("I will die"; "I will have to undergo painful treatment"; "I will lose my job"), but such rumination cannot help them think about how to cope with the upcoming difficulties related to cancer.

Lo et al. (2010) conducted a follow-up study and found that rumination interacted with depressive symptoms to produce an even more pessimistic explanatory style. The researchers argued that people with a pessimistic explanatory style are more likely to exhibit brooding rumination in the face of adversity, which in turn will lead to depressive symptoms (Lo et al., 2010). Brooding rumination and depressive symptoms can trigger more pessimistic attributions of adverse events, creating a vicious circle. Figure 7.2 illustrates these relationships.

Finally, it is helpful to distinguish rumination from coping self-reflection (or self-reflection) (Crane et al., 2019), a beneficial factor related to resilience. Unlike brooding, coping self-reflection involves

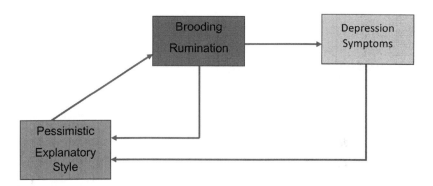

Fig. 7.2 Circular relationships between pessimistic explanatory style, brooding rumination, and depressive symptoms

actively engaging in introspection in the face of stressors to understand the emotional reactions, thoughts, and behaviours associated with coping with adversity. Such active reflection allows you to think about your current situations, your life goals, and ways to achieve them. The two studies mentioned above found that the reflection type of rumination is not related to pessimistic explanatory style and depressive symptoms, although we failed to find any beneficial effects of reflection in these studies (Lo et al., 2008, 2010). Recently, Bucknell et al. (2024) conducted a randomised controlled trial and reported that coping self-reflection training can increase individuals' psychological resilience.

7.5 Constructive Positive Changes

The fourth component of the SHINE framework (i.e. Noticing both Positives and Negatives) emphasises balanced attention to both good and bad things in the environment (Chapter 6). Good and bad things can happen to you or to other people, and they can be due to your efforts or those of other people. When adversity becomes chronic and lasts for a prolonged period, we take the above strategy a step further. We try to see positive changes in ourselves as a result of adversity. Sometimes we even try to gain personal benefit from adversity.

It may seem odd to suggest that we can experience positive change because of adversity. In my professional work, of course, many people have shared with me their suffering during and after trauma. However, it is not uncommon for them to also share some personal positive changes resulting from their trauma. A woman told me that she had a better relationship with her husband after her cancer diagnosis because she saw how much her husband cared for her during her illness. After his disability, a man shared that he developed a stronger connection to his religious beliefs. After her husband died, a woman discovered she could take care of her children on her own, both financially and physically. She considered herself a stronger person than before her husband died. Their positive changes appealed to me because my training in clinical psychology focused almost exclusively on suffering and pathology. The idea that people can draw positive changes from a traumatic encounter was new to me.[1] I searched the literature and found that Tedeschi and

---

[1] This was over 30 years ago. Today, most clinical psychology programmes and other professional training programmes include PTG and related topics in their curriculum.

colleagues (Tedeschi & Calhoun, 1996; Tedeschi et al., 1998a, 1998b; Tedeschi et al., 2017) coined the term "posttraumatic growth" (PTG) to describe the phenomenon of positive changes people report after trauma. I decided to conduct systematic research to understand this phenomenon more deeply and contacted Tedeschi for advice. This decision marked the beginning of a fruitful journey of 20 + years of research on PTG, with some of my projects conducted in collaboration with Tedeschi and his team (Chan et al., 2011; Ho et al., 2021).

In this section, I briefly summarise the major lessons I learnt from my research on PTG. Interested readers can find more details in my latest book chapter (Ho & Cheng, 2023). Next, I explain why I include PTG as a strategy in the Embracing Change component of the SHINE framework.

7.5.1 The Five Dimensions of PTG

Based on the literature, here are the five dimensions of PTG:

Social Dimension: This includes a sense of closeness to others, increased compassion, and improved social resources (Schaefer & Moos, 1992; Tedeschi & Calhoun, 1996).

Cognitive Dimension: Individuals may experience feelings of strength and self-assurance, enhanced self-concept, better problem-solving skills, and increased self-confidence (Collins et al., 1990; Lehman et al., 1993; Schaefer & Moos, 1992).

Emotional Dimension: This encompasses feelings of relaxation, reduced personal demands, greater compassion for the suffering of others, improved emotional expression, and a stronger sense of self-reliance (Tedeschi et al., 1998a).

Physical Dimension: Lifestyle changes may occur, including increased awareness of healthy eating and exercise habits (Epel et al., 1998).

Spiritual/Philosophical Dimension: Individuals may develop a deeper appreciation for life and family and reassess their life priorities (Lehman et al., 1993; Tedeschi et al., 1998a).

Tedeschi and colleagues developed the Posttraumatic Growth Inventory (PTGI) to capture the five growth dimensions discussed above, called Relating to Others, Personal Strength, New Possibilities, Appreciation of Life, and Spiritual Change (Tedeschi & Calhoun, 1996) (Fig. 7.3).

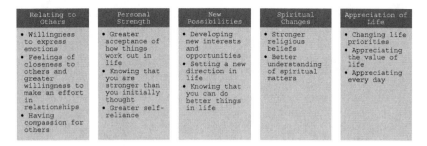

Fig. 7.3 The five domains measured by the PTGI (Tedeschi & Calhoun, 1996)

It is now clearly demonstrated that real positive changes are possible during and after adversity. A study of 1,132 participants who had experienced trauma showed that people reported positive changes whether they experienced the event directly or vicariously (Altinsoy & Aypay, 2023).

One way to maintain resilience in the face of sustained adversity is to be aware that we can change for the better in such situations, no matter how minor. We should embrace change and accept that it is a possible outcome of adversity. Nevertheless, we should keep in mind two points related to PTG.

7.5.2 Constructive Versus Illusory PTG

First, some positive changes are real, while others can be imagined. Imagine you are in a desert for days without water. You are thirsty and you try to find water but in vain. In such a desperate situation, your defence mechanism might create the illusion of an oasis in front of you to soothe your psychological turmoil. However, this illusion cannot solve your problem. Walking towards the "oasis," you find only sand but no water! The same applies to PTG. In prolonged adverse situations, when there seems to be no way out, we can create the illusion of positive changes to make ourselves feel good. Such false positive changes have no effect, or even a negative effect, on resilience.

Zoellner and Maercker (Maercker & Zoellner, 2004; Zoellner & Maercker, 2006) proposed the Janus-face model of PTG to show that there are adaptive and maladaptive types of PTG. They divided PTG into two components: constructive PTG and illusory PTG. Constructive PTG refers to authentic and positive changes associated with healthy psychological adjustments. In contrast, illusory PTG is a coping mechanism that individuals may adopt in response to trauma; it does not reflect real positive change and the benefits it provides are often temporary (Ho, 2016; Pat-Horenczyk et al., 2016).

I conducted a 7-year longitudinal study with psychiatrists and clinical psychologists at the Koo Foundation Sun Yat-Sen Cancer Center (KFSYSC) in Taipei, the only specialised cancer hospital in Taiwan at the time, to investigate PTG in breast cancer survivors. The breast cancer survivors exhibited three types of PTG (Cheng et al., 2018):

Constructive PTG: The survivors in this category reported high levels of PTG and used few maladaptive coping mechanisms.

Illusory PTG: Those exhibiting this pattern also reported high levels of PTG, but relied on more maladaptive coping strategies.

Distressed PTG: This group showed low levels of PTG and relied even more heavily on maladaptive coping mechanisms.

A follow-up study was conducted on the 10th anniversary of the original research, with the same group of breast cancer survivors (Cheng et al., 2020). The findings showed that the survivors with an illusory PTG trajectory exhibited higher levels of anxiety and depressive symptoms and more maladaptive coping strategies (such as hopelessness/helplessness and anxious preoccupation) than those with a constructive PTG trajectory. Overall, these results suggest that illusory PTG may reflect an individual's attempt to cope with post-cancer adjustment by fostering a positive illusion about their experience, while constructive PTG indicates genuine, positive transformation following cancer diagnosis and treatment.

The above studies lead to two related findings. First, people with constructive PTG and illusory PTG have different ways of coping (see Chapter 1). The first group uses adaptive coping, while the second group uses maladaptive coping to deal with adversity. Second, some people have little or no PTG. Our research classified them as "people with a distressed PTG pattern" (Cheng et al., 2018). For various reasons, such as lack of social and financial support, it is normal for some people not to experience PTG. Hence, we should not stigmatise them as low-functioning people.

Furthermore, forcing people to exhibit PTG in the face of adversity is not appropriate. The SHINE framework recommends focusing on developing adaptive coping (and practising the SHINE strategies). At the same

126   S. M. Y. HO

time, people should be sensitive and open to the positive changes they may experience during and after the crisis. If no positive changes are happening, maybe it is not the right time yet and there is nothing wrong with not experiencing PTG.

7.5.3   Growth Versus Depreciation

Participants in my PTG workshop often ask the following questions.

- Can positive changes reduce negative changes during trauma?
- Is it possible for people to experience similar degrees of positive and negative changes at the same time?
- If so, does it represent psychological problems?

It is important to note that *people with PTG are not necessarily free of negative emotions*. People who experience PTG alongside negative emotions tend to be more resilient and better equipped than their counterparts to find "wisdom" in the chaos and unpredictability of life. For instance, Dohrenwend et al. (2004) discovered that Vietnam War veterans who mainly viewed their military experiences through a negative lens felt high levels of alienation. In contrast, those who combined a positive interpretation with their negative feelings demonstrated the best adjustment. Baker et al. (2008) were the first to systematically address the above questions by incorporating 21 negatively worded items into the original 21-item PTGI (Tedeschi & Calhoun, 1996). These new items, which represent negative changes, were called posttraumatic depreciation (PTD) items. For instance, a growth item might state, "I am more likely to try to change things that need to be changed," while a corresponding depreciation item would be, "I am less likely to try to change things that need to be changed."

Later, Taku et al. (2020) added four spiritual–existential change items to the questionnaire of Baker et al. (2008) and developed the 50-item (25 growth items and 25 paired depreciation items) Posttraumatic Growth and Depreciation Inventory–Expanded version (PTGDI-X). In an international study of 10 countries, the researchers reported that the participants reported both PTG and PTD, but that their PTG scores were higher than their PTD scores in all countries. I translated the PTGDI-X into Chinese and administered it to cancer survivors at the KFSYSC in

Taipei (Ho et al., 2021). The results showed that PTG and PTD had five parallel domains similar to the original PTGI (Fig. 7.1). Similar to the results of other studies (Baker et al., 2008; Taku et al., 2020), the breast cancer survivors experienced more PTG than PTD in all five domains. Finally, PTG and PTD showed an inverted U-shaped relationship. More PTG was related to more PTD until it reached a threshold beyond which more PTG was linked to less PTD (Fig. 7.4).

As an analogy to explain the relationship between PTG and PTD, imagine that you are tidying up your house. At the beginning, you discover both trashed and valuable items. You feel distressed when the valuable items cannot offset the trashed items. If you find more valuable articles in the house cleaning process, you will pay less attention to the trashed items and develop more positive feeling. (Ho & Cheng, 2023).

It is therefore normal to experience both positive and negative changes simultaneously in the face of adversity. Keep a log of your positive changes; ultimately, the positive changes will offset the negative changes due to the trauma.

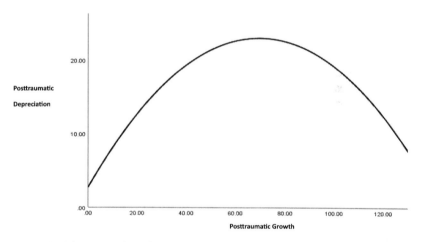

Fig. 7.4 The inverted U-shaped relationship between PTG and PTD (Ho et al., 2021)

128 S. M. Y. HO

7.6 Summary

Some may view Embracing Change as a palliative component of the SHINE framework. The strategies discussed in this chapter serve a "palliative" function by helping us feel better in the face of prolonged adversity. More than that, these strategies can enrich our coping and self-care repertoire, which can help us maintain our psychological well-being and, more importantly, reduce self-harm so that we can bounce back faster and better when the time comes. These strategies include.

1. Developing a self-serving explanatory style to attribute good events to internal, global, and permanent factors, and bad events to external, specific, and temporary factors.
2. Practising self-reflection to replace brooding rumination.
3. Acknowledging and sustaining personal growth in the face of adversity.

The following section introduces practices to help us develop these three strategies.

7.7 Practical Applications

7.7.1 Self-Serving Explanatory Style

a. Explanatory Style Logbook

It may be easier to understand your explanatory style by keeping track of how to explain things that happen to you. Complete the following table every week for at least 1 month.

Instruction. Briefly describe some of the **bad** things that happened to you in the past seven days in Column 1 of the table below.

1	2	3	4	5
The event	Why did this event happen? (briefly describe what caused the event)	To what extent is the cause in Column 2 due to you or other people/circumstances? 1 = Totally because of me 2 = Because of me, to a large extent 3 = Both equally 4 = Because of other people/circumstances to a large extent 5 = Totally because of other people/circumstances	To what extent will the cause of Column 2 happen again in the future? 1 = Will definitely be happened again in the future 2 = Likely to be happened again in the future 3 = Neutral 4 = Unlikely to be happened again in the future 5 = Will definitely not be happened again in the future	To what extent does the cause in Column 2 affect only this event or others in your life? 1 = Affects all areas of my life 2 = Affects most areas of my life 3 = Half and half 4 = Mainly affects only this event, but may also affect other areas of my life 5 = Affects only this event and will not affect other areas of my life

My employer fired me.	I didn't meet the sales quota.	4 (The economy is bad)	4 (I believe the economy will improve soon)	3 (I can continue to be a good husband/father despite my unemployment)

Now do this for good things. Briefly describe some of the **good** things that happened to you in the past seven days in Column 1 of the table below. Then complete the remaining columns.

1	2	3	4	5
The event	Why did this event happen? (briefly describe what caused the event)	To what extent is the cause in Column 2 due to you or other people/circumstances? 1 = Totally because of me 2 = Because of me, to a large extent 3 = Both equally	To what extent will the cause of Column 2 happen again in the future? 1 = Will definitely be happened again in the future 2 = Likely to be happened again in the future	To what extent does the cause in Column 2 affect only this event or others in your life? 1 = Affects all areas of my life 2 = Affects most areas of my life 3 = Half and half

		4 = Because of other people/circumstances to a large extent 5 = Totally because of other people/circumstances	3 = Neutral 4 = Unlikely to be happened again in the future 5 = Will definitely not be happened again in the future	4 = Mainly affects only this event, but may also affect other areas of my life 5 = Affects only this event and will not affect other areas of my life
1 received a job offer.	*My work experience is a perfect match for this job.*	*2 (I have worked hard in the past to gain my current experience)*	*1 (This experience will stay with me forever. No one can take it away from me)*	*2 (With this job offer, I can improve my relationship with my wife and children)*

b. Develop Alternative Explanations

Column 3 represents Internal versus External Explanation, with a higher score indicating a more internal attribution. Column 4 represents Permanent versus Temporary Explanation, with a higher score indicating a more permanent attribution. Column 5 represents Global versus Specific Explanation, with a higher score indicating a more global attribution.

For the negative events described above, find alternative explanations to increase your scores for Columns 3–5 to gradually move towards explaining the causes of the negative events as external, temporary, and specific. In other words, rewrite your explanations by focusing on possible external, specific, and unstable factors.

For the positive events, develop alternative explanations to reduce your scores for Columns 3–5 to gradually explain the causes of the positive events as internal, permanent, and global. In short, rewrite your explanations by focusing on possible internal, general, and stable factors.

7.7.2 Constructive PTG: Expressive Versus Benefit-Finding Condition

Select the worst experience in Sect. 7.7.1 and do the following.

a. Write down your deepest thoughts and feelings about your experiences with the event you have chosen (expressive conditions)

_____

_____

b. Write down the positive changes you observed after the event. If there were no changes before and after the event, write "none." (benefit-finding condition)

_____

_____

c. Share your changes with people you trust and check if they see your positive changes.

_____

_____

REFERENCES

Altinsoy, F., & Aypay, A. (2023). Does the type of exposure to traumatic events make a difference in posttraumatic growth? *Psychological Trauma: Theory, Research, Practice, and Policy, 15*(1), 27–36. https://doi.org/10.1037/tra0001173

Baker, J. M., Kelly, C., Calhoun, L. G., Cann, A., & Tedeschi, R. G. (2008). An examination of posttraumatic growth and posttraumatic depreciation: Two exploratory studies. *Journal of Loss and Trauma, 13*(5), 450–465. https://doi.org/10.1080/15325020802171367

7 EMBRACING CHANGE **133**

Bucknell, K. J., Kangas, M., Karin, E., & Crane, M. F. (2024). A randomized controlled trial comparing the effects of self-reflective writing focused on successful and unsuccessful coping experiences on resilience. *Stress and Health: Journal of the International Society for the Investigation of Stress*, *40*(2). https://doi.org/10.1002/smi.3311

Chan, M. W. C., Ho, S. M. Y., Tedeschi, R. G., & Leung, C. W. L. (2011). The valence of attentional bias and cancer-related rumination in posttraumatic stress and posttraumatic growth among women with breast cancer. *Psycho-Oncology*, 20, 544–552. https://doi.org/10.1002/pon.176

Cheng, C. T., Ho, S. M. Y., Hou, Y. C., Lai, Y., & Wang, G. L. (2018). Constructive, illusory, and distressed posttraumatic growth among survivors of breast cancer: A 7-year growth trajectory study. *Journal of Health Psychology*, 1359105318793199. https://doi.org/10.1177/1359105318793199

Cheng, C. T., Wang, G. L., & Ho, S. M. Y. (2020). The relationship between types of posttraumatic growth and prospective psychological adjustment in women with breast cancer: A follow-up study. *Psychooncology*, 29, 586–588. https://doi.org/10.1002/pon.5312

Collins, R. L., Taylor, S. E., & Skokan, L. A. (1990). A better world or a shattered vision? Changes in life perspectives following victimization. *Social Cognition*, 8, 263–285. https://doi.org/10.1521/soco.1990.8.3.263

Crane, M. F., Searle, B. J., Kangas, M., & Nwiran, Y. (2019). How resilience is strengthened by exposure to stressors: the systematic self-reflection model of resilience strengthening. *Anxiety, Stress, & Coping*, *32*(1), 1–17. https://doi.org/10.1080/10615806.2018.1506640

Dohrenwend, B. P., Neria, Y., Turner, J. B., Turse, N., Marshall, R., Lewis-Fernandez, R., & Koenen, K. C. (2004). Positive tertiary appraisals and posttraumatic stress disorder in U.S. male veterans of the war in Vietnam: the roles of positive affirmation, positive reformulation, and defensive denial. *Journal of Consulting and Clinical Psychology*, *72*(3), 417–433. https://doi.org/10.1037/0022-006x.72.3.417

Epel, E. S., McEwen, B. S., & Ickovics, J. R. (1998). Embodying psychological thriving: Physical thriving in response to stress. *Journal of Social Issues*, *54*(2), 301–322. https://doi.org/10.1111/j.1540-4560.1998.tb01220.x

Ho, S. M. Y. (2016). Posttraumatic growth: Focus on concepts and cross-cultural measurement issues. In C. R. Martin, V. Preedy, & V. B. Patel (Eds.), *Comprehensive guide to post-traumatic stress disorder* (pp. 1831–1848). Springer. https://doi.org/10.1007/978-3-319-08613-2_60-1

Ho, S. M. Y., & Cheng, C.-T. (2023). Illusory versus constructive posttraumatic growth in cancer. In R. Berger (Ed.), *The routledge international handbook of posttraumatic growth* (pp. 21–28). Routledge. https://doi.org/10.4324/9781032208688-4

Ho, S. M. Y., Cheng, C.-T., Shih, S.-M., Taku, K., & Tedeschi, R. G. (2021). The Chinese version of Posttraumatic Growth and Depreciation Inventory—Expanded version (PTGDI-X) for cancer survivors. *Supportive Care in Cancer*, Advance online publication. https://doi.org/10.1007/s00520-021-06223-8

Joseph, S., Yule, W., & Williams, R. (1993). Post-traumatic stress: Attributional aspects. *Journal of Traumatic Stress*, 6(4), 501–513. https://doi.org/10.1002/jts.2490060407

Jolley, S., Garety, P., Bebbington, P., Dunn, G., Freeman, D., Kuipers, E., Fowler, D., & Hemsley, D. (2006). Attributional style in psychosis—The role of affect and belief type. *Behaviour Research and Therapy*, 44, 1597–1607. https://doi.org/10.1016/j.brat.2005.12.002

Lehman, D. R., Davis, C. G., DeLongis, A., Wortman, C. B., Bluck, S., Mandel, D. R., & Ellard, J. H. (1993). Positive and negative life changes following bereavement and their relations to adjustment. *Journal of Social and Clinical Psychology*, 12(1), 90–112. https://doi.org/10.1521/jscp.1993.12.1.90

Lo, C. S. L., Ho, S. M. Y., & Hollon, S. D. (2008). The effects of rumination and negative cognitive styles on depression: A mediation analysis. *Behaviour Research and Therapy*, 46(4), 487–495. https://doi.org/10.1016/j.brat.2008.01.013

Lo, C. S. L., Ho, S. M. Y., & Hollon, S. D. (2010). The effects of rumination and depressive symptoms on the prediction of negative attributional style among college students. *Cognitive Therapy and Research*, 34, 116–123. https://doi.org/10.1007/s10608-009-9233-2

Lo, C. S. L., Ho, S. M. Y., Yu, N. K. K., & Siu, B. P. Y. (2014). Decentering mediates the effect of ruminative and experiential self-focus on negative thinking in depression. *Cognitive Therapy and Research*, 38(4), 389–396. https://doi.org/10.1007/s10608-014-9603-2

Maercker, A., & Zoellner, T. (2004). The Janus face of self-perceived growth: Toward a two-component model of posttraumatic growth. *Psychological Inquiry*, 41–48.

Mezulis, A. H., Abramson, L. Y., Hyde, J. S., & Hankin, B. L. (2004). Is there a universal positivity bias in attributions? A metaanalytic review of individual, developmental, and cultural differences in the self-serving attributional bias. *Psychological Bulletin*, 130(5), 711–747. https://doi.org/10.1037/0033-2909.130.5.711

Nolen-Hoeksema, S. (1991). Responses to depression and their effects on the duration of depressive episodes. *Journal of Abnormal Psychology*, 100, 569–582. https://doi.org/10.1037/0021-843X.100.4.569

Pat-Horenczyk, R., Saltzman, L. Y., Hamama-Raz, Y., Perry, S., Ziv, Y., Ginat-Frolich, R., & Stemmer, S. M. (2016). Stability and transitions in posttraumatic growth trajectories among cancer patients: LCA and LTA analyses. *Psychological Trauma*, 8(5), 541–549. https://doi.org/10.1037/tra0000094

Palacios-Delgado, J., Acosta-Beltrán, D. B., & Acevedo-Ibarra, J. N. (2024). How important are optimism and coping strategies for mental health? Effect in reducing depression in young people. *Psychiatry International*, 5(3), 532–543. https://www.mdpi.com/2673-5318/5/3/38

Peterson, C., & Buchanan, G. M. (1995). Explanatory style: History and evolution of the field. In *Explanatory style* (pp. 1–20). Lawrence Erlbaum Associates, Inc. https://doi.org/10.1017/CBO9780511527937.026

Peterson, C., & Steen, T. A. (2021). Optimistic explanatory style. In C. R. Snyder, S. J. Lopez, L. M. Edwards, & S. C. Marques (Eds.), *The Oxford handbook of positive psychology* (3rd ed., pp. 413–424, 1002 Pages). Oxford University Press.

Reivich, K. (1995). The measurement of explanatory style. In G. M. Buchanan & M. E. P. Seligman (Eds.), *Explanatory Style* (pp. 21–27). Lawrence Erlbaum Associates.

Shamai, M. (2018). Is poverty a collective trauma? A joint learning process with women living in poverty in the city of Haifa in Israel. *British Journal of Social Work*, 48(6), 1718–1735. https://doi.org/10.1093/bjsw/bcx116

Schaefer, J. A., & Moos, R. (1992). Life crises and personal growth. In B. Carpenter (Ed.), *Personal coping: Theory, research, and application* (pp. 149–170). Praeger.

Scheier, M. F., & Carver, C. S. (1988). Dispositional optimism and physical well-being: The influence of outcome expectancies on health. *Journal of Personality*, 55, 169–210. https://doi.org/10.1111/j.1467-6494.1987.tb00434.x

Seligman, M. E. P., Peterson, C., Kaslow, N. J., Tanenbaum, R. L., Alloy, L. B., & Abramson, L. Y. (1984). Attributional style and depressive symptoms among children. *Journal of Abnormal Psychology*, 93, 235–238. https://doi.org/10.1037/0021-843X.93.2.235

Shiloh, S., Peleg, S., & Nudelman, G. (2022). Core self-evaluations as resilience and risk factors of psychological distress during the covid-19 pandemic. *Psychology, Health & Medicine*. https://doi.org/10.1080/13548506.2022.2030480

Taku, K., Tedeschi, R. G., Shakespeare-Finch, J., Krosch, D., David, G., Kehl, D., Grunwald, S., Romeo, A., Di Tella, M., Kamibeppu, K., Soejima, T., Hiraki, K., Volgin, R., Dhakal, S., Zięba, M., Ramos, C., Nunes, R., Leal, I., Gouveia, P., ..., Calhoun, L. G. (2020). Posttraumatic growth (PTG) and posttraumatic depreciation (PTD) across ten countries: Global validation of the PTG-PTD theoretical model. *Personality and Individual Differences*, 110222. https://doi.org/10.1016/j.paid.2020.110222

Tedeschi, R. G., & Calhoun, L. G. (1996). The posttraumatic growth inventory: Measuring the positive legacy of trauma. *Journal of Traumatic Stress*, 9(3), 455–471. https://doi.org/10.1002/jts.2490090305

Tedeschi, R. G., & Calhoun, L. G. (2004). Target Article: Posttraumatic growth: conceptual foundations and empirical evidence. *Psychological Inquiry*, 15(1), 1–18. https://doi.org/10.1207/s15327965pli1501_01

Tedeschi, R. G., Park, C. L., & Calhoun, L. G. (1998a). Posttraumatic Growth: Conceptual issues. In R. G. Tedeschi, C. L. Park, & L. G. Calhoun (Eds.), *Posttraumatic Growth: Positive changes in the aftermath of crisis* (pp. 1–22). Lawrence Erlbaum Associates.

Tedeschi, R. G., Park, C. L., & Calhoun, L. G. (Eds.). (1998b). *Posttraumatic growth: Positive changes in the aftermath of crisis*. Lawrence Erlbaum Associates.

Tedeschi, R. G., Cann, A., Taku, K., Senol-Durak, E., & Calhoun, L. G. (2017). The posttraumatic growth inventory: A revision integrating existential and spiritual change. *Journal of Traumatic Stress*, 30(1), 11–18. https://doi.org/10.1002/jts.22155

Treynor, W., Gonzalez, R., & Nolen-Hoeksema, S. (2003). Rumination reconsidered: A psychometric analysis. *Cognitive Therapy and Research*, 27(3), 247–259. https://doi.org/10.1023/A:1023910315561

Zoellner, T., & Maercker, A. (2006). Posttraumatic growth in clinical psychology - A critical review and introduction of a two component model. *Clinical psychology review*, 26(5), 626–653. https://doi.org/10.1016/j.cpr.2006.01.00

CHAPTER 8

Epilogue

Abstract This chapter reflects on the author's journey in developing the SHINE framework to enhance resilience in the face of increasing global crises and disasters. It revisits the core strategies of the framework, including cultivating character strengths, practising positive and constructive communication, developing hopeful cognition, nurturing a balanced attentional style, and accepting that changes are inevitable. The author advocates integrating the SHINE framework into educational curricula to equip future generations with essential resilience skills. Additionally, the chapter suggests incorporating third-wave cognitive–behavioural therapy techniques, such as mindfulness and acceptance–commitment therapy, in the future development of the SHINE framework.

Keywords Mindfulness · Acceptance–commitment therapy · SHINE revisited

8.1 Introduction

I have been thinking for a few years about writing a book to summarise my research over the past years. I had two ideas. The first idea was about psychology and pottery. Having practised pottery as a hobby for over 30 years and being a professor of psychology, I find it worthwhile to use

© The Author(s), under exclusive license to Springer Nature Switzerland AG 2025
S. M. Y. Ho, *The SHINE Framework*,
https://doi.org/10.1007/978-3-031-89106-9_8

pottery to demonstrate some basic concepts of psychology. The other idea was to write a book about resilience. Ultimately, I found the second book idea timelier given the increasing number of crises and disasters we have witnessed over the past few years. We saw major hurricanes and typhoons, such as Hurricane Helene in the US and Storm Boris in Central Europe. At the start of 2025, devastating wildfires caused major damage to Los Angeles. Floods have occurred in many countries, including Thailand, Tanzania, Kenya, the southern provinces of China, Dubai, and Brazil. Earthquakes in Japan, Taiwan, Turkey, and Morocco have caused severe damage and suffering. Climate change is evident. The economic recovery from the COVID-19 pandemic has also been slower than expected, and many people around the world still live in poverty. We will probably only experience more frequent and severe crises.

Conventional methods for relieving symptoms after a traumatic encounter are effective, but they may not meet all our current needs. In a world of crises, we need to equip ourselves with skills to prepare for adversity, bounce back, and become stronger afterwards. The SHINE framework serves this purpose. The SHINE framework is not a remedial intervention model to produce immediate symptom relief, but instead requires long-term habit-building to achieve the desired outcomes. To a large extent, the SHINE strategies are latent factors of resilience. We may not feel their effects during hay days, but adversity does trigger the SHINE strategies to generate resilience.

8.1.1   The SHINE Framework Revisited

Chapter 1 describes the five components of the SHINE framework (see Fig. 1.2). In this final chapter, I discuss the SHINE framework in another way to summarise its key strategies (Fig. 8.1).

First, as described in Chapter 1, resilience and growth are different (see the central box of Fig. 8.1). Resilience involves a return to the pre-adversity level of functioning, while growth occurs beyond that level (Fig. 1.1, Chapter 1). The SHINE framework focuses primarily on resilience, although it acknowledges that constructive growth does occur after a traumatic encounter (i.e. PTG; see Chapter 7).

Chapter 3 shows that we need to understand and develop our virtues and strengths to call upon them for resilience. There are three major strengths that are universally applicable:

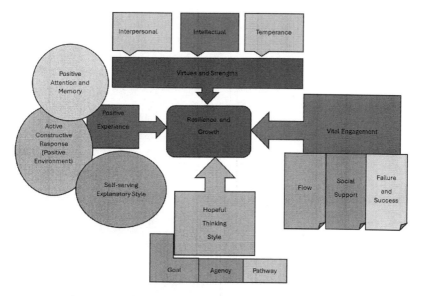

Fig. 8.1 The SHINE framework: A summary of key strategies

Temperance strength is perseverance in achieving goals and exercising self-control.
Interpersonal strength represents love, concern, and gratitude towards others.
Intellectual strength includes curiosity and zest for creativity.

The SHINE frameworks recommend developing habitual vital engagement activities that can bring you flow (i.e. intrinsically rewarding activities that are challenging but within your capabilities) and meaning in life. Long-term engagement in such activities brings you friendships and social support. More importantly, it can give you experiences of failure and teach you to be resilient after failures (see Chapter 3).

Chapter 4 argues that we can develop a future-oriented attitude that allows us to see beyond the current adverse situation. One way to do this is to set realistic goals, generate plausible pathways to achieve these goals and maintain agentic motivation in pursuing these goals. Goal, pathway, and agency thinking together constitute the hopeful thinking component of the SHINE framework. The framework also emphasises goal disengagement and reengagement, as well as regoaling and sub-goaling when external circumstances evolve.

In threatening situations, reinforcing our positive experiences can counteract the effects of negative experiences on us. When someone shares a positive experience with us, we respond by elaborating on the experience (e.g. asking for more details), validating their sharing, and showing that we understand their feelings. ACR, discussed in Chapter 5, describes the above communication style. ACR gives the person who responds the impression that the external environment is not entirely negative (real positive events have happened to the person sharing). It strengthens the sharer's memory of positive events to combat negative events.

Another way to enhance our positive experience is to pay attention to both negative and positive events (Chapter 6). The SHINE framework emphasises balanced attention to positive and negative events. It is important to practise paying more attention to positive stimuli because negative stimuli are abundant in adverse situations (and are therefore easier to notice). More importantly, positive attention and memory can counteract the harmful effects of negative experiences on us.

To take the above strategies one step further, we can develop a self-serving explanatory style, namely, attributing positive events to internal, global, and stable factors and negative events to external, specific, and unstable factors (see Chapter 7).

8.1.2 Building Your Own Psychological Gymnasium

You may go to the gym every day to train your body muscles. Similarly, you can create a psychological gym to train your "mental muscles" and practise regularly to make it a habit. For instance, you can use ACR to communicate with coworkers, friends, and family. You can set goals in different domains of your life, such as work and study, entertainment, and self-improvement, and actively design ways to achieve them. You can use positive self-talk to increase your willpower while pursuing your goals.

Just like exercising at the gym, *Consistency over Intensity* is the golden rule of the SHINE framework.

8.1.3 Future Development of the SHINE Framework

As crises and disasters have become the new normal in our lives, we need to equip the younger generation with the knowledge and skills needed for resilience. Integrating the SHINE framework into primary and secondary education curricula is highly feasible and would enable students to learn and practise SHINE skills from an early age and, more importantly, develop the habit of practising resilience skills.

We should continue to improve the SHINE framework by adding new strategies. Third-wave CBT approaches show promise, such as mindfulness (Kabat-Zinn, 2017) and acceptance–commitment therapy (Hayes et al., 2003). A recent meta-analysis reported a significant relationship between trait mindfulness and resilience (Zhang et al., 2023a, 2023b). It would therefore be useful to integrate these approaches into the SHINE framework.

REFERENCES

Hayes, S. C., Masuda, A., & De Mey, H. (2003). Acceptance and commitment therapy: Een derde-generatie gedragstherapie [Acceptance and Commitment Therapy and the third wave of behavior therapy] [Acceptance and Commitment Therapy and the third wave of behavior therapy]. *Gedragstherapie* (Dutch Journal of Behavior Therapy), *36*(2), 69–96.

Kabat-Zinn, J. (2017). Mindfulness-based interventions in context: Past, present, and future. Routledge/Taylor & Francis Group.

Zhang, J., Mao, Y., Wang, Y., & Zhang, Y. (2023a). The relationship between trait mindfulness and resilience: A meta-analysis. *Personality and Mental Health*, *17*(4), 313–327. https://doi.org/10.1002/pmh.1581

Zhang, L., Rakesh, D., Cropley, V., & Whittle, S. (2023b). Neurobiological correlates of resilience during childhood and adolescence – A systematic review. *Clinical Psychology Review*, *105*, 1–12. https://doi.org/10.1016/j.cpr.2023.102333

REFERENCES

Abdollahi, A., Alsaikhan, F., Nikolenko, D. A., Al-Gazally, M. E., Mahmudiono, T., Allen, K. A., & Abdullaev, B. (2022). Self-care behaviors mediates the relationship between resilience and quality of life in breast cancer patients. *BMC Psychiatry*, *22*(1), 825. https://doi.org/10.1186/s12888-022-04470-5

Abend, R., de Voogd, L., Salemink, E., Wiers, R. W., Pérez-Edgar, K., Fitzgerald, A., White, L. K., Salum, G. A., He, J., Silverman, W. K., Pettit, J. W., Pine, D. S., & Bar-Haim, Y. (2018). Association between attention bias to threat and anxiety symptoms in children and adolescents. *Depression and Anxiety*, *35*(3), 229–238. https://doi.org/10.1002/da.22706

Alex Linley, P., Maltby, J., Wood, A. M., Joseph, S., Harrington, S., Peterson, C., Park, N., & Seligman, M. E. P. (2007). Character strengths in the United Kingdom: The VIA inventory of strengths. *Personality and Individual Differences*, *43*(2), 341–351. https://doi.org/10.1016/j.paid.2006.12.004

Altinsoy, F., & Aypay, A. (2023). Does the type of exposure to traumatic events make a difference in posttraumatic growth? *Psychological Trauma: Theory, Research, Practice, and Policy*, *15*(1), 27–36. https://doi.org/10.1037/tra0001173

American Psychiatric Association. (2000). *Diagnostic and statistical manual of mental disorders (4th ed., text rev.) (DSM-IV-TR)*. Author.

American Psychiatric Association. (2022). *Diagnostic and statistical manual of mental disorders (5th ed., text rev.)*. American Psychiatric Association. https://doi.org/10.1176/appi.books.9780890425787

Aoun, E. G., Brent, D. A., Melhem, N. M., & Porta, G. (2021). Prospective evaluation of the DSM-5 persistent complex bereavement disorder criteria in

© The Author(s), under exclusive license to Springer Nature Switzerland AG 2025
S. M. Y. Ho, *The SHINE Framework*,
https://doi.org/10.1007/978-3-031-89106-9

144 REFERENCES

adults: dimensional and diagnostic approaches. *Psychological Medicine*, *51*(5), 825–834. https://doi.org/10.1017/S0033291719003829

Ayash, S., Lingner, T., Ramisch, A., Ryu, S., Kalisch, R., Schmitt, U., & Müller, M. B. (2023). Fear circuit–based neurobehavioral signatures mirror resilience to chronic social stress in mouse. In *PNAS Proceedings of the National Academy of Sciences of the United States of America* (Vol. 120, No. 17, pp. 1–7). https://doi.org/10.1073/pnas.2205576120

Babyak, M. A., Snyder, C. R., & Yoshinobu, L. (1993). Psychometric properties of the hope scale: A confirmatory factor analysis. *Journal of Research in Personality*, *27*, 154–169. https://doi.org/10.1006/jrpe.1993.1011

Bagby, R. M., & Parker, J. D. (2001). Relation of rumination and distraction with neuroticism and extraversion in a sample of patients with major depression. *Cognitive Therapy and Research*, *25*(1), 91–102. https://doi.org/10.1023/A:1026430900363

Baker, J. M., Kelly, C., Calhoun, L. G., Cann, A., & Tedeschi, R. G. (2008). An examination of posttraumatic growth and posttraumatic depreciation: Two exploratory studies. *Journal of Loss and Trauma*, *13*(5), 450–465. https://doi.org/10.1080/15325020802171367

Banford Witting, A., Tambling, R., & Hobfoll, S. E. (2023). Resource loss, gain, and traumatic stress in couples during COVID-19. *Psychological Trauma: Theory, Research, Practice, and Policy*, *15*(3), 502–510. https://doi.org/10.1037/tra0001276

Bar-Haim, Y., Lamy, D., Pergamin, L., Bakermans-Kranenburg, M. J., & van Ijzendoorn, M. H. (2007). Threat-related attentional bias in anxious and nonanxious individuals: A meta-analytic study. *Psychological Bulletin*, *133*(1), 1–24. https://doi.org/10.1037/0033-2909.133.1.1

Barlow, D. H., Durand, M. V., & Hofmann, S. G. (2023). *Psychopathology: An integrative approach to mental disorders* (9th ed.). Cengage.

Barnhill, J. W., & Zimmerman, M. (2023a). Adjustment Disorders. In *MSD Manual. Professional Version*. Merck & Co., Inc. https://www.msdmanuals.com/professional/psychiatric-disorders/anxiety-and-stressor-related-disorders/adjustmentdisorders#:~:text=Symptoms%20and%20Signs%20of%20Adjustment,%2C%20anxiety%2C%20and%20conduct%20disturbance

Barnhill, J. W. & Zimmerman, M. (2023b). Overview of trauma-and stressor-related disorders. In *MSD Manual. Professional Version*. Merck & Co., Inc. https://www.msdmanuals.com/professional/psychiatric-disorders/anxiety-and-stressor-relateddisorders/overview-of-trauma-and-stressor-related-disorders

Barnhill, J. W. & Zimmerman, M. (2023c). Posttraumatic disorder (PTSD). In *MSD Manual. Professional Version*. Merck & Co., Inc. https://www.msdmanuals.com/professional/psychiatric-disorders/anxiety-and-stressor-related-disorders/posttraumatic-stressdisorder-ptsd?query=ptsd#top

REFERENCES **145**

Barnum, D. D., Snyder, C. R., Rapoff, M. A., Mani, M. M., & Thompson, R. (1998). Hope and social support in psychological adjustment of children who have survived burn injuries and their matched controls. *Children's Health Care, 27*, 15–30. https://doi.org/10.1207/s15326888chc2701_2

Bartone, P. T., McDonald, K., Hansma, B. J., Stermac-Stein, J., Escobar, E. M. R., Stein, S. J., & Ryznar, R. (2023). Development and validation of an improved hardiness measure: The hardiness resilience gauge. *European Journal of Psychological Assessment, 39*(3), 222–239. https://doi.org/10.1027/1015-5759/a000709

Beard, C. (2021, June). 6 Tips for Increasing Social Support. *Psychology Today.* https://www.psychologytoday.com/us/blog/lab-real-world/202106/6-tips-increasing-social-support

Beck, A. T., & Haigh, E. A. P. (2014). Advances in cognitive theory and therapy: The generic cognitive model. *Annual Review of Clinical Psychology, 10*, 1–24. https://doi.org/10.1146/annurev-clinpsy-032813-153734

Beck, A. T., Rush, A. J., Shaw, B. F., & Emery, G. (1979). *Cognitive therapy of depression.* Guildford Press.

Beck, A. T., Weissman, A., Lester, D., & Trexler, L. (1974). The measurement of pessimism: The hopelessness scale. *Journal of Consulting and Clinical Psychology, 42*(6), 861–865. https://doi.org/10.1037/h0037562

Bell, T. R., Langhinrichsen-Rohling, J., & Selwyn, C. N. (2020). Conservation of resources and suicide proneness after oilrig disaster. *Death Studies, 44*(1), 48–57. https://doi.org/10.1080/07481187.2018.1521885

Benight, C. C., Swift, E., Sanger, J., Smith, A., & Zeppelin, D. (1999). Coping self-efficacy as a mediator of distress following a natural disaster. *Journal of Applied Social Psychology, 29*(12), 2443–2464. https://doi.org/10.1111/j.1559-1816.1999.tb00120.x

Bennett, M. P., Knight, R., Patel, S., So, T., Dunning, D., Barnhofer, T., Smith, P., Kuyken, W., Ford, T., & Dalgleish, T. (2021). Decentering as a core component in the psychological treatment and prevention of youth anxiety and depression: A narrative review and insight report. *Translational Psychiatry, 11*(1), 288. https://doi.org/10.1038/s41398-021-01397-5

Berg, C. J., Rapoff, M. A., Snyder, C. R., & Balmont, J. M. (2007). The relationship of children's hope to pediatric asthma treatment adherence. *Journal of Positive Psychology, 2*, 176–184. https://doi.org/10.1080/174397607014 09629

Bonanno, G. A. (2004a). Loss, trauma, and human resilience. Have we underestimated the human capacity to thrive after extremely aversive events? *American Psychologist, 59*(1), 20–28. https://doi.org/10.1037/0003-066X.59.1.20

Bonanno, G. A. (2004b). Loss, trauma, and human resilience: Have we underestimated the human capacity to thrive after extremely aversive events? *The*

146 REFERENCES

American Psychologist, *59*, 20–28. https://doi.org/10.1037/0003-066X.59.1.20

Bonanno, G. A., Galea, S., Bucciarelli, A., & Vlahov, D. (2006). Psychological resilience after disaster: New York City in the aftermath of the September 11th terrorist attack. *Psychological Science*, *17*, 181–186. https://doi.org/10.1111/j.1467-9280.2006.0168

Bonanno, G. A., Galea, S., Bucciarelli, A., & Vlahov, D. (2007). What predicts psychological resilience after disaster? The role of demographics, resources, and life stress. *Journal of Consulting and Clinical Psychology*, *75*(5), 671–682. https://doi.org/10.1037/0022-006X.75.5.671

Bonanno, G. A., Ho, S. M. Y., Chan, J., Kwong, R. S. Y., Cheung, C. K. Y., Wong, C. P. Y., & Wong, V. C. W. (2008). Psychological resilience and dysfunction among hospitalized survivors of the SARS epidemic in Hong Kong: A latent class approach. *Health Psychology*, *27*(5), 659–667. https://doi.org/10.1037/0278-6133.27.5.659

Bonanno, G. A., & Mancini, A. D. (2012). Beyond resilience and PTSD: Mapping the heterogeneity of responses to potential trauma. *Psychological Trauma: Theory, Research, Practice, and Policy*, *4*(1), 74–83. https://doi.org/10.1037/a0017829

Bonanno, G. A., Rennicke, C., & Dekel, S. (2005). Self-enhancement among high-exposive survivors of the September 11th terrorist attack: Resilience or social maladjustment? *Journal of Personality and Social Psychology*, *88*(6), 984–998. https://doi.org/10.1037/0022-3514.88.6.984

Bormans, L. (2016). *The world book of hope: The source of success, strength and happiness*. Lannoo Publishers/Racine. https://books.google.com.hk/books?id=Al-wjwEACAAJ

Brdar, I., & Kashdan, T. B. (2010). Character strengths and well-being in Croatia: An empirical investigation of structure and correlates. *Journal of Research in Personality*, *44*(1), 151–154.https://doi.org/10.1016/j.jrp.2009.12.001

Bucknell, K. J., Kangas, M., Karin, E., & Crane, M. F. (2024). A random- ized controlled trial comparing the effects of self-reflective writing focused on successful and unsuccessful coping experiences on resilience. *Stress and Health: Journal of the International Society for the Investigation of Stress*, *40*(2). https://doi.org/10.1002/smi.3311

Carver, C. S. (1998). Resilence and thriving: Issues, models, and linkages. *Journal of Social Issues*, *54*(2), 245–266. https://doi.org/10.1111/0022-4537.641998064

Carver, C. S., & Connor-Smith, J. (2010). Personality and coping. *Annual Review of Psychology*, *61*, 679–704. https://doi.org/10.1146/annurev.psych.093008.100352

REFERENCES 147

Cawley, M. J., Martin, J. E., & Johnson, J. A. (2000). A virtues approach to personality. *Personality and Individual Differences*, *28*(5), 997–1013. https://doi.org/10.1016/S0191-8869(99)00207-X

Centre for Research on the Epidemiology of Disasters. (2023). *2022 Disasters in numbers: Climate in action*. C. f. R. o. t. E. o. Disasters. https://www.emdat.be/publications/

Chan, M. W. C., Ho, S. M. Y., Law, L. S. C., & Pau, B. K. Y. (2013). A visual dot-probe task as a measurement of attentional bias and its relationship with the symptoms of posttraumatic stress disorder among women with breast cancer. *Advances in Cancer: Research and Treatment*, *2013 (2013)*(Article ID 813339). https://doi.org/10.5171/2013.813339

Chan, M. W. C., Ho, S. M. Y., Tedeschi, R. G., & Leung, C. W. L. (2011). The valence of attentional bias and cancer-related rumination in posttraumatic stress and posttraumatic growth among women with breast cancer. *Psycho-Oncology*, *20*, 544–552. https://doi.org/10.1002/pon.1761

Chang, E. C. (1998). Hope, problem-solving ability, and coping in a college student population: Some implications for theory and practice. *Journal of Clinical Psychology*, *54*, 953–962. https://doi.org/10.1002/(SICI)1097-4679(199811)54:73.0.CO;2-F

Chang, E. C., & DeSimone, S. L. (2001). The influence of hope on appraisals, coping, and dysphoria: A test of hope theory. *Journal of Social and Clinical Psychology*, *20*, 117–129. https://doi.org/10.1521/jscp.20.2.117.22262

Cheavens, J. S., Feldman, D. B., Woodward, J. T., & Snyder, C. R. (2006). Hope in cognitive psychotherapies: On working with client strengths. *Journal of Cognitive Psychotherapy: An International Quarterly*, *20*, 135–145. https://doi.org/10.1891/jcop.20.2.135

Chen, N. T., Clarke, P. J., Watson, T. L., Macleod, C., & Guastella, A. J. (2014). Biased saccadic responses to emotional stimuli in anxiety: An anti-saccade study. *PLoS One*, *9*(2), e86474. https://doi.org/10.1371/journal.pone.0086474

Chen, N. T. M., Clarke, P. J. F., MacLeod, C., & Guastella, A. J. (2012). Biased attentional processing of positive stimuli in social anxiety disorder: An eye movement study. *Cognitive Behaviour Therapy*, *41*(2), 96–107. https://doi.org/10.1080/16506073.2012.666562

Chen, N. T. M., Clarke, P. J. F., MacLeod, C., Hickie, I. B., & Guastella, A. J. (2016). Aberrant gaze patterns in social anxiety disorder: An eye movement assessment during public speaking. *Journal of Experimental Psychopathology*, *7*(1), 1–17. https://doi.org/10.5127/jep.040313

Cheng, C.-T., Ho, S. M. Y., Lai, Y., Zhang, Q., & Wang, G.-L. (2021). Coping profiles predict long-term anxiety trajectory in breast cancer survivors. *Supportive Care in Cancer*. https://doi.org/10.1007/s00520-020-05936-6

148 REFERENCES

Cheng, C.-T., Wang, G. L., & Ho, S. M. Y. (2020). The relationship between types of posttraumatic growth and prospective psychological adjustment in women with breast cancer: A follow-up study. *Psychooncology, 29*, 586–588. https://doi.org/10.1002/pon.5312

Cheng, C. T., Ho, S. M. Y., Hou, Y. C., Lai, Y., & Wang, G. L. (2018). Constructive, illusory, and distressed posttraumatic growth among survivors of breast cancer: A 7-year growth trajectory study. *Journal of Health Psychology.* https://doi.org/10.1177/1359105318793199

Chesney, M. A., Chambers, D. B., Taylor, J. M., Johnson, L. M., & Folkman, S. (2003). Coping effectiveness training for men living with HIV: Results from a randomized clinical trial testing a group-based intervention. *Psychosomatic Medicine, 65*(6), 1038–1046. https://doi.org/10.1097/01.PSY.000 0097344.78697.ED

Chettiar, S., & Terte, I. d. (2022). *The psychological resilience treatment manual: An evidence-based intervention approach.* Taylor & Francis Group. http://ebo okcentral.proquest.com/lib/cityuhk/detail.action?docID=6939704

Cheung, L. K., Loh, J. S. P., & Ho, S. M. Y. (2006). The early psychological adjustment of cleft patients after maxillary distraction osteogenesis and conventional orthognathic surgery: A preliminary study. *Journal of Oral and Maxillofacial Surgery, 64*, 1743–1750. https://doi.org/10.1016/j.joms. 2005.12.060

Cheung, L. K., Loh, J. S. P., & Ho, S. M. Y. (2007). Psychological profile of Chinese with cleft lip and palate deformities. *Cleft Palate-Craniofacial Journal, 44*(1), 79–86. https://doi.org/10.1597/05-053

Cheung, W.-S., & Ho, S. M. Y. (2004). The use of death metaphors to understand personal meaning of death among Hong Kong Chinese undergraduates. *Death Studies, 28*, 47–62. https://doi.org/10.1080/07481180490249265

Cheung, W. S., & Ho, S. M. Y. (2006). Death metaphors in Chinese. In C. L. W. Chan & A. Y. M. Chow (Eds.), *Death, dying and bereavement. A Hong Kong Chinese experience* (pp. 117–126). Hong Kong University Press.

Chin, C. H., Tseng, L. M., Chao, T. C., Wang, T. J., Wu, S. F., & Liang, S. Y. (2021). Self-care as a mediator between symptom-management self-efficacy and quality of life in women with breast cancer. *PLoS ONE, 16*(2), e0246430. https://doi.org/10.1371/journal.pone.0246430

Chua, H. D. P., Ho, S. M. Y., & Cheung, L. K. (2012). The comparison of psychological adjustment of patients with cleft lip and palate after maxillary distraction osteogenesis and conventional orthognathic surgery. *Oral Surgery, Oral Medicine, Oral Pathology and Oral Radiology, 114*(5), S5–S10. https://doi.org/10.1016/j.tripleo.2011.07.047

Collette, A., & Ungar, M. (2020). Resilience of individuals, families, communities, and environments: Mutually dependent protective processes and complex systems. In M. Ochs, M. Borcsa, & J. Schweitzer (Eds.), *Systemic research in*

REFERENCES 149

individual, couple, and family therapy and counseling (pp. 97–111). Springer International Publishing. https://doi.org/10.1007/978-3-030-36560-8_6

Collins, R. L., Taylor, S. E., & Skokan, L. A. (1990). A better world or a shattered vision? Changes in life perspectives following victimization. *Social Cognition, 8,* 263–285. https://doi.org/10.1521/soco.1990.8.3.263

Cordova, M. J., Riba, M. B., & Spiegel, D. (2017). Post-traumatic stress disorder and cancer. *Lancet Psychiatry, 4*(4), 330–338. https://doi.org/10.1016/s2215-0366(17)30014-7

Cornwell, H., Toschi, N., Hamilton-Giachritsis, C., Staginnus, M., Smaragdi, A., Gonzalez-Madruga, K., Mackes, N., Rogers, J., Martinelli, A., Kohls, G., Raschle, N. M., Konrad, K., Stadler, C., Freitag, C. M., De Brito, S. A., & Fairchild, G. (2024). Identifying cortical structure markers of resilience to adversity in young people using surface-based morphometry. *Social Cognitive and Affective Neuroscience, 19*(1). https://doi.org/10.1093/scan/nsae006

Crane, M. F., Searle, B. J., Kangas, M., & Nwiran, Y. (2019). How resilience is strengthened by exposure to stressors: the systematic self-reflection model of resilience strengthening. *Anxiety, Stress, & Coping, 32*(1), 1–17. https://doi.org/10.1080/10615806.2018.1506640

Csikszentmihalyi, M. (1975). Beyond Boredom and Anxiety: Experiencing Flow in Work and Play. Jossey-Bass Publishers.

Csikszentmihalyi, M. (1994). *Flow and the foundations of positive psychology. The collected works of mihaly csikszentmihalyi.* Springer. https://doi.org/10.1007/978-94-017-9088-8

Csikszentmihalyi, M., Abuhamdeh, S., & Nakamura, J. (2005). Flow. In A. J. Elliot & C. S. Dweck (Eds.), *Handbook of competence and motivation* (pp. 598–608, 704 Pages). Guilford Publications.

Csikszentmihalyi, M., & Asakawa, K. (2016). Universal and cultural dimensions of optimal experiences. *Japanese Psychological Research, 58*(1), 4–13. https://doi.org/10.1111/jpr.12104

Davidson, J. E., & Sternberg, R. J. (Eds.). (2003). The psychology of problem solving [doi:10.1017/CBO9780511615771]. Cambridge University Press. https://doi.org/10.1017/CBO9780511615771

de Terte, I., Becker, J., & Stephens, C. (2009). An integrated model for understanding and developing resilience in the face of adverse events. *Journal of Pacific Rim Psychology, 3*(1), 20–26. https://doi.org/10.1375/prp.3.1.20

de Terte, I., Stephens, C., & Huddleston, L. (2014). The development of a three part model of psychological resilience. *Stress and Health, 30*(5), 416–424. https://doi.org/10.1002/smi.2625

Deady, M., Collins, D. A. J., Johnston, D. A., Glozier, N., Calvo, R. A., Christensen, H., & Harvey, S. B. (2021). The impact of depression, anxiety and comorbidity on occupational outcomes. *Occupational Medicine, 72*(1), 17–24. https://doi.org/10.1093/occmed/kqab142

150 REFERENCES

Declercq, F., Vanheule, S., Markey, S., & Willemsen, J. (2007). Posttraumatic distress in security guards and the various effects of social support. *Journal of Clinical Psychology*, *63*(12), 1239–1246. https://doi.org/10.1002/jclp. 20426

Dobson, K. S. (2012). Theory. In *Cognitive therapy* (pp. 11–27, 154 Pages). American Psychological Association. https://doi.org/10.1037/17334-003

Dobson, K. S. (2024). Behavioral activation: Addressing risk factors for depression. In *Clinical depression: An individualized, biopsychosocial approach to assessment and treatment* (pp. 121–148, 291 Pages). American Psychological Association. https://doi.org/10.1037/0000398-008

Dobson, K. S., & Kazantzis, N. (2024). Cognitive theory in psychotherapy. In F. T. L. Leong, J. L. Callahan, J. Zimmerman, M. J. Constantino, & C. F. Eubanks (Eds.), *APA handbook of psychotherapy: Theory-driven practice and disorder-driven practice* (Vol. 1, pp. 175–190, 553 Pages). American Psychological Association. https://doi.org/10.1037/0000353-011

Dohrenwend, B. P., Neria, Y., Turner, J. B., Turse, N., Marshall, R., Lewis-Fernandez, R., & Koenen, K. C. (2004). Positive tertiary appraisals and posttraumatic stress disorder in U.S. male veterans of the war in Vietnam: The roles of positive affirmation, positive reformulation, and defensive denial. *Journal of Consulting and Clinical Psychology*, *72*(3), 417–433. https://doi. org/10.1037/0022-006x.72.3.417

Dong, Y., De Beuckelaer, A., Yu, L., & Zhou, R. (2017). Eye-movement evidence of the time-course of attentional bias for threatening pictures in test-anxious students. *Cognition and Emotion*, *31*(4), 781–790. https://doi. org/10.1080/02699931.2016.1152953

Dorfman, A., Moscovitch, D. A., Chopik, W. J., & Grossmann, I. (2022). None the wiser: Year-long longitudinal study on effects of adversity on wisdom. *European Journal of Personality*, *36*(4), 559–575. https://doi.org/10.1177/ 08902070211014057

Duan, W., & Ho, S. M. Y. (2017). Three-dimensional model of strengths: examination of invariance across gender, age, education levels, and marriage status. *Community Mental Health Journal*, *53*(1), 233–240. https://doi.org/10. 1007/s10597-016-0038-y

Duan, W., & Ho, S. M. Y. (2018). Does being mindful of your character strengths enhance psychological wellbeing? A longitudinal mediation analysis. *Journal of Happiness Studies*, *19*(4), 1045–1066. https://doi.org/10.1007/ s10902-017-9864-z

Duan, W., Ho, S. M. Y., Bai, Y., & Tang, X. (2013). Psychometric evaluation of the Chinese Virtues Questionnaire. *Research on Social Work Practice*, *23*(3), 336–345. https://doi.org/10.1177/1049731513477214

Duan, W., Ho, S. M. Y., Siu, B. P. Y., Li, T., & Zhang, Y. (2015). Role of virtues and perceived life stress in affecting psychological symptoms among Chinese college students. *Journal of American College Health*, *63*(1), 32–39. https://doi.org/10.1080/07448481.2014.963109

Duan, W., Ho, S. M. Y., Tang, X., Li, T., & Zhang, Y. (2014). Character strength-based intervention to promote satisfaction with life in the Chinese university context. *Journal of Happiness Studies*, *15*(6), 1347–1361. https://doi.org/10.1007/s10902-013-9479-y

Duan, W., Ho, S. M. Y., Yu, B., Tang, X., Zhang, Y., Li, T., & Yuen, T. (2012). Factor structure of the Chinese virtues questionnaire. *Research on Social Work Practice*, *22*(6), 680–688. https://doi.org/10.1177/1049731512450074

Dudeney, J., Sharpe, L., & Hunt, C. (2015). Attentional bias towards threatening stimuli in children with anxiety: A meta-analysis. *Clinical Psychology Review*, *40*, 66–75. https://doi.org/10.1016/j.cpr.2015.05.007

Eche, I. J., Eche, I. M., Pires, C., Isibor, C., Achibiri, A., & Aronowitz, T. (2022). A systematic mixed-studies review of hope experiences in parents of children with cancer. *Cancer Nursing*, *45*(1), E43–E58. https://doi.org/10.1097/NCC.0000000000000841

Elliott, T. R., Witty, T. E., Herrick, S., & Hoffman, J. T. (1991). Negotiating reality after physical loss: Hope, depression, and disability. *Journal of Personality and Social Psychology*, *61*(4), 608–613. https://doi.org/10.1037/0022-3514.61.4.608

Epel, E. S., McEwen, B. S., & Ickovics, J. R. (1998). Embodying psychological thriving: Physical thriving in response to stress. *Journal of Social Issues*, *54*(2), 301–322. https://doi.org/10.1111/j.1540-4560.1998.tb01220.x

Eysenck, M. W. (1994). *Individual differences: Normal and abnormal*. Lawrence Erlbaum Associates.

Famodile, E., Stovin, H., & Sumilo, D. (2023). *Impact of COVID-19 (2023)* https://www.nottinghaminsight.org.uk/themes/health-and-wellbeing/joint-strategic-needs-assessment/adults/impact-of-covid-19-2023/

Fearnow-Kenney, M., & Kliewer, W. (2000). Threat appraisal and adjustment among children with cancer. *Journal of Psychosocial Oncology*, *18*, 1–17. https://doi.org/10.1300/J077v18n03_01

Feeny, N. C., Rytwinski, N. K., & Zoellner, L. A. (2014). The crucial role of social support. In *Facilitating resilience and recovery following trauma* (pp. 291–321). The Guilford Press.

Field, N. P., & Filanosky, C. (2010). Continuing bonds, risk factors for complicated grief, and adjustment to bereavement. *Death Studies*, *34*(1), 1–29. https://doi.org/10.1080/07481180903372269

Field, N. P., Gal-Oz, E., & Bonanno, G. A. (2003). Continuing bonds and adjustment at 5 years after the death of a spouse. *Journal of Consulting & Clinical Psychology*, *71*(1), 110–117. https://doi.org/10.1037/0022-006X.71.1.110

152 REFERENCES

Fletcher, D., & Sarkar, M. (2013). Psychological resilience: A review and critique of definitions, concepts, and theory. *European Psychologist*, *18*(1), 12–23. https://doi.org/10.1027/1016-9040/a000124

Folkman, S. (1984). Personal control and stress and coping processes: A theoretical analysis. *Journal of Personality and Social Psychology*, *4*, 839–852. https://doi.org/10.1037/0022-3514.46.4.839

Folkman, S., Lazarus, R. S., Cruen, R. J., & DeLongis, A. (1986). Appraisal, coping, health status, and psychological symptoms. *Journal of Personality and Social Psychology*, *50*, 571–579. https://doi.org/10.1037/0022-3514.50.3.571

Folkman, S., Lazarus, R. S., Dunkel-Schetter, C., DeLongis, A., & Gruen, R. (1986). The dynamics of a stressful encounter: Cognitive appraisal, coping, and encounter outcomes. *Journal of Personality and Social Psychology*, *50*, 992–1003. https://doi.org/10.1037/0022-3514.50.5.992

Forsythe, C. J., & Compas, B. E. (1987). Interaction of cognitive appraisals of stressful events and coping: Testing the goodness of fit hypothesis. *Cognitive Therapy and Research*, *11*(4), 473–485. https://doi.org/10.1007/BF0117 5357

Fredrickson, B. L. (1998). What good are positive emotions? *Review of General Psychology*, *2*, 300–319. https://doi.org/10.1037/1089-2680.2.3.300

Gable, S. L., Gonzaga, G. C., & Strachman, A. (2006). Will you be there for me when things go right? Supportive responses to positive event disclosures. *Journal of Personality and Social Psychology*, *91*(5), 904–917. https://doi.org/10.1037/0022-3514.91.5.904

Gable, S. L., & Haidt, J. (2005). What (and why) is positive psychology? *Review of General Psychology*, *9*(2), 103–110. https://doi.org/10.1037/1089-2680.9.2.10

Gable, S. L., Reis, H. T., & Downey, G. (2003). HE SAID, SHE SAID: A quasi-signal detection analysis of daily interactions between close relationship partners. *Psychological Science*, *14*(2), 100–105. https://doi.org/10.1111/1467-9280.t01-1-01426

Gable, S. L., Reis, H. T., Impett, E. A., & Asher, E. R. (2004). What do you do when things go right? The intrapersonal and interpersonal benefits of sharing positive events. *Journal of Personality and Social Psychology*, *87*(2), 228–245. https://doi.org/10.1037/0022-3514.87.2.228

Gable, S. L., Reis, H. T., Impett, E. A., & Asher, E. R. (2018). What do you do when things go right? The intrapersonal and interpersonal benefits of sharing positive events. In H. Reis (Ed.), *Relationships, well-being and behaviour: Selected works of Harry Reis* (1st ed., pp. 39). Routledge. https://doi.org/10.4324/9780203732496

REFERENCES   153

Gamble, A. L., & Rapee, R. M. (2009). The time-course of attentional bias in anxious children and adolescents. *Journal of Anxiety Disorders, 23*(7), 841–847. https://doi.org/10.1016/j.janxdis.2009.04.001

Gardner, B., Lally, P., & Wardle, J. (2012). Making health habitual: the psychology of 'habit-formation' and general practice. *British Journal of General Practice, 62*(605), 664–666. https://doi.org/10.3399/bjgp12X659466

Gash, H. (2016). Zen and constructivist thinking. In G. E. Lasker & K. Hiwaki (Eds.), *Personal and Spiritual Development in the World of Cultural Diversity*. Vol XIII. (pp. 23–27). International Institute for Advanced Studies.

Gidron, Y. (2013). Trait anxiety. In M. D. Gellman & J. R. Turner (Eds.), *Encyclopedia of Behavioral Medicine* (pp. 1989–1989). Springer New York. https://doi.org/10.1007/978-1-4419-1005-9_1539

Gilman, R., Dooley, J., & Florell, D. (2006). Relative levels of hope and their relationship with academic and psychological indicators among adolescents. *Journal of Social and Clinical Psychology, 25*, 166–178. https://doi.org/10.1521/jscp.2006.25.2.166

Glaesmer, H., Romppel, M., Brähler, E., Hinz, A., & Maercker, A. (2015). Adjustment disorder as proposed for ICD-11: Dimensionality and symptom differentiation. *Psychiatry Research, 229*(3), 940–948. https://doi.org/10.1016/j.psychres.2015.07.010

Grafton, B., & MacLeod, C. (2024). Regulation of anxious emotion through the modification of attentional bias. In J. J. Gross & B. Q. Ford (Eds.), *Handbook of emotion regulation* (3rd ed., pp. 417). The Guilford Press.

Grapin, S. L., Sulkowski, M. L., & Lazarus, P. J. (2016). A multilevel framework for increasing social support in schools. *Contemporary School Psychology, 20*(2), 93–106. https://doi.org/10.1007/s40688-015-0051-0

Grauf-Grounds, C. (2007). Increasing social support to manage chronic illness. In D. Linville & K. M. Hertlein (Eds.), *The therapist's notebook for family health care: Homework, handouts, and activities for individuals, couples, and families coping with illness, loss, and disability* (pp. 19–23, 245 Pages). Haworth Press.

Grewal, P. K., & Porter, J. E. (2007). Hope theory: A framework for understanding suicidal action. *Death Studies, 31*(2), 131–154. https://doi.org/10.1080/07481180601100491

Hall, M. F., & Horvath, S. F. (2015). Micro-skills: Daily practice for mental health providers. In R. H. Witte & G. S. Mosley-Howard (Eds.), *Mental health practice in today's schools: Issues and interventions* (pp. 125–143, 450 Pages). Springer Publishing Company.

Hayes, S. C., Masuda, A., & De Mey, H. (2003). Acceptance and commitment therapy: Een derde-generatie gedragstherapie [Acceptance and Commitment

154 REFERENCES

Therapy and the third wave of behavior therapy] [Acceptance and Commitment Therapy and the third wave of behavior therapy]. *Gedragstherapie* (Dutch Journal of Behavior Therapy), *36*(2), 69–96.

Herrman, H. M. D., Stewart, D. E. M. D., Diaz-Granados, N. M., Berger, E. L. D., Jackson, B. P., & Yuen, T. B. (2011). What is resilience? *Canadian Journal of Psychiatry*, *56*(5), 258–265.

Herth, K. (1989). The relationship between level of hope and level of coping response and other variables in patients with cancer. *Oncology Nursing Forum*, *16*(1), 67–72.

Hewson, H., Galbraith, N., Jones, C., & Heath, G. (2023). The impact of continuing bonds following bereavement: A systematic review. *Death Studies*. https://doi.org/10.1080/07481187.2023.2223593

Ho, S. M. Y. (2011). Resilience, growth, and distress after a traumatic experience. In K. K. Y. Wu, C. S. K. Tang, & E. Y. S. Leung (Eds.), *Healing trauma: A professionals' guide in Hong Kong* (pp. 89–104). HKU Press.

Ho, S. M. Y. (2016a). Adapting goals. In L. Bormans (Ed.), *The world book of hope: The source of success, strength and happiness* (pp. 355–358). Lannoo.

Ho, S. M. Y. (2016b). Posttraumatic growth: Focus on concepts and cross-cultural measurement issues. In C. R. Martin, V. Preedy, & V. B. Patel (Eds.), *Comprehensive guide to post-traumatic stress disorder* (pp. 1831–1848). Springer. https://doi.org/10.1007/978-3-319-08613-2_60-1

Ho, S. M. Y., Chan, I. S., Ma, E. P., & Field, N. P. (2013). Continuing bonds, attachment style, and adjustment in the conjugal bereavement among Hong Kong Chinese. *Death Studies*, *37*(3), 248–268. https://doi.org/10.1080/07481187.2011.634086

Ho, S. M. Y., & Chan, I. S. F. (2018). Externalized and internalized continuing bonds in understanding of grief. In K. Dennis & E. Steffen (Eds.), *Continuing bonds in bereavement. New directions for research and practice* (pp. 129–138). Routledge.

Ho, S. M. Y., Chan, M. W. Y., Yau, T. K., & Yeung, R. M. W. (2011). Relationships between explanatory style, posttraumatic growth and posttraumatic stress disorder symptoms among Chinese breast cancer patients. *Psychology & Health*, *26*(3), 269–285. https://doi.org/10.1080/08870440903287926

Ho, S. M. Y., & Cheng, C.-T. (2023). Illusory versus constructive posttraumatic growth in cancer. In R. Berger (Ed.), *The Routledge international handbook of posttraumatic growth* (pp. 21–28). Routledge. https://doi.org/10.4324/9781032208688-4

Ho, S. M. Y., Cheng, C.-T., Shih, S.-M., Taku, K., & Tedeschi, R. G. (2021). The Chinese version of Posttraumatic Growth and Depreciation Inventory—Expanded version (PTGDI-X) for cancer survivors. *Supportive Care in Cancer*, Advance online publication. https://doi.org/10.1007/s00520-021-06223-8

REFERENCES 155

Ho, S. M. Y., Cheng, J. C. K., Dai, D. W. T., Tam, T., & Hui, O. (2018). The effect of positive and negative memory biases on anxiety and depression symptoms among adolescents. *Journal of Clinical Psychology*, Advance online publication. https://doi.org/10.1002/jclp.22597

Ho, S. M. Y., Chow, A. Y. M., Chan, C. L.-W., & Tsui, Y. K. Y. (2002). The assessment of grief among Hong Kong Chinese: A preliminary report. *Death Studies*, 26, 91–98. https://doi.org/10.1080/074811802753455226

Ho, S. M. Y., Chu, K. W., & Yiu, J. (2008). The relationship between explanatory style and posttraumatic growth after bereavement in a non-clinical sample. *Death Studies*, 32(5), 461–478. https://doi.org/10.1080/074811 80801974760

Ho, S. M. Y., Dai, D. W. T., Mak, C., & Liu, K. W. K. (2018). Cognitive factors associated with depression and anxiety in adolescents: A two-year longitudinal study. *International Journal of Clinical and Health Psychology. Advanced online publication*. https://doi.org/10.1016/j.ijchp.2018.04.001

Ho, S. M. Y., Ho, J. W. C., Bonanno, G. A., Chu, A. T. W., & Chan, E. M. S. (2010). Hopefulness predicts resilience after hereditary colorectal cancer genetic testing: A prospective outcome trajectories study. *BMC Cancer*, 10, 279. https://doi.org/10.1186/1471-2407-10-279

Ho, S. M. Y., Ho, J. W. C., Chan, C. L. W., Kwan, K., & Tsui, Y. K. Y. (2003). Decisional consideration of hereditary colon cancer genetic test results among Hong Kong Chinese adults. *Cancer Epidemiology, Biomarkers & Prevention*, 12(5), 426–432. http://cebp.aacrjournals.org/

Ho, S. M. Y., Ho, J. W. C., Pau, B. K.-Y., Hui, B. P.-H., Wong, R. S.-M., & Chu, A. T.-W. (2012). Hope-based intervention for individuals susceptible to colorectal cancer: A pilot study. *Familial Cancer*, 11, 545–551. https://doi.org/10.1007/s10689-012-9545-3

Ho, S. M. Y., Law, L. S. C., Wang, G.-L., Shih, S.-M., Hsu, S.-H., & Hou, Y.-C. (2013). Psychometric analysis of the Chinese version of the posttraumatic growth inventory with cancer patients in Hong Kong and Taiwan. *Psycho-Oncology*, 22(3), 175–179. https://doi.org/10.1002/pon.3024

Ho, S. M. Y., Li, W. L., Duan, W., Siu, B. P. Y., Yau, S., Yeung, G., & Wong, K. (2016). A brief strengths scale for individuals with mental health issues. *Psychological Assessment*, 28(1), 147–157. https://doi.org/10.1037/pas0000164

Ho, S. M. Y., & Lo, R. S. Y. (2011). Dispositional hope as a protective factor among medical emergency professionals: A preliminary investigation. *Traumatology*, 17, 3–9. https://doi.org/10.1177/1534765611426786

Ho, S. M. Y., Mak, C. W. Y., Ching, R., & Lo, E. T. T. (2017). An approach to motivation and empowerment: The application of positive psychology. In I. H. Amzat & N. P. Valdez (Eds.), *Teacher empowerment towards professional*

156 REFERENCES

development and practices. Perspectives across borders (pp. 167–182). Springer. https://doi.org/10.1007/978-981-10-4151-8

Ho, S. M. Y., Rajandram, R. K., Chan, N., Samman, N., McGrath, C., & Zwahlen, R. A. (2011). The roles of hope and optimism on posttraumatic growth in oral cavity cancer patients. *Oral Oncology, 47,* 121–124. https://doi.org/10.1016/j.oraloncology.2010.11.015

Ho, S. M. Y., Wong, K. F., Chan, C. L.-w., Watson, M., & Tsui, Y. K. Y. (2003). Psychometric properties of the Chinese version of the Mini Mental Adjustment to Cancer (Mini-MAC) scale. *Psycho-Oncology, 12*(6), 547–556. https://doi.org/10.1002/pon.672

Ho, S. M. Y., & Yu, B. (2010). Posttraumatic growth in Chinese culture. In T. Weiss & R. Berger (Eds.), *Posttraumatic growth: A cross-cultural perspective* (pp. 147–156). Wiley.

Ho, S. M. Y., Yuen, A. N. Y., & Siu, B. P. Y. (2013). Hope as a positive cognition against adversity and beyond. In G. M. Katsaros (Ed.), *The psychology of hope* (pp. 91–115). Nova Science Publisher.

Hobfoll, S. E. (1989). Conservation of resources: A new attempt at conceptualizing stress. *American Psychologist, 44*(3), 513–524. https://doi.org/10.1037/0003-066X.44.3.513

Hobfoll, S. E., Freedy, J., Lane, C., & Geller, P. (1990). Conservation of social resources: Social support resource theory. *Journal of Social and Personal Relationships, 7*(4), 465–478.https://doi.org/10.1177/026540759 0074004

Hobfoll, S. E., Halbesleben, J., Neveu, J.-P., & Westman, M. (2018). Conservation of resources in the organizational context: The reality of resources and their consequences. *Annual Review of Organizational Psychology and Organizational Behavior, 5*(1), 103–128. https://doi.org/10.1146/annurev-org psych-032117-104640

Hobfoll, S. E., Palmieri, P. A., Johnson, R. J., Canetti-Nisim, D., Hall, B. J., & Galea, S. (2009). Trajectories of resilience, resistance, and distress during ongoing terrorism: The case of Jews and Arabs in Israel. *Journal of Consulting and Clinical Psychology, 77*(1), 138–148.https://doi.org/10.1037/a0014360

Hobfoll, S. E., Stevens, N. R., & Zalta, A. K. (2015). Expanding the science of resilience: Conserving resources in the aid of adaptation. *Psychological Inquiry, 26*(2), 174–180. https://doi.org/10.1080/1047840x.2015.1002377

Hobfoll, S. E., & Stokes, J. P. (1988). The process and mechanics of social support. In *Handbook of personal relationships: Theory, research and interventions* (pp. 497–517). Wiley.

Hoevenaars, J., & van Son, M. J. M. (1990). New chances for Lewinsohn's social reinforcement theory of depression. In H.-G. Zapotoczky & T. Wenzel (Eds.),

REFERENCES   157

The scientific dialogue: From basic research to clinical intervention (pp. 65–70, 313 Pages). Swets & Zeitlinger Publishers.

Hopwood, M. (2023). Anxiety symptoms in patients with major depressive disorder: Commentary on prevalence and clinical implications. *Neurology and Therapy*, *12*(Suppl 1), 5–12.https://doi.org/10.1007/s40120-023-00469-6

Huen, J. M. Y., Ip, B. Y. T., Ho, S. M. Y., & Yip, P. S. F. (2015). Hope and hopelessness: The role of hope in buffering the impact of hopelessness on suicidal ideation. *PLoS ONE*, *10*(6), e0130073. https://doi.org/10.1371/journal.pone.0130073

Hutchinson, A.-M. K., Stuart, A. D., & Pretorius, H. G. (2011). The relationships between temperament, character strengths, and resilience. In I. Brdar (Ed.), *The human pursuit of well-being: A cultural approach* (pp. 133–144). Springer Netherlands. https://doi.org/10.1007/978-94-007-1375-8_12

Irving, L. M., Snyder, C. K., & Crowson, J. J., Jr. (1998). Hope and coping with cancer by college women. *Journal of Personality*, *66*(2), 195–214. https://doi.org/10.1111/1467-6494.00009

Irving, L. M., Snyder, C. R., Gravel, L., Hanke, J., Hillberg, P., & Nelson, N. (1997). *Hope and the effectiveness of a pre-therapy orientation group for community mental health center client.* Western Psychological Association Convention.

Jackson, D., Firtko, A., & Edenborough, M. (2007). Personal resilience as a strategy for surviving and thriving in the face of workplace adversity: a literature review. *Journal of Advanced Nursing*, *60*(1), 1–9. https://doi.org/10.1111/j.1365-2648.2007.04412.x

Jolley, S., Garety, P., Bebbington, P., Dunn, G., Freeman, D., Kuipers, E., Fowler, D., & Hemsley, D. (2006). Attributional style in psychosis - The role of affect and belief type. *Behaviour Research and Therapy*, *44*, 1597–1607. https://doi.org/10.1016/j.brat.2005.12.002

Jordan, A. H., & Litz, B. T. (2014). Prolonged grief disorder: Diagnostic, assessment, and treatment considerations. *Professional Psychology: Research and Practice*, *45*(3), 180–187. https://doi.org/10.1037/a0036836

Joseph, S., Yule, W., & Williams, R. (1993). Post-traumatic stress: Attributional aspects. *Journal of Traumatic Stress*, *6*(4), 501–513. https://doi.org/10.1002/jts.2490060407

Joyce-Beaulieu, D., & Zaboski, B. A. (2021). Counseling preparation. In D. Joyce-Beaulieu & B. A. Zaboski (Eds.), *Applied cognitive behavioral therapy in schools* (pp. 47–63, 211 Pages). Oxford University Press. https://doi.org/10.1093/med-psych/9780197581384.003.0003

Kabat-Zinn, J. (2017). Mindfulness-based interventions in context: Past, present, and future. Routledge/Taylor & Francis Group.

Kang, H., Na, P. J., Fischer, I. C., Tsai, J., Tedeschi, R. G., & Pietrzak, R. H. (2023). Pandemic-related posttraumatic psychological growth in U.S. military veterans: A 3-year, nationally representative, longitudinal study. *Psychiatry Research, 326*, 1–9. https://doi.org/10.1016/j.psychres.2023.115370

Kashdan, T. B., Pelham, W. E., Lang, A. R., Hoza, B., Jacob, R. G., J.R., J., Blumenthal, J. D., & Gnagy, E. M. (2002). Hope and optimism as human strengths in parents of children with externalizing disorders: Stress in the eye of the beholder. *Journal of Social & Clinical Psychology, 21*, 441–468. https://doi.org/10.1521/jscp.21.4.441.22597

Kelada, L., Schiff, M., Gilbar, O., Pat-Horenczyk, R., & Benbenishty, R. (2023). University students' psychological distress during the COVID-19 pandemic: A structural equation model of the role of resource loss and gain. *Journal of Community Psychology, 51*(7), 3012–3028. https://doi.org/10.1002/jcop.23076

Kelly, L. C., Maratos, F. A., Lipka, S., & Croker, S. (2016). Attentional bias towards threatening and neutral facial expressions in high trait anxious children. *Journal of Experimental Psychopathology, 7*(3), 343–359. https://doi.org/10.5127/jep.052915

Kennedy, F., & Pearson, D. (2021). *Integrating CBT and third wave therapies: Distinctive features*. Routledge/Taylor & Francis Group.

Khosravi, M., & Kasaeiyan, R. (2023). A current challenge in classification and treatment of DSM-5-TR prolonged grief disorder. *Psychological Trauma: Theory, Research, Practice, and Policy*. https://doi.org/10.1037/tra0001510

Klass, D., Silverman, P., & Nickman, S. L. (Eds.). (1996). *Continuing bonds: New understandings of grief*. Taylor & Francis.

Kramper, S., Crosby, E. S., Waitz-Kudla, S. N., Weathers, F., & Witte, T. K. (2023). Highly stressful events and posttraumatic stress disorder symptoms among veterinary professionals: Prevalence and associations with mental health and job-related outcomes. *Psychological Trauma: Theory, Research, Practice, and Policy, 15*(Suppl 2), S275–S285. https://doi.org/10.1037/tra0001432

Lagace-Seguin, D. G., & d'Entremont, M.-R. L. (2010). A scientific exploration of positive psychology in adolescence: The role of hope as a buffer against the influences of psychosocial negativities. *International Journal of Adolescence and Youth, 16*, 69–95. https://doi.org/10.1080/02673843.2010.9748046

Lahad, M., Shacham, M., & Ayalon, O. (2013). *The "BASIC Ph" model of coping and resiliency: Theory, research and cross-cultural application*. Jessica Kingsley Publishers.

Lapierre, S., Chauvette, S., Bolduc, L., Adams-Lemieux, M., Boller, B., & Desjardins, S. (2023). Character strengths and resilience in older adults during the COVID-19 pandemic. *Canadian Journal on Aging, 42*(3), 455–465. https://doi.org/10.1017/S0714980823000089

REFERENCES 159

Lavy, S., & Benish-Weisman, M. (2021). Character strengths as "values in action": Linking character strengths with values theory – An exploratory study of the case of gratitude and self-transcendence. *Frontiers in Psychology*, *12*, 9. https://doi.org/10.3389/fpsyg.2021.576189

Layne, C. M., Warren, J. S., Watson, P. J., & Shalev, A. Y. (2007). Risk, vulnerability, resistance, and resilience: Toward an integrative conceptualization of posttraumatic adaptation. In *Handbook of PTSD: Science and practice* (pp. 497–520). The Guilford Press.

Lazarus, P. S., & Folkman, S. (1984). *Stress, appraisal, and coping*. Springer Publishing Company.

Lehman, D. R., Davis, C. G., DeLongis, A., Wortman, C. B., Bluck, S., Mandel, D. R., & Ellard, J. H. (1993). Positive and negative life changes following bereavement and their relations to adjustment. *Journal of Social and Clinical Psychology*, *12*(1), 90–112. https://doi.org/10.1521/jscp.1993.12.1.90

Leung, Y. Y., Lee, T. C. P., Ho, S. M. Y., & Cheung, L. K. (2013). Trigeminal neurosensory deficit and patient reported outcome measures: The effect on life satisfaction and depression symptoms. *PLoS ONE*, *8*(8), e72891. https://doi.org/10.1371/journal.pone.0072891

Lewis, H. A., & Kliewer, W. (1996). Hope, coping, and adjustment among children with sickle cell disease: Tests of mediator and moderator models. *Journal of Pediatric Psychology*, *21*, 25–41. https://doi.org/10.1093/jpepsy/21.1.25

Li, T., Dong, Y., & Liu, Z. (2020). A review of social-ecological system resilience: Mechanism, assessment and management. *Science of The Total Environment*, *723*, 138113. https://doi.org/10.1016/j.scitotenv.2020.138113

Liang, C.-W., Tsai, J.-L., & Hsu, W.-Y. (2017). Sustained visual attention for competing emotional stimuli in social anxiety: An eye tracking study. *Journal of Behavior Therapy and Experimental Psychiatry*, *54*, 178–185. https://doi.org/10.1016/j.jbtep.2016.08.009

Lim, Y.-J. (2023). Psychometric properties of the brief strengths scale-12 in Korean population. *Sage Open*, *13*(4), 21582440231210045. https://doi.org/10.1177/21582440231210045

Lloyd, T. J., & Hastings, R. (2009). Hope as a psychological resilience factor in mothers and fathers of children with intellectual disabilities. *Journal of Intellectual Disability Research*, *53*, 957–968. https://doi.org/10.1111/j.1365-2788.2009.01206.x

Lo, C. S. L., Ho, S. M. Y., & Hollon, S. D. (2008). The effects of rumination and negative cognitive styles on depression: A mediation analysis. *Behaviour Research and Therapy*, *46*(4), 487–495. https://doi.org/10.1016/j.brat.2008.01.013

Lo, C. S. L., Ho, S. M. Y., & Hollon, S. D. (2010). The effects of rumination and depressive symptoms on the prediction of negative attributional style among college students. *Cognitive Therapy and Research, 34,* 116–123. https://doi.org/10.1007/s10608-009-9233-2

Lo, C. S. L., Ho, S. M. Y., Yu, N. K. K., & Siu, B. P. Y. (2014). Decentering mediates the effect of ruminative and experiential self-focus on negative thinking in depression. *Cognitive Therapy and Research, 38*(4), 389–396. https://doi.org/10.1007/s10608-014-9603-2

Long, L. J., Viana, A. G., Zvolensky, M. J., Lu, Q., & Gallagher, M. W. (2024). The influence of hope and optimism on trajectories of covid-19 stress, health anxiety, and wellbeing during the covid-19 pandemic. *Journal of Clinical Psychology.* https://doi.org/10.1002/jclp.23746

Loper, A. B., Carlson, L. W., Levitt, L., & Scheffel, K. (2009). Parenting stress, alliance, child contact, and adjustment of imprisoned mothers and fathers. *Journal of Offender Rehabilitation, 48*(6), 483–503. https://doi.org/10.1080/10509670903081300

Lopez, S. J., & Snyder, C. R. (2011). *The Oxford handbook of positive psychology.* Oxford University Press.

Lunansky, G., Bonanno, G. A., Blanken, T. F., van Borkulo, C. D., Cramer, A. O. J., & Borsboom, D. (2024). Bouncing back from life's perturbations: Formalizing psychological resilience from a complex systems perspective. *Psychological Review.* https://doi.org/10.1037/rev0000497

Ma, W., Koenig, H. G., Wen, J., Liu, J., Shi, X., & Wang, Z. (2023). The moral injury, posttraumatic stress disorder, and suicidal behaviors in health professionals 1 year after the COVID-19 pandemic peak in China. *Psychological Trauma: Theory, Research, Practice, and Policy, 15*(Suppl 2), S352–S356. https://doi.org/10.1037/tra0001483

Maddi, S. R. (1999). The personality construct of hardiness: I. Effects on experiencing, coping, and strain. *Consulting Psychology Journal: Practice and Research, 51*(2), 83–94. https://doi.org/10.1037/1061-4087.51.2.83

Maddi, S. R. (2002). The story of hardiness: Twenty years of theorizing, research, and practice. *Consulting Psychology Journal: Practice and Research, 54*(3), 173–185. https://doi.org/10.1037/1061-4087.54.3.173

Maddi, S. R., & Kobasa, S. C. (1991). The development of hardiness. In A. Monat & R. S. Lazarus (Eds.), *Stress and coping. An anthology* (3rd ed., pp. 246–257). Columbia University Press.

Maercker, A., & Zoellner, T. (2004). The Janus face of self-perceived growth: Toward a two-component model of posttraumatic growth. *Psychological Inquiry, 41*–48.

Mao, Y., Yang, R., Bonaiuto, M., Ma, J., & Harmat, L. (2020). Can Flow Alleviate Anxiety? The Roles of Academic Self- Efficacy and Self-Esteem in Building Psychological Sustainability and Resilience. *Sustainability, 12*(7), 2987. https://doi.org/10.3390/su12072987

REFERENCES 161

Mak, V. W. M., Ho, S. M. Y., Kwong, R. W. Y., & Li, W. L. (2018). A gender-responsive treatment facility in correctional services: The development of psychological gymnasium for women offenders. *International Journal of Offender Therapy and Comparative Criminology 62*(4), 1062–1079. https://doi.org/10.1177/0306624x16667572

Mak, V. W. M., Ho, S. M. Y., Li, W. L., & Pau, K.-Y. B. (2021). Relationships between hope and mental health among women in prison. *Criminal Behavior and Mental Health, 31*(2), 96–108.https://doi.org/10.1002/cbm.2191

Marchetti, I., & Pössel, P. (2023). Cognitive triad and depressive symptoms in adolescence: Specificity and overlap. *Child Psychiatry and Human Development, 54*(4), 1209–1217. https://doi.org/10.1007/s10578-022-013 23-w

Matthews, G., Lin, J., & Wohleber, R. (2017). Personality, stress and resilience: A multifactorial cognitive science perspective. *Psihologijske Teme, 26*(1), 139–162. https://doi.org/10.31820/pt.26.1.6

McDermott, D., & Snyder, C. R. (1999). *Making hope happen. A workbook for turning possibilities into reality.* New Harbinger.

McGrath, R. E. (2014). Scale- and item-level factor analyses of the VIA inventory of strengths. *Assessment, 21*(1), 4–14. https://doi.org/10.1177/107319111 2450612

McGrath, R. E. (2015). Integrating psychological and cultural perspectives on virtue: The hierarchical structure of character strengths. *The Journal of Positive Psychology, 10*(5), 407–424. https://doi.org/10.1080/17439760.2014. 994222

Mednick, L., Cogen, F., Henderson, C., Rohrbeck, C. A., Kitessa, D., & Streisand, R. (2007). Hope more, worry less: Hope as a potential resilience factor in mothers of very young children with type 1 diabetes. *Children's Healthcare, 36*, 385–396. https://doi.org/10.1080/02739610701601403

Meraj, N., Arbeau, K., Fadiya, B., Ketelaars, T., St. Pierre, J., Swart, G. T., & Zayed, R. (2023). Introducing the Adverse Life Events Inventory for Children (ALEIC): An examination of adverse experiences and related impacts in a large clinical sample of children and youth. *Traumatology: An International Journal, 29*(2), 137–148. https://doi.org/10.1037/trm0000385

Mezulis, A. H., Abramson, L. Y., Hyde, J. S., & Hankin, B. L. (2004). Is there a universal positivity bias in attributions? A meta-analytic review of individual, developmental, and cultural differences in the self-serving attributional bias. *Psychological Bulletin, 130*(5), 711–747. https://doi.org/10. 1037/0033-2909.130.5.711

Miao, M., Zhou, Z., Qi, W., & Zheng, L. (2024). The mediating role of hope in the relationship between benefit finding and anxiety: Insights from the covid-19 pandemic. *Anxiety, Stress & Coping: An International Journal.* https://doi.org/10.1080/10615806.2024.2378864

162   REFERENCES

Michl, L. C., McLaughlin, K. A., Shepherd, K., & Nolen-Hoeksema, S. (2013). Rumination as a mechanism linking stressful life events to symptoms of depression and anxiety: Longitudinal evidence in early adolescents and adults. *Journal of Abnormal Psychology, 122*(2), 339–352. https://doi.org/10.1037/a0031994

Mitchell, A. J., Chan, M., Bhatti, H., Halton, M., Grassi, L., Johansen, C., & Meader, N. (2011). Prevalence of depression, anxiety, and adjustment disorder in oncological, haematological, and palliative-care settings: A meta-analysis of 94 interview-based studies. *The Lancet Oncology, 12*(2), 160–174. https://doi.org/10.1016/S1470-2045(11)70002-X

Mogg, K., & Bradley, B. P. (1998). A cognitive-motivational analysis of anxiety. *Behaviour Research and Therapy, 36*(9), 809–848. https://doi.org/10.1016/s0005-7967(98)00063-1

Mogg, K., & Bradley, B. P. (1999). Selective attention and anxiety: A cognitive–motivational perspective. In T. Dalgleish & M. J. Power (Eds.), *Handbook of cognition and emotion* (pp. 145–170, Chapter xxi, 843 Pages). Wiley.

Mogg, K., & Bradley, B. P. (2016). Anxiety and attention to threat: Cognitive mechanisms and treatment with attention bias modification. *Behaviour Research and Therapy, 87*, 76–108. https://doi.org/10.1016/j.brat.2016.08.001

Moorey, S., & Greer, S. (2012). *Oxford guide to CBT for people with cancer*. Oxford University Press.

Morales, A. S. (2012). *Trait anxiety*. Nova Science Publishers.

Mumm, J., Hearst, M. O., Shanafelt, A., Wang, Q., Leduc, R., & Nanney, M. S. (2017). Increasing social support for breakfast: Project BreakFAST. *Health Promotion Practice, 18*(6), 862–868. https://doi.org/10.1177/1524839917711123

Muris, P., de Jong, P. J., & Engelen, S. (2004). Relationships between neuroticism, attentional control, and anxiety disorders symptoms in non-clinical children. *Personality and Individual Differences, 37*(4), 789–797. https://doi.org/10.1016/j.paid.2003.10.007

Nakamura, J., & Csikszentmihalyi, m. (2003). The construction of meaning through vital engagement. In C. L. M. Keyes & J. Haidt (Eds.), *Flourishing: Positive psychology and the life well-lived*. (pp. 83–104, 335 Pages). American Psychological Association. https://doi.org/10.1037/10594-004

Neal, D. T., Wood, W., Labrecque, J. S., & Lally, P. (2012). How do habits guide behavior? Perceived and actual triggers of habits in daily life. *Journal of Experimental Social Psychology, 48*(2), 492–498. https://doi.org/10.1016/j.jesp.2011.10.011

Nolan, S. A., Roberts, J. E., & Gotlib, I. H. (1998). Neuroticism and ruminative response style as predictors of change in depressive symptomatology. *Cognitive*

REFERENCES 163

Therapy and Research, 22(5), 445–455. https://doi.org/10.1023/A:101876
9531641

Nolen-Hoeksema, S. (1991). Responses to depression and their effects on the duration of depressive episodes. *Journal of Abnormal Psychology*, 100, 569–582. https://doi.org/10.1037/0021-843X.100.4.569

Norris, F. H. (1992). Epidemiology of trauma: frequency and impact of different potentially traumatic events on different demographic groups. *Journal of Consulting and Clinical Psychology*, 60(3), 409–418. https://doi.org/10. 1037//0022-006x.60.3.409

Ntontis, E., Blackburn, A. M., Han, H., Stöckli, S., Milfont, T. L., Tuominen, J., Griffin, S. M., Ikizer, G., Jeftic, A., Chrona, S., Nasheedha, A., Liutsko, L., & Vestergren, S. (2023). The effects of secondary stressors, social identity, and social support on perceived stress and resilience: Findings from the COVID-19 pandemic. *Journal of Environmental Psychology*, 88, 1–11. https://doi. org/10.1016/j.jenvp.2023.102007

O'Donnell, M. L., Agathos, J. A., Metcalf, O., Gibson, K., & Lau, W. (2019). Adjustment disorder: Current developments and future directions. *International Journal of Environmental Research and Public Health*, 16(14). https:// doi.org/10.3390/ijerph16142537

Ogston, P. L., Mackintosh, V. H., & Myers, B. J. (2011). Hope and worry in mothers of children with an autism spectrum disorder or down syndrome. *Research in Autism Spectrum Disorders*, 5, 1378–1384. https://doi.org/10. 1016/j.rasd.2011.01.020

Olatunji, B. O. (Ed.). (2019). *The Cambridge handbook of anxiety and related disorders*. Cambridge University Press. https://doi.org/10.1017/978110814 0416

Onwuegbuzie, A. J. (1998). Role of hope in predicting anxiety about statistics. *Psychological Reports*, 82, 1315–1320. https://doi.org/10.2466/pr0.1998. 82.3c.1315

Or, D. Y. L., Lam, C. S., Chen, P. P., Wong, H. S. S., Lam, C. W. F., Fok, Y. Y., Chan, S. F. I., & Ho, S. M. Y. (2021). Hope in the context of chronic musculoskeletal pain: relationships of hope to pain and psychological distress. *Pain Reports*, 6(4), e965. https://doi.org/10.1097/pr9.0000000000000965

Pai, A., Suris, A. M., & North, C. S. (2017). Posttraumatic stress disorder in the DSM-5: Controversy, change, and conceptual considerations. *Behavioral Sciences (Basel)*, 7(1). https://doi.org/10.3390/bs7010007

Palacios-Delgado, J., Acosta-Beltrán, D. B., & Acevedo-Ibarra, J. N. (2024). How important are optimism and coping strategies for mental health? Effect in reducing depression in young people. *Psychiatry International*, 5(3), 532–543. https://www.mdpi.com/2673-5318/5/3/38

164 REFERENCES

Park, C. L., & Folkman, S. (1997). Meaning in the context of stress and coping. *Review of General Psychology*, *1*(2), 115–144. https://doi.org/10.1037/1089-2680.1.2.115

Park, C. L., Folkman, S., & Bostrom, A. (2001). Appraisals of controllability and coping in caregivers and HIV+ men: Testing the goodness-of-fit hypothesis. *Journal of Consulting and Clinical Psychology*, *69*(3), 481–488. https://doi.org/10.1037/0022-006X.69.3.481

Park, N., Peterson, C., & Seligman, M. E. P. (2004). Strengths of character and well-being: A closer look at hope and modesty. *Journal of Social and Clinical Psychology*, *23*(5), 628–634. https://doi.org/10.1521/jscp.23.5.628.50749

Pat-Horenczyk, R., Saltzman, L. Y., Hamama-Raz, Y., Perry, S., Ziv, Y., Ginat-Frolich, R., & Stemmer, S. M. (2016). Stability and transitions in post-traumatic growth trajectories among cancer patients: LCA and LTA analyses. *Psychological Trauma*, *8*(5), 541–549. https://doi.org/10.1037/tra0000094

Perkonigg, A., Lorenz, L., & Maercker, A. (2018). Prevalence and correlates of ICD-11 adjustment disorder: Findings from the Zurich adjustment disorder study. *International Journal of Clinical and Health Psychology*, *18*(3), 209–217. https://doi.org/10.1016/j.ijchp.2018.05.001

Peterson, C., & Buchanan, G. M. (1995). Explanatory style: History and evolution of the field. In *Explanatory style* (pp. 1–20). Lawrence Erlbaum Associates, Inc. https://doi.org/10.1017/CBO9780511527937.026

Peterson, C., Park, N., Pole, N., D'Andrea, W., & Seligman, M. E. (2008). Strengths of character and posttraumatic growth. *Journal of Traumatic Stress*, *21*(2), 214–217. https://doi.org/10.1002/jts.20332

Peterson, C., & Seligman, M. E. P. (2004). *Character strengths and virtues: A handbook and classification.* American Psychological Association.

Peterson, C., & Steen, T. A. (2021). Optimistic explanatory style. In C. R. Snyder, S. J. Lopez, L. M. Edwards, & S. C. Marques (Eds.), *The Oxford handbook of positive psychology* (3rd ed., pp. 413–424, 1002 Pages). Oxford University Press.

Peterson, C., Stephens, J. P., Park, N., Lee, F., & Seligman, M. E. P. (2010). Strengths of character and work. In P. A. Linley, S. Harrington, & N. Garcea (Eds.), *Oxford handbook of positive psychology and work.* Oxford University Press.

Quick, J. C., Wright, T. A., Adkins, J. A., Nelson, D. L., & Quick, J. D. (2013). Primary prevention for individuals: Managing and coping with stressors (2nd ed., pp. 147–163, 247 Pages). American Psychological Association. https://doi.org/10.1037/13942-010

Quigley, L., & Dobson, K. S. (2017). Behavioral activation treatments for depression. In S. G. Hofmann & G. J. G. Asmundson (Eds.), *The science of cognitive behavioral therapy* (pp. 291–318, 610 Pages). Elsevier Academic Press. https://doi.org/10.1016/B978-0-12-803457-6.00012-X

Quigley, L., Russell, K., Yung, C., Dobson, K. S., & Sears, C. R. (2024). Associations between attentional biases for emotional images and rumination in depression. *Cognition and Emotion.* https://doi.org/10.1080/02699931.2024.2434158

Rajandram, R. K., Ho, S. M. Y., Samman, N., Chan, N., McGrath, C., & Zwahlen, R. A. (2011). Interaction of hope and optimism with anxiety and depression in a specific group of cancer survivors: A preliminary study. *BMC Research, 4,* 519.

Rand, K. L. (2009). Hope and optimism: Latent structures and influences on grade expectancy and academic performance. *Journal of Personality, 77*(1), 231–260.

Raugh, I. M., & Strauss, G. P. (2023). Integrating mindfulness into the extended process model of emotion regulation: The dual-mode model of mindful emotion regulation. *Emotion.* https://doi.org/10.1037/emo0001308

Reisig, V., & Wildner, M. (2008). Prevention, primary. In W. Kirch (Ed.), *Encyclopedia of public health* (pp. 1141–1143). Springer Netherlands. https://doi.org/10.1007/978-1-4020-5614-7_2759

Reivich, K. (1995). The measurement of explanatory style. In G. M. Buchanan & M. E. P. Seligman (Eds.), *Explanatory Style* (pp. 21–27). Lawrence Erlbaum Associates.

Russo, S. J., Murrough, J. W., Han, M.-H., Charney, D. S., & Nestler, E. J. (2012). Neurobiology of resilience. *Nature Neuroscience, 15*(11), 1475–1484. https://doi.org/10.1038/nn.3234

Sacco, A., Pössel, P., & Roane, S. J. (2023). Perceived discrimination and depressive symptoms: What role does the cognitive triad play? *Journal of Clinical Psychology, 79*(4), 985–1001. https://doi.org/10.1002/jclp.23452

Sajquim de Torres, M., & Dura, L. (2019). Habits as building blocks for the resilience of vulnerable populations: Two positive deviance case studies from the U.S.–Mexico Border Region. *Health Promotion Practice, 20*(6), 793–797. https://doi.org/10.1177/1524839919855392

Salisbury, E. J., & Van Voorhis, P. (2009). Gendered pathways: A quantitative investigation of women probationers' paths to incarceration. *Criminal Justice and Behavior, 36*(6), 541–566. https://doi.org/10.1177/009385480 9334076

Schaefer, J. A., & Moos, R. (1992). Life crises and personal growth. In B. Carpenter (Ed.), *Personal coping: Theory, research, and application* (pp. 149–170). Praeger.

Scheier, M. F., & Carver, C. S. (1985). Optimism, coping, and health: Assessment and implications of generalized outcome expectancies. *Health Psychology, 4,* 219–247.

Scheier, M. F., & Carver, C. S. (1988). Dispositional optimism and physical well-being: The influence of outcome expectancies on health. *Journal of*

Personality, 55, 169–210. https://doi.org/10.1111/j.1467-6494.1987.tb0 0434.x

Scheier, M. F., Carver, C. S., & Bridges, M. W. (1994). Distinguishing optimism from neuroticism (and trait anxiety, self-mastery, and self-esteem): A reevaluation of the life orientation test. *Journal of Personality and Social Psychology*, 67(6), 1063.

Scher, C. D., Ingram, R. E., & Segal, Z. V. (2005). Cognitive reactivity and vulnerability: empirical evaluation of construct activation and cognitive diatheses in unipolar depression. *Clinical Psychology Review*, 25(4), 487–510. https://doi.org/10.1016/j.cpr.2005.01.005

Segerberg, T. S. S., Ozenne, B., Dam, V. H., Köhler-Forsberg, K., Jørgensen, M. B., Frokjaer, V. G., Knudsen, G. M., & Stenbæk, D. S. (2024). Rumination in patients with major depressive disorder before and after antidepressant treatment. *Journal of Affective Disorders*, 360, 322–325. https://doi.org/10.1016/j.jad.2024.05.135

Seligman, M. E. P. (1990). *Learned optimism*. Random House Australia.

Seligman, M. E. P., & Csikszentmihalyi, M. (2000). Positive psychology. An introduction. *American Psychologist*, 55(1), 5–14.

Seligman, M. E. P., Peterson, C., Kaslow, N. J., Tanenbaum, R. L., Alloy, L. B., & Abramson, L. Y. (1984). Attributional style and depressive symptoms among children. *Journal of Abnormal Psychology*, 93, 235–238. https://doi.org/10.1037/0021-843X.93.2.235

Shakespeare-Finch, J., & Obst, P. L. (2011). The development of the 2-way social support scale: A measure of giving and receiving emotional and instrumental support. *Journal of Personality Assessment*, 93(5), 483–490. https://doi.org/10.1080/00223891.2011.594124

Shamai, M. (2018). Is poverty a collective trauma? A joint learning process with women living in poverty in the city of Haifa in Israel. *British Journal of Social Work*, 48(6), 1718–1735. https://doi.org/10.1093/bjsw/bcx116

Shiloh, S., Peleg, S., & Nudelman, G. (2022). Core self-evaluations as resilience and risk factors of psychological distress during the covid-19 pandemic. *Psychology, Health & Medicine*. https://doi.org/10.1080/13548506.2022.2030480

Shoychet, G., Kimber, M., Weiss, J., Honest, O., & Prime, H. (2023). Empirical support for a model of risk and resilience in children and families during covid-19: A systematic review & narrative synthesis. *Development and Psychopathology*. https://doi.org/10.1017/S0954579423000767

Shryack, J., Steger, M. F., Krueger, R. F., & Kallie, C. S. (2010). The structure of virtue: An empirical investigation of the dimensionality of the virtues in action inventory of strengths. *Personality and Individual Differences*, 48(6), 714–719. https://doi.org/10.1016/j.paid.2010.01.007

Siegel, J. T., Alvaro, E. M., Crano, W. D., Lienemann, B. A., Hohman, Z. P., & O'Brien, E. (2012). Increasing social support for depressed individuals: A cross-cultural assessment of an affect-expectancy approach. *Journal of Health Communication*, *17*(6), 713–732. https://doi.org/10.1080/108 10730.2011.635775

Siegel, P., & Peterson, B. S. (2024). "All we have to fear is fear itself": Paradigms for reducing fear by preventing awareness of it. *Psychological Bulletin*, *150*(9), 1118–1154. https://doi.org/10.1037/bul0000437

Sin, N. L., & Lyubomirsky, S. (2009). Enhancing well-being and alleviating depressive symptoms with positive psychology interventions: A practice-friendly meta-analysis. *Journal of Clinical Psychology*, *65*(5), 467–487. https://doi.org/10.1002/jclp.20593

Sinclair, R. R., & Tetrick, L. E. (2000). Implications of item wording for hardiness structure, relation with neuroticism, and stress buffering. *Journal of Research in Personality*, *34*(1), 1–25. https://doi.org/10.1006/jrpe.1999.2265

Sisto, A., Vicinanza, F., Campanozzi, L. L., Ricci, G., Tartaglini, D., & Tambone, V. (2019). Towards a transversal definition of psychological resilience: A literature review. *Medicina (Kaunas)*, *55*(11). https://doi.org/10.3390/medicina55110745

Snook, D. W., Kaczkowski, W., & Fodeman, A. D. (2023). Mask on, mask off: Risk perceptions for COVID-19 and compliance with COVID-19 safety measures. *Behavioral Medicine*, *49*(3), 246–257. https://doi.org/10.1080/08964289.2021.2021384

Snyder, C. R. (1994). *The psychology of hope: You can get there from here*. Free Press.

Snyder, C. R. (2000). *Handbook of hope: Theory, measures, and applications*. Access Online via Elsevier.

Snyder, C. R. (2002). Hope theory: Rainbows in the mind. *Psychological Inquiry*, *13*(4), 249–275.

Snyder, C. R., Harris, C., Anderson, J. R., Holleran, S. A., Irving, L. M., Sigmon, S. T., Yoshinobu, L., Gibb, J., Langelle, C., & Harney, P. (1991). The will and the ways: Development and validation of an individual-differences measure of hope. *Journal of Personality and Social Psychology*, *60*(4), 570–585.

Snyder, C. R., Hoza, B., Pelham, W. E., Rapoff, M., Ware, L., Danovsky, M., Highberger, L., Rubinstein, H., & Stahl, K. J. (1997). The development and validation of the children's hope scale. *Journal of Pediatric Psychology*, *22*, 399–421.

Snyder, C. R., Shorey, H. S., Cheavens, J. S., Pulvers, K. M., Adams, V. H., & Wiklund, C. (2002). Hope and academic success in college. *Journal of Educational Psychology*, *94*, 820–826.

Snyder, C. R., Sympson, S. C., Michael, S. T., & Cheavens, J. (2000). The optimism and hope constructs: Variants on a positive expectancy theme. In E. C. Chang (Ed.), *Optimism and Pessimism* (pp. 103–124). American Psychological Association.

Snyder, C. R., Sympson, S. C., Ybasco, F. C., Borders, T. F., Babyak, M. A., & Higgins, R. L. (1996). Development and validation of the state hope scale. *Journal of Personality and Social Psychology, 70,* 321–335.

Southwick, S., & Watson, P. (2015). The emerging scientific and clinical literature on resilience and psychological first aid. In N. C. Bernardy & M. J. Friedman (Eds.), *A practical guide to PTSD treatment: Pharmacological and psychotherapeutic approaches* (pp. 21–33, 194 Pages). American Psychological Association. https://doi.org/10.1037/14522-003

Southwick, S. M., & Charney, D. S. (2022). *Resilience: The science of mastering life's greatest challenges.* Cambridge University Press. http://ebookcentral.pro quest.com/lib/cityuhk/detail.action?docID=1024995

Southwick, S. M., Charney, D. S., & DePierro, J. M. (2023). *Resilience: The science of mastering life's greatest challenges* (3rd ed.). Cambridge University Press.

Stanton, A. L., Danoff-Burg, S., Cameron, C. L., Bishop, M., Collins, C. A., Kirk, S. B., Sworowski, L. A., & Twillman, R. (2000). Emotionally expressive coping predicts psychological and physical adjustment to breast cancer. *Journal of Consulting and Clinical Psychology, 68,* 875–882.

Steger, M. F., Hicks, B. M., Kashdan, T. B., Krueger, R. F., & Bouchard Jr, T. J. (2007). Genetic and environmental influences on the positive traits of the values in action classification, and biometric covariance with normal personality. *Journal of Research in Personality, 41*(3), 524–539. https://doi.org/10.1016/j.jrp.2006.06.002

Stroebe, M., & Schut, H. (2005). To continue or relinquish bonds: A review of consequences for the bereaved. *Death Studies, 29,* 477–494. https://doi.org/10.1080/07481180590962659

Stroebe, M., Schut, H., & Boerner, K. (2010). Continuing bonds in adaptation to bereavement: Toward theoretical integration. *Clinical Psychology Review, 30*(2), 259–268. https://doi.org/10.1016/j.cpr.2009.11.007

Stroebe, M. S., Hansson, R. O., & Stroebe, W. (Eds.). (2001). *Handbook of bereavement research: Consequences, coping, and care* (1st ed.). American Psychological Association.

Suen, K. S., Lai, Y., Ho, S. M. Y., Cheung, L. K., & Choi, W. S. (2018). A longitudinal evaluation of psychosocial changes throughout orthognathic surgery. *PLoS ONE, 13*(9), e0203883. https://doi.org/10.1371/journal.pone.020 3883

REFERENCES 169

Swartzman, S., Booth, J. N., Munro, A., & Sani, F. (2017). Posttraumatic stress disorder after cancer diagnosis in adults: A meta-analysis. *Depress Anxiety*, *34*(4), 327–339. https://doi.org/10.1002/da.22542

Snyder, C. R., Cheavens, J. S., & Michael, S. T. (2005). Hope Theory: History and elaborated model. In J. Eliott (Ed.), *Interdisciplinary perspective on hope* (pp. 101–118). Nova Science Publishers.

Taku, K., Tedeschi, R. G., Shakespeare-Finch, J., Krosch, D., David, G., Kehl, D., Grunwald, S., Romeo, A., Di Tella, M., Kamibeppu, K., Soejima, T., Hiraki, K., Volgin, R., Dhakal, S., Zięba, M., Ramos, C., Nunes, R., Leal, I., Gouveia, P., ... Calhoun, L. G. (2020). Posttraumatic growth (PTG) and posttraumatic depreciation (PTD) across ten countries: Global validation of the PTG-PTD theoretical model. *Personality and Individual Differences*, 110222. https://doi.org/10.1016/j.paid.2020.110222

Tam, C. K., McGrath, C. P., Ho, S. M. Y., Pow, E. H. N., Luk, H. W. K., & Cheung, L. K. (2014). Psychosocial and quality of life outcomes of prosthetic auricular rehabilitation with CAD/CAM technology. *International Journal of Dentistry*, *2014*(Article ID 393571), 12. https://doi.org/ https://doi.org/10.1155/2014/393571

Taylor, C. T., Bomyea, J., & Amir, N. (2010). Attentional bias away from positive social information mediates the link between social anxiety and anxiety vulnerability to a social stressor. *Journal of Anxiety Disorders*, *24*(4), 403–408. https://doi.org/10.1016/j.janxdis.2010.02.004

Taylor, C. T., Bomyea, J., & Amir, N. (2011a). Malleability of attentional bias for positive emotional information and anxiety vulnerability. *Emotion*, *11*(1), 127–138. https://doi.org/10.1037/a0021301

Taylor, C. T., Bomyea, J., & Amir, N. (2011b). Malleability of attentional bias for positive emotional information and anxiety vulnerability. *Emotion*, *11*, 127–138. https://doi.org/10.1037/a0021301

Teasdale, J. D. (1983). Negative thinking in depression: Cause, effect, or reciprocal relationship. *Advances in Behaviour Research & Therapy*, *5*(1), 3–25. https://doi.org/10.1016/0146-6402(83)90013-9

Teasdale, J. D., & Dent, J. (1987). Cognitive vulnerability to depression: An investigation of two hypotheses. *British Journal of Clinical Psychology*, *26*(2), 113–126. https://doi.org/10.1111/j.2044-8260.1987.tb00737.x

Tedeschi, R. G., & Calhoun, L. G. (1996). The posttraumatic growth inventory: Measuring the positive legacy of trauma. *Journal of Traumatic Stress*, *9*(3), 455–471. https://doi.org/10.1002/jts.2490090305

Tedeschi, R. G., & Calhoun, L. G. (2004). Posttraumatic growth: Conceptual foundations and empirical evidence. *Psychological Inquiry*, *15*(1), 1–18. https://doi.org/10.1207/s15327965pli1501_01

Tedeschi, R. G., Cann, A., Taku, K., Senol-Durak, E., & Calhoun, L. G. (2017). The posttraumatic growth inventory: A revision integrating existential and spiritual change. *Journal of Traumatic Stress*, 30(1), 11–18. https://doi.org/10.1002/jts.22155

Tedeschi, R. G., Park, C. L., & Calhoun, L. G. (1998a). Posttraumatic growth: Conceptual issues. In R. G. Tedeschi, C. L. Park, & L. G. Calhoun (Eds.), *Posttraumatic growth: Positive changes in the aftermath of crisis* (pp. 1–22). Lawrence Erlbaum Associates.

Tedeschi, R. G., Park, C. L., & Calhoun, L. G. (Eds.). (1998b). *Posttraumatic growth: Positive changes in the aftermath of crisis*. Lawrence Erlbaum Associates.

Treynor, W., Gonzalez, R., & Nolen-Hoeksema, S. (2003). Rumination reconsidered: A psychometric analysis. *Cognitive Therapy and Research*, 27(3), 247–259. https://doi.org/10.1023/A:1023910315561

Truitt, M., Biesecker, B., Capone, G., Bailey, T., & Erby, L. (2012). The role of hope in adaptation to uncertainty: the experience of caregivers of children with down syndrome. *Patient Education and Counseling*, 87, 233–238.

Tse, D. C. K., Nakamura, J., & Csikszentmihalyi, M. (2022). Flow Experiences Across Adulthood: Preliminary Findings on the Continuity Hypothesis. *Journal of Happiness Studies*, 23(6), 2517–2540. https://doi.org/10.1007/s10902-022-00514-5

Van Bockstaele, B., Verschuere, B., Tibboel, H., De Houwer, J., Crombez, G., & Koster, E. H. W. (2014). A review of current evidence for the causal impact of attentional bias on fear and anxiety. *Psychological Bulletin*, 140(3), 682–724.

van Eeden, C., Wissing, M. P., Dreyer, J., Park, N., & Peterson, C. (2008). Validation of the Values in Action Inventory of Strengths for Youth (VIA-Youth) among South African learners. *Journal of Psychology in Africa*, 18(1), 143–154.

Vrijen, C., Hartman, C. A., & Oldehinkel, A. J. (2019). Reward-related attentional bias at age 16 predicts onset of depression during 9 years of follow-up. *Journal of the American Academy of Child and Adolescent Psychiatry*, 58(3), 329–338. https://doi.org/10.1016/j.jaac.2018.06.009

Wagner, L., Gander, F., Proyer, R. T., & Ruch, W. (2020). Character strengths and PERMA: Investigating the relationships of character strengths with a multidimensional framework of well-being. *Applied Research in Quality of Life*, 15(2), 307–328. https://doi.org/10.1007/s11482-018-9695-z

Wagnild, G. M., & Young, H. M. (1993). Development and psychometric evaluation of the resilience scale. *Journal of Nursing Measurement*, 1(2), 165–178.

Wang, B., Ni, C., Chen, J., Liu, X., Wang, A., Shao, Z., Xiao, D., Cheng, H., Jiang, J., & Yan, Y. (2011). Posttraumatic stress disorder 1 month after 2008 earthquake in China: Wenchuan earthquake survey. *Psychiatry Reearch*, 187(3), 392–396. https://doi.org/10.1016/j.psychres.2009.07.001

Wang, L., Zhang, Y., Shi, Z., & Wang, W. (2009). Symptoms of posttraumatic stress disorder among adult survivors two months after the Wenchuan earthquake. *Psychological Reports*, *105*(3 Pt 1), 879–885.https://doi.org/10.2466/pr0.105.3.879-885

Wang, L., Zhang, Y., Wang, W., Shi, Z., Shen, J., Li, M., & Xin, Y. (2009). Symptoms of posttraumatic stress disorder among adult survivors three months after the Sichuan earthquake in China. *Journal of Traumatic Stress*, *22*(5), 444–450. https://doi.org/10.1002/jts.20439

Wang, T., & Pavelko, R. (2024). Increasing social support for women via humanizing postpartum depression. *Health Communication*. https://doi.org/10.1080/10410236.2024.2361582

Waters, A. M., Henry, J., Mogg, K., Bradley, B. P., & Pine, D. S. (2010). Attentional bias towards angry faces in childhood anxiety disorders. *Journal of Behavior Therapy and Experimental Psychiatry*, *41*(2), 158–164. https://doi.org/10.1016/j.jbtep.2009.12.001

Waters, A. M., Lipp, O. V., & Spence, S. H. (2004). Attentional bias toward fear-related stimuli: An investigation with nonselected children and adults and children with anxiety disorders. *Journal of Experimental Child Psychology*, *89*(4), 320–337. https://doi.org/10.1016/j.jecp.2004.06.003

Waters, A. M., Mogg, K., Bradley, B., & Pine, D. (2008). Attentional bias for emotional faces in children with generalized anxiety disorder. *Journal of the American Academy of Child and Adolescent Psychiatry*, *47*(4), 435–442. https://doi.org/10.1097/CHI.0b013e3181642992

Watkins, E., & Teasdale, J. D. (2001). Rumination and overgeneral memory in depression: Effects of self-focus and analytic thinking. *Journal of Abnormal Psychology*, *110*(2), 353–357. https://doi.org/10.1037/0021-843X.110.2.333

Watson, M., Greer, S., Young, J., Inayat, Q., Burgess, C., & Robertson, B. (1988). Development of a questionnaire measure of adjustment to cancer: The MAC scale. *Psychological Medicine*, *18*, 203–209.

Watson, M., Law, M., dos Santos, M., Greer, S., Baruch, J., & Bliss, J. (1994). The Mini-MAC: Further development of the mental adjustment to cancer scale. *Journal of Psychosocial Oncology*, *12*(3), 33–46.

Wellman, J. (2022). Living in vivid color with "vital engagement". *Psychology Today*. https://www.psychologytoday.com/intl/blog/4000-mondays/202212/living-in-vivid-color-with-vital-engagement

Williams, J. M. G., Watts, F. N., MacLeod, C., & Mathews, A. (1988). *Cognitive psychology and emotional disorders*. Wiley.

Williams, R., Ntontis, E., Alfadhli, K., Drury, J., & Amlôt, R. (2021). A social model of secondary stressors in relation to disasters, major incidents and conflict: Implications for practice. *International Journal of Disaster Risk Reduction*, *63*, 102436. https://doi.org/10.1016/j.ijdrr.2021.102436

172 REFERENCES

Wong, S. S., & Lim, T. (2009). Hope versus optimism in Singaporean adolescents: Contributions to depression and life satisfaction. *Personality and Individual Differences, 46*(5), 648–652.

World Health Organization. (2022). *ICD-11: International classification of diseases (11th revision).* https://icd.who.int/.

World Health Organization. (2023a). *Number of COVID-19 deaths reported to WHO (cumulative total).* Retrieved January 16, 2024, from https://data.who.int/dashboards/covid19/deaths?n=c

World Health Organization. (2023b). WHO Director-General's opening remarks at the media briefing – 5 May 2023. Retrieved Janurary 2, 2024, from https://www.who.int/director-general/speeches/detail/who-director-general-s-opening-remarks-at-the-media-briefing---5-may-2023

World Health Organization. (2024). *Health promotion and disease prevention through population-based interventions, including action to address social determinants and health inequity* https://www.emro.who.int/about-who/public-health-functions/health-promotion-disease-prevention.html

World Health Organization, War Trauma Foundation, & World Vision International. (2011). *Psychological first aid: Guide for field workers.* Geneva. https://iris.who.int/bitstream/handle/10665/44615/9789241548205_eng.pdf?sequence=1#:~:text=Suggested%20citation%3A%20World%20Health%20Organization,WHO%3A%20Geneva

Worrell, F. C., & Hale, R. L. (2001). The relationship of hope in the future and perceived school climate to school completion. *School Psychology Quarterly, 16*, 370–388.

Wright, K. B. (2009). Increasing computer-mediated social support. In J. C. Parker & E. Thorson (Eds.), *Health communication in the new media landscape* (pp. 243–265, Chapter xxxiii, 460 Pages). Springer Publishing Company.

Xanthopoulos, M. S., & Daniel, L. C. (2013). Coping and social support. In A. M. Nezu, C. M. Nezu, P. A. Geller, & I. B. Weiner (Eds.), *Handbook of psychology: Health psychology* (Vol. 9, 2nd ed., pp. 57–78, 686 Pages). Wiley.

Yeung, D. Y., Ho, S. M. Y., & Mak, C. W. Y. (2015). Attention to positive information mediates the relationship between hope and psychosocial well-being of adolescents. *Journal of Adolescence 42*, 98–102. https://doi.org/10.1016/j.adolescence.2015.04.004

Yuan, J., Shi, G., Zhang, Q., & Cui, L. (2024). Visual search attentional bias modification reduced the attentional bias in socially anxious individuals. *Psychophysiology, 11*. https://doi.org/10.1111/psyp.14724

Yuen, A. N. Y., Ho, S. M. Y., Chan, C. K. Y., Chiang, A., Lee, V., Yuen, H. L., & Ling, S. C. (2013). The relationship between hope, rumination response styles, rumination content and psychological adjustment among childhood cancer patients and survivors. *Pediatric Blood & Cancer, 60*(S3), S180. Article P-0542. https://doi.org/10.1002/pbc.24719

Zalta, A. K. (2023). Dianne L. Chambless (1948–2023). *American Psychologist.* https://doi.org/10.1037/amp0001291

Zhang, J., Mao, Y., Wang, Y., & Zhang, Y. (2023a). The relationship between trait mindfulness and resilience: A meta-analysis. *Personality and Mental Health, 17*(4), 313–327. https://doi.org/10.1002/pmh.1581

Zhang, L., Rakesh, D., Cropley, V., & Whittle, S. (2023b). Neurobiological correlates of resilience during childhood and adolescence – A systematic review. *Clinical Psychology Review, 105*, 1–12. https://doi.org/10.1016/j.cpr.2023.102333

Zhang, Y., & Ho, S. M. Y. (2011). Risk factors of posttraumatic stress disorder among survivors after the 512 Wenchuan earthquake in China. *PLoS ONE, 6*(7), e22371. https://doi.org/10.1371/journal.pone.0022371

Zhu, Q., Wang, Q., & Yang, S. (2024). Does mindfulness matter in the development of character strengths? A RCT study comparing mindfulness-based strengths practice and character strengths-based intervention. *The Journal of Positive Psychology, 19*(5), 900. https://doi.org/10.1080/17439760.2023.2257678

Zinbarg, R. E., Schmidt, M., Feinstein, B., Williams, A. L., Murillo, A., Echiverri-Cohen, A. M., Enders, C., Craske, M., & Nusslock, R. (2023). Personality predicts pre-COVID-19 to COVID-19 trajectories of transdiagnostic anxiety and depression symptoms. *Journal of Psychopathology and Clinical Science, 132*(6), 645–656. https://doi.org/10.1037/abn0000803

Zoellner, T., & Maercker, A. (2006). Posttraumatic growth in clinical psychology - A critical review and introduction of a two component model. *Clinical psychology review, 26*(5), 626–653.

INDEX

A

abandoning, 38, 83
absolute reality, 14
academic/work setbacks, 2
academic distress, 73
academic domain, 81
acceptance, 11, 15
acceptance–commitment therapy, 141
accidents, 2, 7, 32
accomplishments, 61
across the lifespan, 17
active constructive communication matrix, 100
active constructive responding (ACR), 15, 97, 99, 101, 102, 140
active constructive response, 100, 101
active coping, 9–11
acute stress disorder, 30–33
adaptive, 9, 14, 39, 56, 75, 84, 97, 124
adaptive cognition, 68
adaptive cognitive triad of hope, 68
adaptive coping, 8, 9, 125
adaptive habit-building, 54, 56, 57

adaptive health practices, 8, 10
adjustment, 6, 7, 9, 14, 31, 37, 39, 73, 74, 83, 125, 126
adjustment disorder, 30, 32, 33
adolescents, 11, 34, 73, 95
adversity, ix, 2–12, 14–17, 30, 32, 33, 35–37, 40, 52, 53, 56, 60, 69, 70, 72, 73, 75, 76, 78, 80, 83, 84, 93–100, 102, 108–110, 112, 113, 118, 120–122, 124, 125, 127, 128, 138
advice, 49, 84, 85, 95, 123
aetiology, 36
affect regulation, 10
affirmations, 85
agency, 48, 52, 68–70, 72, 74–80, 82, 86, 139
agoraphobia, 36
alterations in arousal, 32
altered gene, 74
ambitious goals, 68, 78, 82, 83
American Psychiatric Association, 30–33, 36, 37, 40
angry outbursts, 32

© The Author(s), under exclusive license to Springer Nature
Switzerland AG 2025
S. M. Y. Ho, *The SHINE Framework*,
https://doi.org/10.1007/978-3-031-89106-9

176 INDEX

anhedonia, 32, 33
anxiety, viii, 7–9, 12, 30, 33, 36, 37, 40, 54, 74–76, 108, 110, 111, 125
anxiety disorders, 6, 36, 110, 111
anxious individuals, 37, 108, 110, 111
apathy, 54
appetite, 34
appreciation of beauty, 49
appreciation of life, 123
apprehensive expectation, 37
approaching, 68
Asian, 15, 119
assessment, viii, ix, 30, 54, 57
assessment of strengths, 51
attention, 7, 11, 14, 37, 40, 76, 99, 100, 102, 108–113, 127, 140
attentional bias, viii, 6, 8, 36, 37, 110, 111
attention deployment, 108, 109
Australia, 36
autogenic, 54
automatic, 16, 17, 56, 57, 61
automatic detection, 37, 108
automatic habits, 16
avoidance, 32, 36, 37, 109
avoidance coping, 9
avoiding, 16, 68
awareness, 38, 49, 84, 123

B
balanced attention, 76, 99, 109, 110, 112, 122, 140
BASIC Ph, 10, 11, 15, 16
Beck's cognitive triad of depression, 34
behavioural activation, 36
belief, 10, 49, 50, 84, 122
benefit finding, 118, 132
benefits, 73, 122, 125
bereavement, 38, 39

bio-neurological, 37
blame, 95, 96
blaming, 120
blessings, 61, 112
body muscles, 76, 140
body posture, 98
Bonanno, G.A., vii, 3, 4, 6–8
Bone marrow transplantation, viii
Book of Changes, 13
boredom, 54
Bormans, L., viii, 70
bottom-up, 37, 108
bounce back, 3, 128, 138
brain structure, 5
bravery, 49, 50, 61
Brazil, 138
breast cancer, 10, 96, 111, 125
Brief Strength Scale (BSS-12), 50–52, 58
broaden-and-build theory, 100
brooding, 35, 121, 128

C
Calhoun, L.G., vii, 4, 123, 124, 126
calm, 53, 97
cancer, vii, viii, 4, 9, 10, 31, 33, 74, 75, 96, 108, 111, 121, 122, 125
carers, 73
caring, 48, 52, 94
carriers, 73
catastrophic events, 2
cautiousness, 50, 52, 53
challenge, 2, 6, 7, 11, 54–57, 60, 61, 70, 86, 108
challenging, 54, 56, 62, 76, 82, 139
change, 6, 8, 13, 15, 40, 69, 70, 74, 78, 83, 84, 95, 123, 124, 126, 127, 138
character strengths, viii, 15, 48–50, 52, 53, 57, 70, 112, 118
Cheung, L.K., 74, 75

Cheung, W.S., 38, 39
children, vii, 3, 30, 73–75, 94, 95, 99, 110, 111, 122
Children's Cancer Foundation, 75
Children's Hope Scale, 78
Chinese, 9, 13, 38, 39, 50, 51, 79, 94
chronic, 32, 33, 95, 122
chronic dysfunction, 74
Citizenship, 49
cleft lip, 75
clinical psychologist, vii, viii, 75, 125
cognition, 8, 12, 14, 32, 36, 72, 75, 80
cognitive, viii, 14, 17, 34, 36, 37, 68, 69, 77, 110, 123
cognitive avoidance, 9, 10
cognitive-behavioural approaches, 75
cognitive behavioural therapy, viii
cognitive control, 37, 108
cognitive functioning, 34
cognitive preoccupation, 38
cognitive processing factors, 37
cognitive psychology, viii, ix, 14, 78
cognitive strategies, 7
cognitive theory, 14
cognitive theory of hope, viii, 12, 68
cognitive triad of depression, 14, 34
colleagues, vii, 3, 4, 10, 54, 78, 99, 111, 123
collective trauma, 118
commitment, 6
community, 34, 38, 49, 51, 76, 95
comorbidity, 36
complete, 7, 15, 38, 53, 55, 57, 61, 79, 128, 130
comprehensive, 10, 11, 17
concentration, 34, 55
conditions, 2, 7, 15, 31, 54, 76, 78, 132
confidence, 83, 85
confidential, 98
confronting, 9

conscientiousness, 9, 48, 52
conscious, 68, 78, 85
conscious awareness, 14, 110
conservation of resources (COR), 7, 8, 16, 17, 52, 94
constructive, ix, 118, 124, 138
constructive PTG, 124, 125, 132
constructive self-talk, 85
constructivism, 14
constructivist approach, 15
contextual prompts, 56
continuing bonds (CBs), 38, 39
control, 6, 8, 37, 55, 61, 77, 84, 108
controllability, 9
controllable situations, 9
control measures, 3
convergent, 79
coping, 5, 9, 10, 16, 95, 118, 121, 122, 125, 128
coping effectiveness training, 8
core strengths, 51, 53
Coronavirus Disease 2019 (COVID-19), 2, 3, 6, 8, 11, 16, 31, 38, 53, 56, 71, 94, 97, 118, 138
correctional institutions, 75, 76
courage, 6, 48, 49, 53
creativity, 49, 50, 52, 53, 58, 61, 139
criticism, 95, 96
Csikszentmihalyi, M., viii, 15, 54–56
cultural, 15, 52, 98
curiosity, 11, 49, 50, 52, 53, 58, 139
curricula, 141
cut-off score, 80

D
daily hassles, 2
daily stress, 85
death, 31, 38, 39, 94
deceased, 37–40
decentring, 36

178 INDEX

delayed dysfunction, 74
delayed expression, 31
dementia, 7
dental, 74
dentist, 74
dentofacial deformities, 74, 75
depreciation, 126
depressed mood, 33–36
depression, viii, 7–9, 12, 30, 33–36, 38, 40, 71, 74–76, 95, 111, 118, 121
developmental milestones, 33
diagnosis, 9, 30, 31, 36, 38, 96, 111, 122, 125
Diagnostic and Statistical Manual of Mental Disorders (DSM-5-TR), 30–33, 36, 37, 40
difficulty concentrating, 37
dimension, 6, 48, 119, 123
disasters, vii, 2, 7, 11, 14, 17, 93, 94, 138, 141
disciplinary workers, 11
discomfort, 2
discrete events, 33
discriminant validity, 79
disengagement, 9, 83
disinhibited social engagement disorder, 30
dispositional, 2, 6, 8, 9, 78
distancing, 3, 9
distorted, 55
distortion, 14
distress, 3, 6, 16, 30, 39, 72, 94, 96–98, 111, 118
distressed PTG, 125
divorce, 31, 32
Dobson, K.S., viii, 14, 36
Dohrenwend, B.P., 126
doubt, 95, 96
downward regoaling, 69, 70, 78, 118
dreams, 32, 81
drought, 2

dual process theory, 38
Dubai, 138
dynamic personal factors, 8, 9, 11
dysfunctional, 4

E

earthquake, 2, 32, 94, 138
Eastern, 99
economic hardship, 2
economic recovery, 138
education, ix, 81, 141
effortless, 55, 57
electronic media, 31
Embracing Change, viii, 11, 13, 15, 17, 40, 72, 118, 123, 128
emotional, 10, 37–39, 52, 86, 95, 100, 122, 123
emotional instability, 6
emotionally threatening stimuli, 6
emotional social support, 10
emotion-focused, 9, 10, 95
emotion regulation, 8, 10
empathic understanding, 102
energies, 7, 38, 81, 84, 85, 96, 102
engagement, 9, 54, 139
epigenetic, 5
escape-avoidance, 9
excessive arousal, 32
exercise, ix, 10, 12, 16, 54, 57, 61, 74, 75, 81, 84, 85, 112, 123
expanded model of hope, 69–71
explanatory style, 119, 120, 128
exposure, 31, 32, 94, 118
expressive, 132
external, 3, 8, 10, 14, 56, 69, 70, 78, 95, 118, 119, 128, 131, 140
externalised CBs, 39
extraversion, 9
eye contact, 98, 102

F

facial expression, 98
factor structure, 50, 51, 79
fairness, 49, 50
family, 10, 81, 94, 95, 102, 123, 140
family domain, 81
famines, 2
fatalism, 10
fatigue, 37, 85
fear, 6, 11, 74, 97, 110
fear of fear, 37
female offenders, 16, 75, 76
Field, N.P., 38
fighting spirit, 9, 10
512 Wenchuan Earthquake, 94
five-part model, 8
flashbacks, 32
flexibility, 10, 11, 84
flexible, 70
floods, 2, 138
flow, 12, 13, 15, 54–57, 61, 139
focus attention, 37, 108
Folkman, S., 8–10, 95
forgiveness, 49, 50, 61
fostering, 125
4L, 98, 99, 101, 102
Fredrickson, B.L., 100
friends, 10, 61, 81, 94–98, 140
fulfilling, 15, 55, 81, 82
functional, 86
functioning, 2–5, 14, 68, 125, 138
future-oriented, 36, 70, 72, 139
Future Scale, 79, 80

G

Gable, S.L., 15, 97, 99, 100
gender-responsive, 75, 76
generalisation, 36
generalised anxiety disorder, 36
generic, 11, 97
genetic, 5, 74

genetic colon cancer screening, 73
Geopolitical tensions, vii
gift, 61
global, 119, 121, 128, 131, 132, 140
goal, 12, 36, 40, 49, 50, 52, 56–58, 61, 68–70, 72, 74–86, 112, 118, 139, 140
goal disengagement, 12, 70, 72, 74, 78, 83, 140
goal-oriented, 68
goal reengagement, 70, 78
goal setting, 56, 72, 75, 76, 84, 112
good diet, 68
goodness-of-fit hypothesis, 9, 10
good news, 97, 100–102
good nutrition, 84
good thing, 9, 49, 61, 70, 97, 112, 118, 130
gratitude, 15, 49, 50, 52, 58, 61, 113, 139
grief, 38–40, 95
growth, 4–6, 11, 16, 17, 30, 40, 83, 123, 126, 128, 138
guilt, 33, 38

H

habit-building, ix, 16, 17, 138
habitual practice, 10
happy, 99, 100, 111
hardiness, 6, 7
hardship, 3
hardy, 6, 7
harms, 12, 73, 76
Hayes, 141
healing, 15
health and physical fitness domain, 81
healthcare professional, 85
health-related, 72, 73
healthy, 4, 38, 49, 68, 108, 110, 125
healthy eating, 84, 123
healthy habits, 84

180 INDEX

healthy lifestyle, 84
heat waves, 2
hereditary colorectal cancer (HCRC), 73, 74, 80
HIV+, 8
hobby, 95, 137
Ho, J.W.C., 73
hope, ix, 15, 36, 49, 50, 61, 68–80, 111, 118
hope-based intervention, 74, 76, 80
hopeful thinking, viii, 11, 14, 17, 56, 68, 72, 78, 112, 118, 139
hopeless, 76, 118
hopelessness, 33, 76, 77, 125
Horne, David, viii
Ho, S.M.Y., viii, 4, 9, 10, 12, 31, 32, 38, 39, 48, 50–52, 58, 70–74, 79, 80, 94, 103, 111, 123, 125, 127
humanity, 48, 49
humility, 49
humour, 49, 50
hurricane, 7, 138
hypervigilance, 32

I
idiosyncratic, 14
illusory, 12, 111
illusory PTG, 124, 125
imagination, 10
incarceration, 75
infection, 4, 31, 97
inquisitiveness, 50, 52
inspire, 61, 81
instrumental, 84, 86, 95
instrumental functions, 10
instrumental social support, 10
integrated cognitive model, 37, 108
integrated model of resilience, 10
integrity, 49
intellectual, 52, 58, 60, 61, 68

intellectual strength, 50, 51, 53, 58, 139
interacting, 6
internal, 7, 95, 119, 121, 128, 131, 132, 140
internalised CBs, 39
internal reliability, 79
interpersonal, viii, 50–53, 58, 60, 61, 93–95
Interpersonal communication and support, 11, 12, 15, 17, 86
interpersonal strength, 49, 50, 139
interpretation, 14, 126
intervention, vii, ix, 8, 10, 11, 16, 36, 53, 54, 73, 74, 138
intrinsic, 55
intrinsically, 54, 139
intrusion, 32
intrusive, viii, 4, 74
involuntary, 32
irritability, 32, 37
Israeli, 8

J
Janus-face model, 124
joy, 32
justice, 48, 49

K
Kabat-Zinn, 141
Kenya, 138
key strategies, 8, 138, 139
Kindness, 49, 50, 61
knowledge, 7, 14, 49, 50, 53, 98, 141

L
latent factors, 138
Lazarus, P.S., 8–10, 95
Lazarus, R.S., 9, 95
leadership, 49, 50

INDEX   181

learn, 6, 9, 16, 37, 53, 72, 83, 95, 97–99, 101, 141
learnable cognition, 70
leisure, 55, 81
leukaemia, 108
life experiencer, 53, 54
life goals, 78, 122
life-saving, 73
life-threatening, 31
link, 97–99, 101
listen, 97–99, 101
loneliness, 38
longitudinal study, 8, 10, 74, 125
long-term, ix, 16, 17, 68, 70, 74, 138, 139
look, 98, 99, 101
Los Angeles, 138
loss, 6, 7, 30, 36–38, 52, 68
loss-focused tasks, 38
loss of interest, 33
love, 49, 50, 52, 58, 61, 81, 139
Love of Learning, 49

M
Maercker, A., 124
major depressive disorder, 33
Mak, V.W.M., 16, 73, 75, 76, 79
maladaptive, 6, 9, 35, 124, 125
maladjustment, 6
male-oriented approach, 75
manageable, 54, 70, 82
man-caused disaster, 2
mastery, 55, 82
meaning, 11, 14, 36, 49, 54–56, 61, 70, 78, 139
meaningful experience, 55
meaningless, 38
medical, 4, 31, 36, 68, 70, 73, 74, 94
memory bias, 111
memory(ies), 7, 32, 36, 37, 68, 70, 99, 112, 140

mental health, 2, 3, 50, 75
mental muscles, 140
mental targets, 68
mercy, 49
meta-analysis, 7, 9, 15, 31, 119, 141
meta-analytic commonality analysis approach, 34
micro-skills, 97
mindful, 15, 53
mindfulness, viii, 141
mindfulness-based, 8
mindset, 85
Mini-Mental Adjustment to Cancer Scale (Mini-MAC), 9
misconduct, 33
misfortunes, 2
moderator, 7
modesty, 49, 50
moody pondering, 35, 121
moral compass, 11
morale, 6, 85
Morocco, 138
motivational, 69
mourning, 38, 39
multiple events, 33
muscle tension, 37

N
Nakamura, J., 54–56
natural disasters, vii, 2, 94
negative alterations, 32
negative attentional bias, 109–112
negative cognitive style, 35
negative events, 2, 12, 35, 36, 96, 109, 112, 118–121, 131, 140
negative information, 75, 76, 108, 109, 112
negative social support, 95, 96, 98
negative thinking styles, 34
negative views, 34, 35
neurobiological, 5

182 INDEX

neuroticism, 6, 7, 9
neurotransmitters, 5
new possibilities, 123
new skills, 16, 54, 83
New York, vii, 4
9/11, vii, 4
non-conscious, 68
non-judgemental, 36
non-specific, 68
nonverbal behaviour, 98
nonverbal responses, 102
normal functioning, 3, 40
norms, 98
noticing both positives and negatives,
    viii, 11, 14, 17, 109, 122
nuclear meltdowns, 2
nurturing, 12
nutrient-rich diet, 84
nutrition, 10, 85

O
objective, 14, 36, 82, 83
offenders, 75
ongoing challenges, 33
online platforms, 95
open mind, 84
open-mindedness, 49
openness, 9
optimal functioning, 15
optimism, 8, 9, 11, 70–72, 118
optimistic, 9, 118, 120
optimistic belief, 11
optimistic explanatory style, 119, 120
oracle, 38, 39
oral cancer, 75
outcomes, 2–10, 12, 14, 36, 38, 53,
    60, 69, 71, 74, 75, 124, 138
outcome trajectory, 3, 4, 17, 74
outpatients, 121
overdiagnosis, 31

P
Paediatric oncology, vii
palate deformities, 75
palliative, 128
pandemic, vii, 2, 3, 6, 8, 11, 53, 56,
    71, 94, 97, 118, 138
panic disorder, 36
passive recycling, 121
pathology, 15, 122
pathway, 68–70, 72, 74–80, 82, 83,
    86, 139
perception, 14, 34, 55
persistence, 35, 49, 50, 52, 58, 112
persistent depressive disorder, 33
personal characteristics, 7, 52
personal factors, 8
personal growth and development
    domain, 81
personal health, 2
personality, 5–8, 74
personal resources, 52, 100
personal strength, 112, 123
perspective, 2, 49, 50
pessimistic, 118, 121
pessimistic explanatory style, 119–122
pet, 95
Peterson, B.S., 110
Peterson, C., 15, 48–50, 53, 57, 70,
    118
pharmaceutical treatment, 35
philosophical, 70, 123
physical, 7, 16, 37, 39, 52, 61, 68,
    84, 85, 94, 98, 123
physical fatigue, 33
physical gym, 16
physical harm, 31
physical health, 83, 84
physical illnesses, 11
physical objects, 7
physical well-being, 10, 76
physiology, 10
planful problem-solving, 9

INDEX 183

pleasure, 32, 33, 56
population-based, 16, 77
positive adaptation, 2, 3, 5, 8
positive attention, 36, 112, 113, 140
positive attentional bias, 109–112
positive changes, vii, ix, 4, 96, 118, 122–127
positive communication, viii, 99
positive emotions, 32, 100
positive energy, 69
positive events, 36, 37, 112, 113, 119, 120, 132, 140
positive experiences, 15, 96, 99, 102, 112, 113, 140
positive psychology, viii, 14, 15, 17, 48, 49
positive psychology intervention, 15, 75
positive reappraisal, 9
positive self-talk, 69, 85, 140
post-intervention, 54, 74
Posttraumatic Growth Inventory (PTGI), 123, 124, 126
posttraumatic growth (PTG), vii, 4, 96, 122–127, 138
posttraumatic stress disorder, 30–33, 38, 93
posttraumatic symptomatology, 31
potentially traumatic experiences, 2
potential threats, 36, 110
potential trauma events, 4, 6
poverty, 118, 138
practical applications, viii, 16, 112, 120, 128
practise, ix, 16, 53, 56, 74, 78, 82, 85, 113, 140, 141
practitioners, ix, 10, 48
pre-intervention, 54, 74
present-focus, 36
prevalence rate, 31–33
primary, 94, 141
primary prevention, 11, 16

primary stressors, 94
proactively, 6
problem-focused, 9, 72, 95, 118
problem-solving skills, 72, 82, 123
process, 2, 15, 37, 54, 68, 83, 108, 120, 127
prolonged grief disorder, 30, 37, 38
prosocial, 76
prudence, 49, 50, 61
psychiatric, 31, 121
psychiatric disorders, 30
psychological, vii, ix, 4–8, 14, 16, 17, 30, 32, 36, 37, 40, 53, 55, 73–76, 102, 110, 122, 124, 126, 140
psychological adjustment, 74, 76, 125
psychological disorders, 6, 16, 80
psychological distress, 73
psychological first aid (PFA), 96, 97, 99
psychological gymnasium (PSY GYM), 16, 17, 76, 140
psychological well-being, 10, 16, 53, 128
psychological wellness, 76
psychologist, viii, 73
psychometric properties, 51, 79
psychopathology, 6, 14, 30, 40, 110, 112, 120
psychosocial stressors, 31
pull factors, 56

Q
quadrant model of flow, 54, 55

R
reaching out, 95
reactive adjustment disorder, 30
reactive attention, 37, 108
reactivity, 32
realistic model, 14

184 INDEX

recover, vii, 85
recovery, 2, 4, 16, 17, 38, 74, 97, 108
recurring, 32
reengagement, 12, 72, 74, 83, 140
reflection, 122
rehabilitation, 75, 76
reinforcement, 36
rejuvenation, 85
relating to others, 123
relaxation, 54, 123
religious, 11, 70, 95, 122
remedial, ix, 138
remorse, 38
resilience, vii–ix, 2–12, 14–17, 30–32, 37, 40, 50, 52–54, 56, 72–76, 80, 83–86, 94, 97, 99, 108–112, 118–122, 124, 138, 141
resilience–resistance, 4
resilience quadrant, 4
Resilience Scale, 53
resilient resources, 17
resistance, ix, 4, 5, 12, 16, 17
resource gain, 7
resource loss, 7, 8, 17, 52
responding to negative experiences, 97, 103
responding to positive experiences, 99, 103
rest, 84, 85
restlessness, 37
restoration-focused tasks, 38
retirement, 7
reward, 55
rewarding, 54, 139
role models, 11
romantic domain, 81
rumination, 35, 36, 75, 118, 120–122, 128

S
sadness, 30

savour, 102
schemas, 14, 35
secondary, 71, 141
secondary stressors, 38, 94
self-assuredness, 48, 52
self-blame, 32
self-care behaviour, 10
self-compassion, 10
self-control, 6, 48, 50, 52, 58, 139
self-destructive behaviour, 32
self-esteem, 7, 8
self-help, 3
self-perceived positive changes, 111
self-reflection, 121, 122, 128
self-regulation, 49
self-serving bias, 119
self-serving explanatory style, 72, 128, 140
self-statements, 68
self-talk, 68
self-worth, 94
Seligman, M.E.P., viii, 9, 15, 48–50, 53, 57, 70, 119
sense of caring, 94
severity, 32, 35, 53
sexual violence, 31
shifting, 7
SHINE, viii, ix, 2, 5, 11, 13–17, 33, 40, 48, 50–54, 56–58, 68, 70, 72, 78, 86, 95–97, 99, 108, 110–112, 118, 120, 122, 123, 125, 128, 138–141
short-term memory, 68
Sichuan province, 32, 94
signs, 83, 84, 98, 108, 109
sleep, 34
sleep disturbances, 32, 34
sleep problems, 37
smile, 61
Snyder, C.R., 12, 68–70, 73, 76–80
sociability, 48, 52
social, 3, 10, 49, 52, 70, 98, 123, 125

social anxiety disorder, 36
social conflict, 2
social domain, 81
social factors, 5
social identity, 94
social intelligence, 49, 50
social interaction, 12, 94
social network, 38, 94
social support, 8, 10, 11, 15, 37, 86, 93–99, 139
social support resource theory (SSRT), 94
social work, 68
sociocultural, 10
socioenvironmental, 7, 37
solving problems, 6, 10
specific, 3, 14, 68, 85, 119, 128, 131, 140
specific phobia, 36
specific populations, 11
spiritual, 11, 123
spiritual–existential change, 126
spiritual change, 123
spirituality, 49
stable, 4, 5, 8, 11, 119, 121, 132, 140
stamina, 85
State Hope Scale, 78
storms, 2, 138
Strength-based habit-building, viii, 11, 12, 15, 17, 50, 54, 112
strengths, 12, 15, 40, 49–54, 56–58, 60–62, 70, 74, 76, 102, 123, 138, 139
strength training, 53, 54
stress, 6, 8, 31, 53, 71, 85, 94, 95, 119
stress coping, 8
stress management, 16
Strobe, 38
stroke, 68

students, ix, 3, 8, 34, 51, 53, 54, 68, 71, 111, 121, 141
sub-goaling, 12, 69, 70, 72, 82, 140
subjective "reality", 14
substance-free, 85
substance use, 10
succumbing, 3
suffering, 2, 10, 16, 118, 122, 123, 138
suicidal ideation, 76, 77
suicide, 76, 78
support group, 95
survival with impairment, 3
symptomatology, 4
symptom presentation, 36
symptom relief, 138
symptoms, ix, 4, 8, 15, 16, 30–38, 53, 55, 74, 108, 110, 111, 119–122, 125, 138
Szer, Jeff, viii

T
Taiwan, 10, 111, 125, 138
Taku, K., 126, 127
Tanzania, 138
task performance, 37, 108
Taylor, C.T., 37, 111
technological devices, 68
Tedeschi, R.G., vii, 4, 122–124, 126
temperance, 48–52, 58, 60, 61, 70, 139
Templeton Fellows Programme, viii
terrorism, 2
Thailand, 138
Therapeutic psychology, vii
third wave, 14, 15
threat detection system, 37, 108
threatening stimuli, 37, 108, 110
three-dimensional model of virtue, 50
three-factor model of virtue, 48
three-part model (3-PR), 8–10, 15, 16, 52

186 INDEX

thriving, 3, 4
top-down, 37, 108
trait, 2, 5–8, 48, 78, 79, 141
trait anxiety, 6
Trait Hope Scale, 78, 79
trait–stressor–outcome (TSO), 6
transactional model of stress (TMS),
    8, 95
transcendence, 48, 49, 53
trauma, vii, viii, 2–4, 6, 30–33, 94,
    108, 122–127
trauma and stress-related disorders,
    30, 40
trauma-based behaviours, 118
trauma-like symptoms, 31
trust, 97, 100
Turkey, 138

U
uncertainties, 68, 74, 78
uncontrollable situations, 9
underwater oil fracking, 2
undesirable goals, 76
unemployment, 2, 7, 31, 32, 56, 83
unstable, 4, 119, 131, 140
uplifting ideas, 85
upward regoaling, 69, 70
US, viii, 8, 34, 48, 119, 138

V
vaccination, 16
Values in Action Inventory of
    Strengths (VIA-IS), 48, 50, 53
virtue, 48–51, 53, 138
virtues in action (VIA), 48, 50, 57, 70

visual images, 68
vital engagement, 54, 55, 57, 61, 62,
    139
vitality, 49, 50, 52, 53, 61
volunteer, 95

W
wars, 2
Waters, A.M., 111
waypower, 12, 68, 82–84
weaknesses, 15, 83, 84
well-being, 11, 12, 52, 71, 72, 84,
    110, 118
Wenchuan County, 32, 94
wildfires, 138
willpower, 12, 49, 69, 70, 72, 84, 85,
    140
wisdom and knowledge, 48
work domain, 82
work-related, 31, 55
World Book of Hope, 70
World Health Organization (WHO),
    2, 3, 16, 30, 38, 97, 99
worry, 36, 96, 98
worthlessness, 33

Y
yin and yang, 13
Yip, 76
younger generation, 141

Z
Zen Buddhism, 15
Zoellner, T., 124

Printed in the United States
by Baker & Taylor Publisher Services